D0087312

# The Words and Music of David Bowie

THE PRAEGER SINGER-SONGWRITER COLLECTION

# The Words and Music of David Bowie

James E. Perone

PRAEGER

Westport, Connecticut
London

**Library of Congress Cataloging-in-Publication Data**

Perone, James E.
    The words and music of David Bowie / James E. Perone.
        p.   cm. — (The Praeger singer-songwriter collection, ISSN 1553–3484)
    Includes bibliographical references (p.   ), discography (p.   ), and index.
    ISBN-13: 978–0–275–99245–3 (alk. paper)
    ISBN-10: 0–275–99245–4 (alk. paper)
    1. Bowie, David—Criticism and interpretation.   I. Title.
ML420.B754P47 2007
782.42166092—dc22   2007008323

British Library Cataloguing in Publication Data is available.

Copyright © 2007 by James E. Perone

All rights reserved. No portion of this book may be
reproduced, by any process or technique, without the
express written consent of the publisher.

Library of Congress Catalog Card Number: 2007008323
ISBN-13: 978–0–275–99245–3
ISBN-10: 0–275–99245–4
ISSN: 1553–3484

First published in 2007

Praeger Publishers, 88 Post Road West, Westport, CT 06881
An imprint of Greenwood Publishing Group, Inc.
www.praeger.com

Printed in the United States of America

The paper used in this book complies with the
Permanent Paper Standard issued by the National
Information Standards Organization (Z39.48–1984).

10  9  8  7  6  5  4  3  2  1

# Contents

# Series Foreword

Although the term, *Singer-Songwriters,* might most frequently be associated with a cadre of musicians of the early 1970s such as Paul Simon, James Taylor, Carly Simon, Joni Mitchell, Cat Stevens, and Carole King, the Praeger Singer-Songwriter Collection defines singer-songwriters more broadly, both in terms of style and in terms of time period. The series includes volumes on musicians who have been active from approximately the 1960s through the present. Musicians who write and record in folk, rock, soul, hip-hop, country, and various hybrids of these styles will be represented. Therefore, some of the early 1970s introspective singer-songwriters named above will be included, but not exclusively.

What do the individuals included in this series have in common? Some have never collaborated as writers. But, while some have done so, all have written and recorded commercially successful and/or historically important music *and* lyrics at some point in their careers.

The authors who contribute to the series also exhibit diversity. Some are scholars who are trained primarily as musicians, while others have such areas of specialization as American studies, history, sociology, popular culture studies, literature, and rhetoric. The authors share a high level of scholarship, accessibility in their writing, and a true insight into the work of the artists they study. The authors are also focused on the output of their subjects and how it relates to the their subject's biography and the society around them; however, biography in and of itself is not a major focus of the books in this series.

Given the diversity of the musicians who are the subject of books in this series, and given the diversity of viewpoint of the authors, volumes in the series will differ from book to book. All, however, will be organized chronologically around the compositions and recorded performances of their subjects. All of the books in the series should also serve as listeners' guides to the music of their subjects, making them companions to the artists' recorded output.

James E. Perone
Series Editor

# Acknowledgments

This book could not have been written without the valuable assistance of a number of people. I wish first to thank Karen Perone for offering moral and technical support throughout this and all of my book projects for Greenwood Press and Praeger Publishers, and for offering much-needed input at every stage of every project. In the case of this project, I wish particularly to acknowledge her ability to endure repeated hearings of David Bowie's pre-fame song "The Laughing Gnome."

Over the course of writing several books, the entire staff of the Greenwood Publishing Group has been most helpful and cooperative. I wish to extend special thanks to Editor Daniel Harmon for his assistance in putting this book together and for his continuing support in the development of the Praeger Singer-Songwriter Collection, and to all the copy and production editors for helping me in the fine-tuning of this book. I also wish to thank Eric Levy and Rob Kirkpatrick for their assistance in getting the Praeger Singer-Songwriter Collection off the ground over the course of the first few years of the twenty-first century.

I also wish to send a special shout of thanks out to photographer Chris Walter (www.photofeatures.com) for the photographs of David Bowie that appear in the photo essay in this book.

Despite my own best efforts and the assistance of those named above there are bound to be errors in this book: they are solely my responsibility.

# Introduction

## David Bowie as a Musician and Cultural Icon

Born David Robert Jones in a London suburb in 1947, David Bowie changed his name in the 1966–67 period to avoid confusion with the singer David (Davy) Jones of the Monkees. This name change turned out to be highly symbolic: Bowie would become the most notorious musical changeling of the rock era. The popular, cliché perception of Bowie is that he is a musical chameleon. Evidence of the widespread nature of this description—that of a chameleon—can be found in its inclusion in the first line of the *Wikipedia* (the Internet free encyclopedia that enjoys wide use) article on Bowie.[1] However, as often as Bowie acts like a chameleon, taking on the characteristics of his surroundings, he also sometimes finds himself wildly at odds with current trends in pop music.

By incorporating the widest variety of styles of virtually any performer of the past forty years, Bowie would become the rock musician most likely to confound the critics. For example, *All Music Guide*'s Stephen Thomas Erlewine has written, "Even when he was out of fashion in the '80s and '90s, it was clear that Bowie was one of the most influential musicians in rock, for better or worse."[2] Erlewine—and other critics—would also credit Bowie with not only taking up, but in some cases anticipating such styles as folk, punk, new wave, goth rock, grunge, and electronica. Brock Helander, a contributor to *Baker's Biographical Dictionary of Musicians,* on the other hand, wrote, "David Bowie has pursued an erratic career based very much on image, as opposed to musical substance."[3] Regardless of their critical reaction to Bowie's compositions and recordings, though, virtually all critics agree that he has made a tremendous impact on rock music through his combinations of various rock styles with theater and a narrative poetic style that can be traced back to the American Beat poets of the 1950s. But, Bowie's craft also includes references to such diverse styles as vaudeville, jazz, the British music hall, and the musical avant-garde.

Although Bowie has been primarily an album artist, his recordings of "Fame," "Golden Years," "Let's Dance," "China Girl," "Blue Jean," and "Dancing in the Streets" all made it into the *Billboard* top 10 pop singles charts. Of these, all but one was written or co-written by Bowie. Even more notable are the songs he wrote and recorded that made an impact far in excess of their chart standing. These include "Space Oddity," "Rebel, Rebel," "Changes," "Modern Love," and "Young Americans." From his early 1970s albums such as *Hunky Dory* and *The Rise and Fall of Ziggy Stardust and the Spiders from Mars*—in both of which he established the character of the fictional, androgynous Ziggy Stardust—to *Diamond Dogs,* "*Heroes,*" *Tin Machine, Black Tie White Noise,* and *Heathen,* Bowie's albums generated both significant on-the-street, word-of-mouth interest and some of the most contentious critical reactions of any artist of the rock era. Due in large part to his early success in the glam rock subgenre and his claims of homosexuality (dismissed by some writers as a ploy to generate public interest and record sales), Bowie raised serious issues about sexual orientation in rock music, regardless of whether or not his claimed homosexuality was genuine or part of his stage "character."[4] His regular use of theatrical personae also raise interesting issues concerning authenticity and the perception of authenticity in rock music. David Bowie was inducted into the Rock and Roll Hall of Fame in 1996. Bowie continues to record into the twenty-first century, and continues to explore new musical styles through collaborations with younger artists.

## THE SCOPE AND ORGANIZATION OF THIS BOOK

The focus of this volume is on the music, lyrics, and recordings of David Bowie; therefore, the book is arranged chronologically and has biographical information woven into the discussion of Bowie's songs and recordings. I have also included a concluding chapter devoted to discussion of an assessment of Bowie's work within the context of performance art, and narrative and theatrical traditions.

With few notable exceptions, Bowie wrote or co-wrote nearly every song he has recorded over the past forty years. With over twenty-five full-length albums of new studio material, a thorough study of every individual Bowie composition would be too difficult to accomplish in the context of a book of this size. Therefore, my discussion will focus on the overall gestalt of each of Bowie's albums, with the most detailed analysis being of his most important and best-known individual songs.

The bibliography includes many sources for further information on Bowie and his work. Since the focus of this volume is on Bowie's work as a recording artist, I have not included references to concert reviews, with a few notable exceptions. Likewise, I will not give detailed attention to Bowie's work as a film actor, although I will discuss some of the highlights of his acting career. I have included annotations for most, but not all of the bibliographical citations.

Note that in the selected discography I have included information pertaining to the principal medium for each album release (33-1/3 rpm vinyl record or compact disc). Some of Bowie's albums were also issued in various tape media (1-7/8 ips cassette and 3-3/4 ips 8-track tape). I have not included information pertaining to these tape releases because of the fact that tape was not the primary medium through which the music was sold by Bowie's record companies, and because of the unfortunate fact that cassettes and 8-tracks of the early 1970s through the 1980s are not likely to have survived into the twenty-first century to the extent that vinyl and CDs have. Because of what might be called the more transitory nature of singles (they are very difficult to find in their original format in the digital age), I have not included them in the discography.[5]

I have included an index of names, places, and song titles. Song titles include those written and recorded by David Bowie, as well as songs by others that I discuss in relationship to Bowie's compositions and recordings. It should be noted that I have included only the most extensive and most important discussions of Bowie's work in the various subheadings of his entry in the index.

# From David Jones
# to David Bowie

The musician who came to be known as David Bowie was born on January 8, 1947 in Brixton, London, United Kingdom, as David Robert Jones. Reportedly the young David Robert Jones endured a rough childhood, including a history of mental illness in his family and schoolyard fights, one of which left him with a permanently dilated left pupil. Along the way, however, he took up the saxophone and guitar and showed both musical and artistic promise. As a teenager, Jones worked as a commercial artist and played saxophone in a number of rock bands, none of which made significant commercial or critical impact.[1] By the year 1966, the made-for-television band the Monkees had begun to make an impact not only on American television, but also on the record charts. In order to avoid confusion with the Monkees's Manchester, England-born singer Davy Jones, David Robert Jones took on the pseudonym David Bowie. It was at this time that he recorded several singles with a group named the Lower Third, after having spent time various bands such as the Manish Boys and the King Bees. Although Bowie had recorded one single as the lead singer of the King Bees back in 1964, his post-name change recordings of 1966 represent the real start of the story of singer-songwriter David Bowie.

## THE EARLY PYE SINGLES

Released in January 1966 on the Pye label by David Bowie and the Lower Third, "Can't Help Thinking About Me" (Pye 7N 17020) marks the recording debut of Bowie as a singer and songwriter. The song finds Bowie exploring the 1965 mod style of the early Who, with a hint of the musical and lyrical style of the Kinks. The singer longs for the innocence of childhood, since the young man has now apparently been found guilty of some indiscretion (exactly what, however, is not specified), which has embarrassed his family. He has decided to leave town in order to make it on his own and to escape the whispers of neighbors. With this single, Bowie establishes a pattern of portraying characters that are aliens, outsiders, and outcasts from conventional society. The song also establishes Bowie as a composer who is able to assimilate a prevailing musical style.

The B-side, "And I Say to Myself," begins with an introduction with chromatic harmonic changes that suggest some of the harmonically advanced songs of the day, such as songs by the Beatles and the Dave Clark Five. This opening material also serves as a chorus later in the song. The verses use the I (tonic), vi (submediant), IV (subdominant), V (dominant) progression,[2] something that was a carry over from the early rock and doo-wop vocal harmony songs of the 1950s. However, this conventional chord progression also served as the basis for some of the popular mid-1960s songs written by Mike Smith, Dave Clark, and Lenny Davidson of the Dave Clark Five. Musically, then, Bowie points in the direction of a different popular British rock style of the day, turning away from the A-side's references to the Who and the Kinks. The song's lyrics are more conventional than those of the other five songs on his 1966 Pye releases. Here, the singer of the song has been rejected by a girl who he is convinced is wrong in her assessment of him and their relationship.

The single "Can't Help Thinking About Me"/"And I Say to Myself" is symptomatic of the problem that dogged David Bowie until he finally rose to international fame as part of the glam movement in rock half a dozen years later: his compositions and performances were so wide ranging stylistically that it is difficult to define the Bowie style. Eventually, Bowie successfully used his powers of anticipation of musical trends and assimilation of trends that were in the air to his advantage so that he could be one of the leading musicians of the next several decades. As an emerging artist, however, these early singles seem like too much of a shotgun approach.

"Do Anything You Say" (Pye 7N 17079) is the least memorable of the three Bowie A-sides released by Pye in 1966. The basic gist of the song is that Bowie's character is crying after having been rejected by his girlfriend. As he watches couples walk by hand in hand he decides that he will completely submit himself to his girlfriend's will and do anything that she tells him to do so that he can get her back again. Lyrically, the song is interesting enough: Bowie's character exudes codependency; however, the music itself does not make a particularly strong impression.

The B-side, "Good Morning Girl," in sharp contrast to "Do Anything You Say," is stronger musically, but finds Bowie steering into yet another direction. In this song he references jazz, evoking the feeling of Van Morrison. Not so much the work of Morrison as the lead singer of the group Them, but the work for which Morrison is best known: later songs such as "Brown Eyed

Girl" (1967) and "Moondance" (1970). Bowie's "Good Morning Girl" also suggests the upbeat jazz-influenced swing of the Dave Clark Five's "I Need Love." Bowie provides some tasty scat vocals and a fluid rhythmic approach in singing the song's lyrics. Curiously, of all the styles Bowie explored over the following forty years, jazz was one that he turned to only a handful of times. "Good Morning Girl" betrays an affinity for jazz, which he didn't explore again until the 1993 album *Black Tie White Noise*.

From its opening electric organ licks, Latin percussion, and chunky rhythm guitar chords, the "I Dig Everything" single (Pye 7N 17157) exudes the swinging London sound of the mid-1960s. It is not so much a rock song, as a rock-inspired pop song. Bowie's lyrics paint him as a loveable loser who, despite his youth and poor economic circumstances, can find beauty in everything he sees around him in the city. In addition to the beauty he finds in what some people might not find conventionally beautiful, he expresses the importance of the friends that he has, suggesting that his community of other poor youths enjoys a genuine connection. That the song effectively captures the musical spirit of swinging 1960s London is evidenced by the fact that the recording appears from time to time even in the twenty-first century. For example, I heard it played in a disc jockey's rotation of mid-sixties English pop at a British car show in Perrysburg, Ohio, on June 4, 2006. Alongside the Bowie recording the DJ's rotation played such well-known songs as "Please Please Me," "She Loves You," and a couple of other Beatles songs; "Needles and Pins" and "Love Potion No. 9" by the Searchers; Donovan's "Mellow Yellow"; and the Kinks' "A Well Respected Man." The Bowie recording, despite its relative obscurity, held its own as an example of contemporary British pop of the period.

More than that, however, the song "I Dig Everything" really forms the basis for David Bowie's entire career. He has continued to play the roles of the social outsider and outcast in song after song. Like his character in "I Dig Everything," who finds interest, beauty, and significance in that which mainstream society downplays or even rejects, the so-called real life David Bowie has explored perhaps the widest range of subjects, psychological states, and lifestyle choices and circumstances of any artist in pop music. Like the character of "I Dig Everything," the lifestyle choices that Bowie explores tend to be well on the fringes of society. In fact, I believe that to the extent that David Bowie represents a stage persona for David Jones, Bowie's entire recording, acting, and concert career can be understood as a big, decades-long performance art piece that continues to play out the basic themes of "I Dig Everything."

In many respects, "I'm Not Losing Sleep," the B-side of the "I Dig Everything" single, is even more musically interesting than the A-side. Here, Bowie is addressing someone who has made headlines by making money. His friend has left the old gang behind and has taken up people of the upper socioeconomic class. Bowie's character states that he is not losing any sleep over his friend's newfound fortune, nor over the fact that they no longer run in the same circles. He is fully content with his lot in life. While not as fully developed musically even as some of Bowie's songs of the next couple of years, "I'm Not Losing Sleep" is memorable, catchy, and up to the standards of the pop-rock of the day.

While none of Bowie's three Pye singles enjoyed commercial success, these six early compositions anticipate a couple of significant characteristics of Bowie's compositions and performances of the 1970s through the present, including: his playing the role of the social outsider; his incorporating a rare sense of theater into pop music; his ability to write melodies with strong, recognizable hooks; and his ability to adopt diverse contemporary musical styles and make them his own. Fortunately, despite the relative obscurity of these early singles, the music is still available today. In 1989, Castle Communications released the material on an album. Castle brought these six songs into the twenty-first century with the 2001 compact disc *I Dig Everything: The 1966 Pye Singles* (Castle 06076 81130–2).

## THE EARLY DERAM SINGLES

Although the first of Bowie's three singles on Pye had been released in January 1966, Decca signed him to their subsidiary, Deram Records before the year was out. Bowie's first release on Deram consisted of the single "Rubber Band"/"The London Boys" (Deram DM 107). Both songs had been recorded as part of Bowie's October 1966 audition for Decca,[3] and both stand in sharp contrast lyrically and musically to Bowie's Pye recordings of the same year. "Rubber Band" finds Bowie adopting a vocal style that he had clearly derived from the British musical theater star Anthony Newley. Newley sang with an exaggerated vibrato and an affected pronunciation. He was perhaps best known in the United States for his movie appearances and his 1962 recording of the song "What Kind of Fool Am I," from the show *Stop the World—I Want to Get Off.* Starting with the "Rubber Band" single, not only does Bowie's vocal performance take on these stylistic traits, but his writing leaps far beyond whatever sense of theater he exhibited on his early-1966 recordings.

"Rubber Band" begins with the sound of tuba, trumpet, and oboe playing in a style that suggests a stylized, small pit orchestra musical-theater version of early twentieth-century concert band music. Bowie—in his best Anthony Newley voice—sings of a band that used to serenade him and his lover in the early days of their relationship. His character, however, went off to war. When he returned, he found that his lover was now married to the leader of the band. Bowie's lyrics place this as an event that took place in the early twentieth century: hence the instrumental accompaniment references to John Philip Sousa-era band music. Bowie's melody for each verse is in a relatively simple a-a-a-a form (each of the four phrases is essentially the same) built on a short, easily memorable motive. This helps him quickly advance the story line, and also makes the melody of the chorus contrast quite sharply with that of the verses.

As an example of the type of music that was likely to break a nineteen-year-old singer-songwriter into the big time of pop music in the mid-1960s, "Rubber Band" is a most curious and commercially unsuccessful choice. As a sample of the development of the sense of music as theater of a nineteen-year-old songwriter, however, it represents a remarkable achievement, and it sets the stage for the role-playing that would mark the great David Bowie work of the early 1970s. Bowie's lyrics and music fit the historical style perfectly. The main problems with the song are that his vocal style clearly is entirely based on Newley and that the composition and arrangement are so completely divorced from the pop hits of 1966 that there was no way that "Rubber Band" was ever going to break him as a solo artist, except possibly as a cabaret singer or in the London theater world.

The B-side, "The London Boys," uses the same type of chamber wind ensemble to supplement the more typical instruments of a rock band (bass guitar, drums, electronic organ). Bowie's lyrics concern a seventeen-year-old girl who has left home to go to the big city: London. In the process of getting to know the London boys, she turns to taking pills in order to fit in. Bowie directs one verse to the London boys themselves, speaking with disdain of their flashy clothes and their concern with having fun (apparently at others' expense). It is not at all a pretty picture of urban teen life in England's capital city. The musical accompaniment is fairly minimal and Bowie speaks the lyrics as much as he sings them. His vocal line nearly sobs with regret at the plight of the girl and with the ultimate fate of her and her new "friends," the London boys. It is not a pleasant song to listen to, and clearly presents the flip side of the stereotypical perception of the so-called swinging London of the mid-1960s. Melodically, the song is fairly abstract, at least for a pop song. It does, however, foreshadow one of the more notable characteristics of Bowie's better-known songs of the 1970s: Bowie's melodies appear on the surface to be simple, but they actually are difficult to sing, because of unusual skips and sometimes-unconventional harmonic support.

Deram turned in an entirely different direction for David Bowie's next (again self-composed) single: "The Laughing Gnome"/"The Gospel According to Tony Day" (Deram DM 123). These two songs were recorded during the sessions for Bowie's debut album, but were released in advance of the album itself. "The Laughing Gnome," like Bowie's first Deram single and many of the songs of his forthcoming album, again features the curious combination of rock band instruments and traditional orchestral woodwind and brass instruments that marked his audition recordings for Deram.

"The Laughing Gnome," a peppy, up-tempo number, is a humorous romp that revolves around Bowie's encounter with a laughing gnome with whom he trades vaudeville-style puns. Without giving too much away, some of them involve jokes about the "Rolling Gnomes" (Rolling Stones) and "metrognomes" (metronomes). No, it is not very sophisticated material, but is not entirely out of the ballpark in terms of the whimsical British humor of the period. Certainly, it was no sillier and the puns were no worse than those in a song such as the somewhat dreary Monkees's recording of "Gonna Buy Me a Dog," a song in which one of the punsters ironically is the *other* David Jones, the one whose popularity caused Bowie to have to adopt a stage name. And, it wasn't just the Monkees's record and Bowie's "The Laughing Gnome" that represented the vaudeville-influenced British music hall style of the day; the New Vaudeville Band's recording of "Winchester Cathedral"—a record that suggests the singer Rudy Vallee—made it to the top of the American pop charts in late 1966, and Herman's Hermits's recording of "I'm Henry VIII, I Am" was a remake of an actual vaudeville-era song. As a pop composition, "The Laughing Gnome" is far better than its lack of chart success would suggest. The melody is catchy; in fact, the chorus is one of those tunes that one can't get out of one's head, whether one wants to or not.

Like "The Laughing Gnome," "The Gospel According to Tony Day" features the unlikely sound of rock bassoon. In fact, there is even a blues-influenced improvised bassoon solo in "The Gospel According to Tony Day," which is perhaps the only time such a thing has been heard on a commercial recording prior to the recent work of the eclectic double-reed quartet, the Bassoon Brothers. The lyrics in this rather heavy, dark song describe several characters who suffer from alienation brought on by their having their own individual gospels, or narrowly focused paths to what they believe to be the Truth (with a capital "T"). Unlike what he would do in the 1970s, here Bowie is not the outsider: he is the dispassionate social observer. The alienation of the characters, however, reflects what was to become a pervasive theme in Bowie's writing.

## DAVID BOWIE

While the Deram album *David Bowie* was not the commercial breakthrough for which a singer-songwriter or record company might have hoped, it provides plenty of evidence of Bowie's quickly developing compositional, lyrical, conceptual, and vocal skills. In the case of a few songs, notably "Love You Till Tuesday" and "Sell Me a Coat," Bowie exhibits strong commercial potential: certainly these songs are as hook-filled and convincingly performed as much material that was on the 1966–1967 American and British pop charts. Some of the other songs present strong thematic and theatrical constructs, but are musically or lyrically outside the scope of pop commerciality. Due to the relative obscurity of *David Bowie* today (and certainly at the time of its release), I will discuss several representative songs that stand as particularly significant examples of Bowie's prefame work as a singer-songwriter.

Let us begin with possibly the two most commercially viable songs on the album: "Sell Me a Coat" and "Love You Till Tuesday." "Sell Me a Coat" uses the metaphor of standing coatless in the winter cold to express the feelings that his character has since his lover has left him. The sentiments are fairly predictable, but the lyrics are rich with imagery. Bowie's music exhibits strong melodic contrast between verse (in which his lyrics explore the feelings of icy coldness now that his girlfriend has rejected him) and chorus (in which he requests that someone sell him a coat—bring him metaphorically into a new loving relationship—to warm him). The lower-range melody of the verses help Bowie the performer express a feeling of resignation that matches his lyrics, while the higher range and shorter phrases of the chorus highlight the urgency of his character's need for the metaphorical "coat." The melodic, harmonic, and rhythmic material is all easily memorable and shows strong commercial potential. And, the combination of music and lyrics, and use of metaphor resemble other successful British pop material of the day. In particular, the Graham Goulding song "No Milk Today," popularized by the group Herman's Hermits, comes to mind, not because of any foreground resemblance, but because the two songs seem to belong within the same basic metaphorical genre. That, along with the richness of Bowie's vocal work on the recording, makes this one of his best prefame songs. Bowie's melodic and harmonic writing also bears some resemblance to the folkish progressive rock ballads composed by Justin Hayward of the Moody Blues.

The song "Love You Till Tuesday" finds Bowie singing in an exaggerated accent that emphasizes the Englishness of the song. Again, the comparison to Herman's Hermits is inescapable: one need only think of the band's lead singer, Peter Noone, and his delivery on "I'm Henry VIII, I Am" to get a sense of the overt Englishness of the Bowie performance. The "da-da-da-dum" chorus and the melodic and harmonic material of the verses is strong in the hook department. One could easily imagine one of the top-40 British pop bands of the day—most obviously, Herman's Hermits—including this as an album track, or even as a viable single.

Quite possibly, part of the problem for David Bowie in gaining a commercial following early in his career was that the album *David Bowie,* like Bowie's earlier singles, is just too disparate stylistically. Bowie's lyrics on the album range from funny, to whimsical, to dark, to sarcastic. The character types he observes and portrays in the songs include lovable losers, social outcasts, introspective near-philosophers, and brash Hitler-esque types. The music ranges from up-tempo top-40 pop, to waltz, to rock, to dark brooding, nearly monothematic melodies. As a collection of songs, the album tends to come off as a shotgun approach to writing: let's try a whole bunch of approaches and see what strikes a chord with the public. In the context of a bunch of 45-rpm singles that approach might work, but in the context of an album it proves too confusing for the listener.

Among those songs that contrast most sharply with material such as "The Laughing Gnome," "Love You Till Tuesday," and "Sell Me a Coat," let us consider two others: "We Are Hungry Men" and "Little Bombardier." "We Are Hungry Men" is about the closest thing to a rock (as opposed to pop) song on the album. Bowie's lyrics, however, are anything but conventional. He portrays a character who is part of the master race, and who would legalize and endorse mass abortions in order to cure the overpopulation problem. The basic gist of the song is that by wiping out those who are the less desirable members of society, the hungry men of the song's title, will ensure that they have enough. Between Bowie's portrayal of a strange, twisted character in the lyrics, the cheesy sound of the Farfisa organ, and up-tempo pace of the song, "We Are Hungry Men" anticipates the themes and sounds of the post-punk, new wave bands of the late 1970s: some of the songs on the first two Talking Heads albums—*Talking Heads: 77* and *More Songs About Buildings and Food*—for example, are natural descendants of this Bowie song. Incidentally, the ties between David Bowie and David Byrne, principal songwriter and lead singer of Talking Heads, would reemerge in the late 1970s.

The main character of "Little Bombardier" is a former war hero who eventually is forced to leave town because of suspicions about his possible inappropriate relationships with children. Bowie develops the character gradually over the course of the song, so that his perversions aren't immediately made clear. Bowie leaves the specifics of the Little Bombardier's unnaturally close relationship with the children of the neighborhood somewhat hazy, so that the song is not overly lurid. As a character, the Bombardier fits in squarely with Ziggy Stardust, several of the characters of the album *Outside,* the Diamond Dogs, and the other social/sexual outcasts of Bowie's later, better-known songs.

It is in the combination of character type, lyrics, and music, however, that "Little Bombardier" becomes more than just an off-the-wall song about a war hero who is exiled from town because of his proclivity toward pedophilia. Bowie sets his tale to waltz music that is both disarming and reminiscent of the music of the grand age of ballroom dancing in the late nineteenth and early twentieth century. Melodically, rhythmically, and harmonically, this music would not be at all out of place in a 1920s or 1930s dance hall. And, the arrangers and producers with whom Bowie worked on his debut album orchestrate the song in a style entirely appropriate for the ballroom era. In fact, Bowie's approach falls within a tradition of setting lyrics that deal with difficult or controversial topics to music that provides irony by means of its completely disarming character. One need only consider some of the work of Gustav Mahler in setting texts that deal with death to child-like melodies, or—an even closer antecedent to the entire gestalt of the "Little Bombardier"—one of the great collaborations of Kurt Weill and Bertold Brecht in the musical *The Three-Penny Opera.* The song "Moritat: Mack the Knife," with its tale of a serial murder who favored prostitutes as victims set to perky jazz-influenced cabaret music, immediately comes to mind.

Some of the other songs on *David Bowie* are not so successful. While Bowie had struck a balance between singing the verses of the single version of "Rubber Band" in the lower and upper octaves, the album version of the song finds him singing more of the material in the upper octave. This makes his voice sound forced and renders the mood progression of the song less effective than that in the earlier recording. The lyrics of the song "When I Live My Dream" rely on images of slaying dragons and other childhood dreams, whereas the music would not be out of place in a 1960s

Broadway musical starring a particularly naïve character. The song as a whole ends up sounding too much like something from the 1964–1965 British Invasion (or a not-too-great early 1960s musical) to be completely effective. The songs in which Bowie reflects back farther in time lyrically or musically ("Little Bombardier" and "Rubber Band," for example) are much more effective than in a song such as "When I Live My Dream" that just ends up sounding a year or two out of fashion.

The use of classical orchestral instruments, especially the woodwinds (bassoon, oboe, English horn, and piccolo) and brasses (tuba, trumpet, and French horn) that Bowie's producers at Deram chose both for his audition recordings and for many of the songs on this album may seem like a somewhat strange choice: they decidedly were *not* commonly heard on pop records of the day. However, I believe that there is another way to look at the arrangements on *David Bowie*. I tend to hear the album as part of a larger corporate plan at Deram to find a commercially viable way to merge classical and pop. This was the same company, after all, that would release the groundbreaking *Days of Future Passed*—on which the Moody Blues was joined by the London Festival Orchestra—in 1967 (the same year as the release of *David Bowie*) complete with album liner notes that, frankly, make a big deal out of the "fusion" of the two styles.[4] The combination of folk, pop, rock, and classical on *David Bowie* might not have been as commercial accessible as that of *Days of Future Passed*, but there are some ties between the two. In fact, in a few songs, notably "Sell Me a Coat" and the album version of "Rubber Band," the classical, pop, folk combination is more fully integrated than in parts of *Days of Future Passed*, particularly because of the chamber music nature that runs through the Bowie album. Despite its lack of commercial and critical success, Bowie's debut album shows a young singer-songwriter exploring a wide variety of styles, and generally to good effect.

Once David Bowie became a star, the Deram album was reissued, as was a follow-up album that consisted of post-*David Bowie* singles and several recordings that had been left unissued at the time of Bowie's departure from the record label. Deram has reissued the album's material on compact disc as part of the single-CD collection *The Deram Anthology 1966–1968* (Deram 844 784–2, 1997). Despite of, or perhaps because of, the sharp contrast between these recordings (particularly in composition and orchestration) and Bowie's post-Deram work, this collection is a must-have for any serious David Bowie fan that wants to experience the full range of Bowie's talents.

## THE LATER DERAM RECORDINGS

In the wake of David Bowie's debut album, Deram issued "Love You Till Tuesday"/"Did You Ever Have a Dream" as a single (Deram DM 135). While substantially the same as the versions of the song found on the album, at least from the standpoint of Bowie's vocal performance, the single version of "Love You Till Tuesday" features orchestral woodwinds and strings.

While this kind of orchestration worked quite well on songs such as "Rubber Band" and "The Laughing Gnome," here it seems superfluous, even unnatural. Ultimately, it just sounds too different from the pop music of the day, and for no immediately understandable reason having to do with the nature of the story; the album version of the song probably would have been a better choice for release. The B-side of the single, "Did You Ever Have a Dream" is not one of Bowie's most distinguished prefame songs and is not nearly as memorable as the best of his work of the period.

While this third Deram single was issued in Europe, South Africa, and the United States, in addition to Bowie's native United Kingdom,[5] it was not a great commercial success. This single, however, was not a case of three strikes and you're out for David Bowie. He would continue to record more new material for Deram into 1968. Perhaps the most important thing to come out of the post-*David Bowie* recordings for Deram was Bowie's association with record producer Tony Visconti, with whom Bowie would collaborate on his famous recordings of the early 1970s, and with whom he would resume collaborations in the twenty-first century.

The most notable of these late Deram recordings was the song "Let Me Sleep Beside You," a cut produced by Visconti. Bowie's music eliminates the references to the music hall, to old ballroom dance music, and to Herman's Hermits–style pop; here, he places himself firmly in the rock sphere. His melodic material is based primarily on one short motive, in sharp contrast to the more expansive phrases of Bowie's so-called retro songs. Visconti's production and the arrangement (in particular the use of the cello section) suggest the Moody Blues's *Days of Future Passed* and stand in contrast to the emphasis on orchestral winds found on the *David Bowie* album and on the previous singles. Bowie's lyrics also represent a break with some of the more conventional pop sentiments of what appeared to be designed as potential breakthrough top-40 hits. The lyrics are a little more impressionistic than those in his earlier songs, but also find Bowie expressing intimacy in a somewhat unusual way. Rather than focusing on emotional attachment, or on kissing, holding hands, intercourse, or some other sexual attachment (all staples of pop songs), he focuses on the act of sleeping together—in what seems to be the literal sense of the phrase. This interesting turn of expression anticipates some of Bowie's later songs, perhaps most directly the mid-1970s song "Be My Wife," probably the only marriage proposal in which the word "love" never appears. What Bowie effectively does in songs such as "Let Me Sleep Beside You" and "Be My Wife" (which I will discuss in chapter 5) is to express the possibility that love and attachment are sometimes not best defined in stereotypical, cliché ways, but sometimes through the less-frequently expressed, but very real other associated emotional needs.

The end of Bowie's time with Deram also found him recording an early version of the song "Space Oddity," the song that (in its 1969 version) became one of his best-remembered and most frequently heard oldies into the twenty-first century. Many of the substantial ingredients of the definitive version of "Space Oddity" can be heard in the early recording: the melody, instrumental harmony, harmony vocals, and form are the same. The lyrics of the original Deram version are a bit different, in that the verses are in a different order (the order on the famous 1969 version makes more sense from a narrative standpoint). The most important difference is in the arrangement and overall performance. The early recording is not as tight vocally or instrumentally, which makes it sound like a demo, rather than a fully produced, ready-to-be-released recording. The arrangement is also considerably thinner, which confirms the demo-like nature of the Deram version. Once Bowie's post-Deram recording of "Space Oddity" became a success in the United Kingdom in 1969, Deram put together an album made up of over a dozen tracks, including several of the recordings Bowie had recorded for the label after the *David Bowie* album. *The World of David Bowie* (Deram PA58) was issued in 1970.

Bowie's activities at the end of and following his two years with Deram Records suggests that he was looking for another outlet for his creativity and may have been considering options outside the sphere of pop music. He spent a couple of months in a Buddhist monastery in Scotland, and then became involved in mime, studying with the Lindsay Kemp Mime Troupe. Bowie then formed his own mime troupe, as well as an experimental arts group. It was in an effort to fund these new creative activities that Bowie recorded his next album, one that would find him moving in a fundamentally different direction musically from anything that he had recorded for Pye or Deram.

## MAN OF WORDS, MAN OF MUSIC (SPACE ODDITY)

Originally released by Mercury in 1969 as *Man of Words, Man of Music,* this album is best known today under the title *Space Oddity,* for it is under that moniker that it was reissued by RCA in 1972 and in subsequent vinyl and late twentieth-century compact disc reissues on RCA, Rykodisc, and Virgin.

The album begins with its best-remembered track, and one of David Bowie's best-known songs ever: "Space Oddity." The story of Bowie's text concerns Major Tom, an astronaut on a doomed mission. When Major Tom's ground crew warns him that something has gone wrong with his spacecraft, he either does not hear the message or is so lost in his awe of what he sees around him in space that he never understands the urgency of the message. The genius of Bowie's lyrics is that Major Tom can so easily be understood as a literal character and as a metaphor for those people who are blissfully unaware of the world as it is, or either because they do not make the effort to observe, or because through no fault of their own, they are unable to interpret the world around them. Major Tom is the first of Bowie's famous alienated characters.

Musically, "Space Oddity" also finds David Bowie in fine form. He uses very basic harmonic materials, and clear contrasts from section to section in his melodies. Even within the sections (verse, chorus, and middle eight), Bowie makes effective use of repetition and contrast. Bowie's vocal performance on the recording is also particularly effective. He sets the material that comes from the voice of the ground crew in the lowest part of his vocal register (occasionally multi-tracked an octave higher) when all is going well in the mission. In this register, which Bowie does not use all that often, his voice has an almost crooner-like richness. When the ground crew tries to let Major Tom know that they have instrument readings that indicate a catastrophe on board the Major's spacecraft, Bowie writes contrasting melodic material that places him in the middle, more powerful and urgent part of his vocal range. The general range of the melodic material that comes from the voice of Major Tom contrasts both with the calm material and the urgent material from the ground crew. In short, "Space Oddity," more obviously than anything else David Bowie had previously written and recorded, sounds like Bowie writing for Bowie the singer. Some of the theatricality of his earlier songs is apparent, but the execution of the song as a performance is more assured and subtle than in his earlier songs.

Significantly, "Space Oddity" is the one track on the album that was not produced by Tony Visconti; Gus Dudgeon handled the chores. The arrangement, which was written by Bowie and Paul Buckmaster, and Dudgeon's production are much richer and ethereal than that of the rest of the album. This tends to make "Space Oddity" seem a bit like the odd song out. But, it is the strongest, most accessible, and easily best-known song of the album. This creates a structural problem for the *Space Oddity* album: it starts out on a high and never quite comes back again.

After "Space Oddity," the album starts to move in the direction of the Scottish folk and psychedelic musician Donovan. The song "Unwashed and Somewhat Slightly Dazed" begins with a twelve-string acoustic guitar introduction that echoes the introduction to "Space Oddity." In addition to late-1960s folk-rock references in the music, Bowie makes musical reference to a variation on the famous so-called Bo Diddley rhythm associated with the early rock and roll pioneer of the same name. The lyrics are impressionistic and describe a Bob Dylan-esque scene of desperation, sickness, poverty, and lust. In establishing the impressions of a not-at-all-pleasant scene, it is an effective track. "Unwashed" is followed by "(Don't Sit Down)," which is really just a brief excerpt from a jam by Bowie and his backing musicians that breaks down into laughter.

The song "Letter to Hermione" returns to the folk style, again suggesting Donovan. Bowie's text represents a letter written by a young man to his former lover. Although Bowie's character never says it directly, he clearly is writing as much for catharsis and out of an intense loneliness as he is to communicate with Hermione. By and large Bowie's lyrics resemble the text of a letter; the lyrics, for the most part, avoids rhyme, and the musical setting avoids short melodic motives, both of which contribute to the letter-like narrative style. In fact, in starting with the song "Letter to Hermione" Bowie begins to abandon the kinds of formulaic poetic structures, subjects, and situations that were heard in so many top-40 records of the 1970s. "Letter to Hermione" might just be a sample, but Bowie's lyrics of the 1970s set him apart from most other rock writers: his lyrics can stand up far better as poems, if the music is taken away, than those of most of his contemporaries.

"Cygnet Committee," another folkish impressionistic song, is less effective. For one thing, Bowie is not as convincing singing this type of material, particularly in the middle-to-upper part of his vocal range. He performs the song in a fairly expressionless manner—something that is part of the introspective folk singer-songwriter style—and the impressionistic lyrics are quite lengthy; this makes it difficult for the listener to establish a clear mood or overall meaning to the song. When Bowie began making his most famous music a couple years later, he would still sometimes create impressions, but almost always with a clearer focus and with less meandering texts. At nine-and-a-half minutes, "Cygnet Committee" is quite a lot to take in and digest.

"Janine" uses a more conventional rock song structure, harmony, melodic shapes, and rhythms; however, the verses again find Bowie fitting in quite a lot of text. It is more effective, however, than "Cygnet Committee." "An Occasional Dream" returns to a more gentle folk-pop style. The rhyme scheme is not consistent from verse to verse, which helps Bowie to create the unpredictable dreamlike atmosphere of the song.

Aside from "Space Oddity," very little of *Man of Words, Man of Music* found its way into later Bowie releases—greatest hits studio albums or concert albums—with the notable exceptions of "Wild Eyed Boy from Freecloud" and "God Knows I'm Good." "Wild Eyed Boy from Freecloud" paints an impressionistic picture of a young man who does not fit into the world around him. Bowie's lyrics contain numerous references to a world of almost medieval fantasy. It is interesting to note that this kind of Medieval or Renaissance world of fantasy, mysticism, and mythology was quite popular in British music in the late 1960s and early 1970s, in particular in a folk-influenced rock style—think, for example, of Led Zeppelin's "Stairway to Heaven" or Traffic's album *John Barleycorn Must Die*, or Donovan's "Atlantis." Certainly, one of the things that makes this recording more effective than some of the other songs on *Man of Words, Man of Music* is Bowie's vocal work, which exhibits more emotional connection to the text than on some of the other more taciturn performances.

"God Knows I'm Good" finds Bowie cast in the role of social observer. He describes watching a poor old woman who has to steal food in order to survive. Bowie contrasts the woman's plight with the sound of cash machines and the clean-cut affluent people around her. He allows the listener to interpret the ultimate meaning of his song, since he does not offer commentary on the situation. It is successful because of this, and because it is more lyrically direct than most of the songs on the album. Another important feature of the song is its instrumental rhythmic connection to "Unwashed and Somewhat Slightly Dazed" by means of the use of a Bo Diddley–variant rhythm.

The sharp contrast between the impressionistic, fantasy-laden songs of *Man of Words, Man of Music* and an observational piece such as "God Knows I'm Good" gets blurred in later recordings, especially the work from his Berlin period in the late 1970s. In the song "Heroes," for example, Bowie takes a scene that he actually observed at the Berlin Wall and weaves it into a metaphorical tale. That kind of narrative development does not come through nearly as clearly on *Man of Words, Man of Music:* the songs here tend to be either clearly observational or highly impressionistic; there's not a great deal of development in between songs, nor is there a great deal of development within songs.

"Memory of a Free Festival" presents Bowie's impressions of the Beckenham Free Festival (at which he performed), which took place in August 1969. From his lyrics, it sounds as if the festival was a Woodstock-type love, peace, drugs, near-Utopian stereotypical late-1960s experience. The song is structured in two main sections, each of which accounts for almost exactly half of the seven-minutes-plus run time of the recording. The first section is an almost stream-of-consciousness account of the festival, recounted primarily through psychedelic imagery. Bowie's voice is accompanied primarily with a chord organ, which he plays. The melodic material freely floats over the sparse accompaniment, adding to the dream-like effect. The second half of the song is a repeated run-out chorus sung by what sounds like an assembled multitude. The effect is reminiscent of the second half of the Beatles's "Hey Jude" and the closing, sung part of Donovan's "Atlantis."

While the song "Space Oddity" generated interest in the United Kingdom, *Man of Words, Man of Music* remained fairly obscure until its reissue in 1972, after Bowie had established himself as a well-known artist. It was not for lack of some strong work from Bowie or for lack of strong support from his accompanying musicians that the album pretty much languished. With luminaries such as John Lodge of the Moody Blues on bass, Paul Buckmaster on violoncello, and Rick Wakeman (later of the band Yes) on keyboards, *Man of Words, Man of Music* certainly found David Bowie working with some of the leading figures in British progressive rock. In listening to this album decades after its initial release, it would seem that perhaps *Man of Words, Man of Music* was not commercially successful in part because it did not come from a consistent, definable voice. Bowie's next albums would find him developing different artistic personae that would resonant more strongly with listeners and would make him stand apart from the crowd; here—with the notable exception of "Space Oddity"—he was aiming at a sort of niche audience, one for which he was not as well-equipped vocally or conceptually as he would be for his later incarnations. In addition, a fair number of the songs of *Man of Words, Man of Music* feature meandering melodies, which are entirely appropriate for the impressionistic fantasy-folk style, but which generally do not make the kind of immediate impact on audiences as the types of pop hooks Bowie was writing in the 1966–1968 period, or the hooks he would write after *Man of Words, Man of Music*. A more direct approach to melody, harmony, and rhythm, and a less folk-oriented approach was soon to come.

# Becoming Ziggy Stardust

David Bowie's singles with bands such as the King Bees, the Mannish Boys, the Lower Third, and his singles and albums as a soloist between 1964 and 1969 may not have met with critical or commercial success, but they established Bowie as a singer-songwriter who was adaptable and willing to take musical chances. The next phase of his career found Bowie moving toward and adopting an otherworldly, androgynous performance persona—one that would help to make him stand apart from the crowd of early 1970s acts and secure him a sizeable fan base. He successfully combined several of the individual aspects that had marked his earlier work, including an ability to write memorable, easily recognizable music; a conscious desire to combine theater and rock-pop music; and a lyrical fascination with the outsider, whether that outsider be someone seen through his eyes or a first-person alter ego.

## THE MAN WHO SOLD THE WORLD

No, *The Man Who Sold the World* was not the album that proved to be David Bowie's big breakthrough. The 1971 album, however, represented a crucial step along the way to worldwide fame. The album found Bowie developing an androgynous, bisexual performance persona; incorporating heavy metal, guitar-based rock; writing in a melodically, harmonically, and rhythmically more accessible way than he had in folk-oriented compositions of a couple of years previous; and (most importantly) putting together a team of collaborators that would form perhaps his most famous band.

Let us first consider this team. Tony Visconti, with whom Bowie had been associated since his Deram days, produced *The Man Who Sold the World*. Even though *Man of Words, Man of Music* (which Visconti also produced) was not a hit, he seemed to be one producer who could collaborate with Bowie to create a recorded soundscape that matched the style of Bowie's words and music. Just as Visconti had matched the folkish feel of *Man of Words, Man of Music* with the open feeling of space, in *The Man Who Sold the World* Visconti incorporates an immediacy of instruments and voices, along with sound compression to create an effective heavy metal sound. Although he would not continue on as a member of Bowie's famous Spiders from Mars band, Visconti also played bass guitar on *The Man Who Sold the World*.

Drummer Mick Woodmansey and guitarist Mick Ronson are the other two principals of the new Bowie team. Woodmansey added a new virtuosity to the percussion part of the Bowie sound, something that was especially important on *The Man Who Sold the World,* given the importance of instrumental virtuosity in the heavy metal genre. The most famous member of the new team, however, was Mick Ronson, whose burning lead guitar would play an important role over the course of Bowie's next several albums.

Even before one hears the music of *The Man Who Sold the World,* one can tell that this album is not about the 1966 mod David Bowie, or about the folkie, Donovan-esque David Bowie of 1969: Bowie appears on the album cover in a long satin-looking dress, posed on a daybed, looking very much like the American actress Lauren Bacall. This album cover, incidentally, would be banned when the album was released in the United States, so controversial was cross-dressing in America at the time.[1] This gender and sexuality ambiguity, however, was an essential component in the new glam rock (sometimes called glitter rock) style.

Diehard fans of David Bowie and diehard fans of Marc Bolan, the leader of the band T. Rex, continue to argue into the twenty-first century about which of their heroes invented the glam rock style. Certainly both performers were developing along similar lines with respect to stylized gender ambiguity, lyrics that reflect fantasy worlds and sex, and music that combined the disparate styles of hard rock and acoustic folk. *The Man Who Sold the World* fits squarely in the style, and despite the impact of Bolan—particularly in the United Kingdom—it would be Bowie who would bring this particularly British style to a much wider audience. Although this wide dissemination of glam rock was not to take place for another couple of years, this album is clear evidence of Bowie's development of the style as early as 1970.

Black Sabbath's 1970 album *Paranoid* has been acknowledged as one of, if not the, earliest classic heavy metal albums. Led Zeppelin had also made an important contribution to the hard rock and heavy metal genre with their heavily electric blues–oriented 1969 albums *Led Zeppelin* and *Led Zeppelin II.* The David Bowie album *The Man Who Sold the World* is not *Paranoid,* nor does it sound exactly like a product of Led Zeppelin, but it is in the same ballpark. In particular, some of the near-classical and folk influences on the Bowie album resemble the contemporary work of Led Zeppelin. So, while David Bowie did not invent heavy metal, he was integrating the style into his personal musical repertory just as metal was developing. As it would turn out, one of the weaknesses of *The Man Who Sold the World* was that in some of the songs Bowie adopted some of the most obvious and easy-to-parody aspects of heavy metal. This led to a few of the tracks remaining effective for years, while some became near cartoon images of early metal within a short time.

The first track on the album, "The Width of a Circle," is a prototypical metal/glam song, and is one of the tracks that holds up pretty well. Bowie forsakes the meandering melodies of *Man of Words, Man of Music,* and instead turns to more conventional musical phrase structure. He also turns to more conventional phrase and rhyme structures in his lyrics. He adopts a near-sneer in his vocal texture; he does not sing with the intensity of Led Zeppelin's Robert Plant, nor with the laser beam edge of Black Sabbath's Ozzy Osbourne on a song such as *Paranoid*'s "War Pigs," but this is clearly a different David Bowie timbre (i.e., the tone and color of his voice) than anything heard on his previous recordings. All of this is set to virtuosic electric guitar and bass guitar–heavy accompaniment that exudes heavy metal.

It is in the lyrics of "The Width of a Circle" that the sexual ambiguity of the glam style comes out. In fact, Bowie's lyrics suggest a nightmarish fantasy of homosexual intercourse, with Bowie's character playing the submissive role. Unlike the so-called mature glam style, which generally included a good deal of camp, this piece does not play up or glamorize the gay sexual encounter; it resembles a dark nightmare. Likewise, Bowie has not yet adopted the campy, stereotypical so-called gay voice (if there really is such a thing) that would emerge over the course of the next couple of years.

Musically, "The Width of a Circle" is divided into two principal parts, each with unique melodic, harmonic, and rhythmic material. Since Bowie recaps just a little bit of the first section at the conclusion of the eight-minute song, there is a hint at a classical A-B-A rhyme structure. The "A" section is marked by metrical changes, which are handled precisely by Bowie (on acoustic guitar) and the rest of the band.

In "All the Madmen," Bowie's persona—an outcast from society—says that he would rather be with those who are considered to be "mad" (i.e., insane) rather than being with those who society considers normal. Like the famous Led Zeppelin song "Stairway to Heaven," Bowie's "All the Madmen" juxtaposes the sounds of Renaissance music—including a recorder consort—with the heavy electric guitar of the metal genre. Unfortunately, Bowie affects a Cockney-esque dialect in the Renaissance-style sections. While this might suit his societal outcast character, it tends to be one of the features of early heavy metal that would be prone to parody. The juxtaposition of Renaissance-style music and the electronic pompousness of heavy metal is another one of the features of the music of this time period that would eventually be subjected to parody. For example, this song, as well as the song "After All," another highly sectional song with exaggerated dialect (in chantey-style echo phrases) and an overly dramatic heavy metal style, sound like the very kind of thing that the writers of the 1984 film *This Is Spinal Tap* had in mind in the hilarious

Stonehenge sequence—the funniest send up of the juxtaposition of Renaissance fantasy with electric blues-influenced metal of the early 1970s ever committed to film.

The song that comes between "All the Madmen" and "After All," "Black Country Rock" fares better today. With only two verses of text, it is easily the shortest set of lyrics on the album. The piece is the sort of electric blues-heavy metal mix that populated the early Led Zeppelin albums. The whole point of the piece is the heavy musical groove. The best David Bowie songs that feature memorable, catchy instrumental grooves from later in his career, also feature more substantial lyrics than this song. Bowie just had not quite yet put the whole package together yet.

"Running Gun Blues" contains some of the stylistic contrasts and unexpected metrical changes typical of heavy metal. The most interesting thing about the song, however, is the character Bowie portrays in the song—a soldier who mourns the end of the Vietnam War. This soldier still has a gun and wants to go out and shoot a few "gooks" (a racist reference to the Vietnamese of the still-ongoing Vietnam conflict) for good measure. Bowie's soldier is so extreme and utterly despicable that "Running Gun Blues" becomes clearly an anti-war song. The unspoken message seems to be, "look at what war has done to this fellow."

"Saviour Machine" concerns a politician (President Joe) who becomes convinced that the world needs a "saviour machine" in order to be saved from destruction. The merits of this technology, however, are quite open to debate, since Bowie delivers the contrary message that the world cannot and should not depend on such a machine for its survival. It's not that "Saviour Machine" is an anti-technology song. The point that Bowie seems to be making is that humankind cannot rely on a machine, leader, political system or any one thing to be its savior: every individual is responsible for the survival of the species. The song is notable for its eerie harmonic progression and difficult-to-sing melody. This type of harmonic progression and snaky melody continue to be heard in David Bowie's music right up to his most recent albums in the twenty-first century: *Heathen* and *Reality*. And, despite the contours of the melody, Bowie sings it utterly without falter.

"She Shook Me Cold" brings up the great glam-metal irony of sexual identity. On one hand, Bowie appears in drag on the album cover, and the album's first song is clearly about a homosexual encounter. On the other hand, Bowie's character in "She Shook Me Cold," is a insatiable lothario who, despite having deflowered numerous female virgins along the way, has now met his match with a woman who has an even stronger sex drive than his own. Ultimately, this is really what glam and heavy metal are all about: exploring extremes and the dark fringes of sexuality.

The title song "The Man Who Sold the World" is far less direct. Here, Bowie encounters the title character, but it is not clear just what the phrase means, or exactly who this man is. The music is not as memorable as the best songs on the album. The main thing that the song does is to paint—however elusively—the title character as another example of the societal outcasts who populate the album. The album's final track, "The Supermen," returns to the mythology that marked a couple of the earlier songs. The song consists of the kind of stereotypical metal sound and lyrics that, while fashionable in 1970, would become almost a self-parody in the not-too-distant future.

Ultimately, *The Man Who Sold the World* was not a huge commercial success for David Bowie, nor did it establish the heavy metal style as his milieu. However, the album was an important step along the way for Bowie's career, in that it proved that he could adopt diverse styles. It also allowed him to explore the themes of sexuality and gender roles that only a few of his earlier songs had done. Although Bowie's next project would find him steering clear of hard rock and heavy metal, he would return to some, highly selective elements of the style in his later work. Gone would be the more cliché aspects of metal, but remaining would be the electric guitar emphasis and the emphasis on sexual ambiguity.

## HUNKY DORY

David Bowie's *Man of Words, Man of Music* may not have been a hit when it was first released, but it became successful when reissued after the single "Space Oddity" hit the charts. The 1970 hard rock and heavy metal album *The Man Who Sold the World* was also not an enormous success at first. Bowie's next album, the 1971 *Hunky Dory,* found the musician moving in new directions as a songwriter and as a performer, and taking the first steps toward the establishment of a new fictional character, Ziggy Stardust. *Hunky Dory* perhaps is best known for its highly successful single, "Changes," but the album runs much deeper than just that one song. It was the first album on which Bowie would discernibly and successfully merge the widely disparate styles and influences that had marked his work since the mid-1960s. In *Hunky Dory* Bowie makes observations about the social scene; continues to raise questions about sexual identity and gender roles; features his saxophone playing for the first time; more fully incorporates his dry wit; and creates a unique blend of folk, pop, glam, and progressive rock that would go a long way in separating him from other early 1970s musicians.

David Bowie had moved from memorable and easy-to-sing pop material in the mid-1960s to more dramatic, but less hook-oriented melodies on his folk-psychedelia (*Man of Words, Man of Music*) and heavy metal (*The Man Who Sold the World*) albums. The pop tunesmith in Bowie returns in full force with the first track on *Hunky Dory:* "Changes." Here, Bowie uses traditional British pop song structure, with clearly defined verse, chorus, and middle-eight sections. Bowie's melody, harmonic progression, and the instrumental accompaniment are all memorable, easily identifiable, and truly catchy. However, unlike some of his catchy songs of the 1960s, "Changes" features some thought-provoking and clearly autobiographical lyrics.

The first verse of "Changes" is concerned with the idea of self-recognition. The implication is that the narrator of the song had not previously been able to come to grips with his true identity. Part of this failure in self-recognition seems to be because he has believed in his public image, rather than allowing his true identity to come forward; Bowie's character refers to himself as a "faker." Given the number of pre-*Hunky Dory* musical styles Bowie had tried, it is very easy to interpret this verse of the song as a public acknowledgement that his earlier attempts at securing an elusive breakthrough in pop music had been cases of adopting styles that were not the true David Bowie style. Given the ambiguity of sexual identity that runs through *Hunky Dory* and that had run through *The Man Who Sold the World*, the lyrics could possibly be interpreted as being a reference to a proverbial coming out of the closet, however, there is not much else in the song that suggests that Bowie is making reference to sexual identity. In the second verse, Bowie deals with the struggle between generations and urges parents of teenagers to allow their children to be themselves.

One of the easiest-to-overlook lyrical references in "Changes" is to the aging of "rock and rollers." With nothing to back this up save circumstantial evidence, I believe that it is quite possible that Bowie is addressing the rock stars who came to prominence in the early 1960s. At the time of this song, in 1971, the Beatles were no more, and Jimi Hendrix, Janis Joplin, and Jim Morrison had all died. Interestingly, the Rolling Stones, who back in the mid-1960s were singing that "time [was] on their side," in an American rhythm and blues song they had covered ("Time Is on My Side"), were within a year of Bowie's *Hunky Dory* acknowledging that "time waits for no one," in their song of the same title. Bowie at once acknowledges that time marches on and that people had better be prepared to accept that fact. In retrospect, this small part from the last iteration of the chorus of "Changes" seems especially ironic, for, over the years David Bowie has been one of the few rock stars to have successfully integrated styles from the 1960s through the twenty-first century in his music. In doing so, he has proven himself to be perhaps the rock star least affected by age. Interestingly, Bowie's most recent three albums, *hours...*, *Heathen*, and *Reality*, deal with the subjects of aging and mortality. The main difference between "Changes" and his later albums is his own age: Bowie turned 50 a couple of years before the release of the 1999 album *hours...*, whereas on "Changes," he was all of 25.

Although David Bowie's previous recordings had sometimes featured him as a rhythm guitarist, sometimes including some twelve-string acoustic guitar work, "Changes" represents the first feature of David Bowie as saxophonist in his solo recordings. Bowie's background work on saxophone on "Changes" is easy to lose in the rich texture of the song, but his tenor sax solo at the end of the song is fully out front. Although Bowie plays just briefly, he proves himself to be a fully functional jazz-inspired rock saxophonist. It should be noted, however, that generally Bowie's work on tenor saxophone is superior to his alto sax playing, which tends not to be as well in tune.

"Oh! You Pretty Things" finds Bowie reworking a lyrical premise from his obscure "We Are Hungry Men" single. On the song "We Are Hungry Men" he had explored the issue of the establishment of a master race to rule the earth. "Oh! You Pretty Things" pinpoints the younger generation, the "pretty things" of the song's title, as a master race that will eventually establish its rule. The premise with which Bowie is working is an interesting one. On the one hand it suggests such things as the desire for a pure Aryan race during the Nazi period in twentieth-century Germany, as well as other notorious cases of ethnic genocide, but on the other hand, it can be seen as a rather colorful and thought-provoking way of describing the generational changeover and the desire of each generation that life will be better for the next. And yet—because Bowie does not specify the gender of the "pretty things"—he could be addressing "pretty" boys, the song could be interpreted to be about homosexuality. Like some of Bowie's best lyrics, the references here are just vague enough, with just enough potential double entendre built in to allow the listener to hear several possible meanings, each of which can be supported as the so-called correct interpretation.

The song's music includes a strong melodic hook in the chorus, which contrasts nicely with a rather understated, lower-pitched melody in the verses. Bowie's performance involves a touch of his old Anthony Newley-style singing, which though notably absent from the earlier album *The Man Who Sold the World*, works well in several *Hunky Dory* songs as a way of enhancing the theatricality of the project.

With a chord progression that is reminiscent of the Rolling Stones' ballad "Wild Horses," which was in fact recorded in the same year as *Hunky Dory,* "Eight Line Poem" is a fairly conventional gentle, country-blues rock song—at least musically. The text is, as the song's title implies, an eight-line, highly impressionistic poem in free verse style. Of all the songs on *Hunky Dory,* this is perhaps the least evocative and the least essential.

In "Life on Mars?" Bowie paints the movie theater as an escape for a girl who is at odds with her parents and wanders through town in search for some sort of brief escape from reality. The real meat of the lyrics, though, is in the way in which Bowie weaves together a long series of disconnected images that one might find in watching random films from different eras. Musically, he contrasts the narrow range and thin texture of the rather plaintive verses—it is in the first of the two verses that we learn of the girl and her travails in making sense out of her life and her relationship with her parents—with an expansive and fully orchestrated chorus, in which he presents the cinematic images.

The title line of "Life on Mars?" is just one of the many cinematic images found in the song. It is worth noting, however, that with the release of the next Bowie album after *Hunky Dory,* Bowie's band would take on the identity of the Spiders from Mars. Certainly, the science fiction character that Bowie and company would soon adopt is theatrical and cinematic. It would seem to germinate from the twin kernels of the fleeting image in "Life on

Mars?" and the androgynous outcast Bowie had earlier portrayed on *The Man Who Sold the World*.

One of the features of *Hunky Dory* that really helps the album to work effectively is Bowie's use of ever-changing frames of reference. Some of the songs are observational (the plight of the main character in "Life on Mars?," for example), some address groups of people (parents and his fellow rock and rollers in "Changes," for example), and some find Bowie addressing or observing celebrities ("Song for Bob Dylan" and "Andy Warhol"). The song "Kooks" finds Bowie addressing an individual of indeterminate gender who seems to be on the receiving end of an invitation from Bowie's character to move in with Bowie and his lover (who also is of non-specified gender). Could this be an invitation to a ménage à trois? Is this an invitation to someone that the couple would simply like to help get back on his or her feet? It could be either, since Bowie's lyrics are just vague enough that the nature of the relationship of the three is open to interpretation.

The British music hall music in "Kooks," as well as Bowie's dialect, evokes images of that other David Jones, the Monkees star. This was a musical style that had been noticeably absent from Bowie's work since he'd moved into folk music on *Man of Words, Man of Music* and hard rock and heavy metal on *The Man Who Sold the World*. His recapturing of a style that he had used very early in his career—in the Deram years—shows that Bowie was well on his way to creating a full composite voice, one in which he would integrate a wide variety of musical and lyrical styles. As an album, *Hunky Dory* is a significant step along that path; however, though the musical heaviness that had been the hallmark of *The Man Who Sold the World* is almost completely absent, it would take Bowie one more album to achieve a classic balance.

In the song "Quicksand," Bowie portrays a tragic character that essentially has given up all hope for the future. It is only through death that his character's self knowledge can come. With his reference to the unrealized potential that he has to be "Superman," the song represents a darker side of "Oh! You Pretty Things." Musically, the song features elements of folk, classical, and a touch of hard rock music. One of the stronger features is Bowie's effective use of the kind of chromatic harmony that marks the most memorable songs that George Harrison was writing at the end of the 1960s and in the early 1970s. The almost anthem-like quality of the song, though, stands in sharp relief to the rather depressing lyrical sentiments. While in some cases this sort of contradiction can force the listener into hearing an inner meaning to the song, one filled with irony, "Quicksand" tends to leave the listener more with a feeling of confusion.

"Fill Your Heart," which was written by Biff Rose and Paul Williams, is the sole non-Bowie song on *Hunky Dory*. A jazzy, music hall number, its music and playful message of happiness seem not to fit the overall focus of the album particularly well. Bowie, however, does offer some nice saxophone playing on the song.

Co-producers Ken Scott and "the actor" (Bowie) transform the last saxophone notes of "Fill Your Heart" into the beginning of a brief segue into the song "Andy Warhol." The segue includes some processed studio dialogue that suggests the way in which Warhol incorporated found objects, such as the famous Campbell's soup can, into his art. This is a much more successful and substantial song than the preceding three *Hunky Dory* tracks. Bowie makes reference to Warhol's paintings, silk screens, films, and live performance pieces, which captured consumerism and the dark side of life. Bowie was aware of the famous paintings, as they were part of worldwide pop culture at the time, but he was also familiar with the voyeuristic side of Warhol's film and live-performance pieces, having seen a production of *Andy Warhol's Pork* in London. It was this production that inspired the song "Andy Warhol."[2] Bowie's minor-key folk-rock music enhances the dark undercurrent of the verses of the song.

Interestingly, when David Bowie traveled to New York shortly after the release of *Hunky Dory,* he had the opportunity to meet Warhol, hear Warhol's project, Lou Reed's band, the Velvet Underground, and to play the song "Andy Warhol" for Warhol and his entourage. According to Warhol biographers, the artist was offended by Bowie's reference to Warhol's appearance as "a scream."[3] A thorough listening to Bowie's lyrics would seem to suggest that to Bowie, Warhol himself is not as interesting as an artist as the real life objects and people Warhol observes and tries to recreate. However, Warhol's biographers do not mention this interpretation of the song in reference to the offense their subject took with the song.

Incidentally, Bowie's meeting with Lou Reed would prove to be important for both artists, as they mutually were drawn to dark subjects. Bowie would perform as a guest vocalist on Reed's 1972 album *Transformer* (RCA Victor LSP-4807), and the two musicians would continue to be linked through the singer-songwriter Iggy Pop for years. Bowie would also later be linked with Warhol, however, in a way that never could have been predicted back in the early 1970s: Bowie would portray the artist in the 1996 film *Basquiat.* Interestingly, the man who in 1971 characterized Warhol's appearance as "a scream" would don one of Warhol's white wigs in this film a quarter-century later.

Within the whole gestalt of pop music performance (writing, arranging, playing, and singing), David Bowie is characterized by writer after writer as a chameleon. While the stereotype of Bowie as chameleon is a bit dubious, it is safe to say that Bowie has explored many different musical and lyrical styles. The thing that is of utmost importance to remember is that all of the different musical styles, character portrayals, and rhetorical styles require a more expressive—or at least adaptable—vocal technique than just singing the notes, syllables, and rhythms. Bowie's "Song for Bob Dylan" is a rare example of Bowie overtly imitating another singer. He hits the mark quite well vocally and incorporates a number of Dylanesque touches in his lyrics and music.

Bowie's lyrics in "Song for Bob Dylan" clearly differentiate between Robert Zimmerman—Dylan's real name—and Bob Dylan. It is as though Bowie sees Dylan as being a character that Zimmerman portrays. Although it is possible to make too much of this, the same could be said of the relationship between David Jones and David Bowie: one, the real man, and the other, the public performance persona. Bowie paints Dylan's importance as a generational voice, but also projects the feeling that Dylan's importance as someone who raises questions about political and social values has been on the wane. In large part, the song asks Zimmerman to bring back the relevant Dylan of old.

The simple descending bass line that accompanies Bowie's folk-rock chord progression in "Song for Bob Dylan" suggests 1965–1966 Dylan. One of the musical highpoints of the song, however, is the unexpected key change and texture change for the chorus section. In the chorus sections, Rick Wakeman's virtuoso piano playing and Mick Ronson's expressive lead guitar drive the song along. Melodically, too, Bowie's writing reflects the influence of Dylan with its stark contrasts between a narrow-range verse and soaring chorus. More than a mere imitation of Dylan as a writer and singer, however, Bowie's song raises issues about the artistic direction Dylan/Zimmerman had taken, and about the needs of both social groups and individuals to have artists who represent them and are able to give them a pop culture voice.

In the next song on *Hunky Dory*, "Queen Bitch," Bowie portrays a character whose male roommate—or lover—turns to picking up a drag queen on the street after Bowie's character refuses his advances. Bowie observes both characters from an apartment window and, in remarking about the drag queen's exaggerated (and stereotypical) mannerisms, concludes that he "could do better than that." However, this is another of those Bowie songs about either homosexuality or bisexuality that is just vague enough that it is unclear exactly what the orientation of Bowie's character really is. Perhaps the most likely reading of the lyrics, supported by Bowie's affected voice, is that the character regrets not being the current object of the roommate's lust.

Since so much of *Hunky Dory* reflects an acoustic guitar, folkish flavor as well as either Rick Wakeman or Bowie on piano on most songs, generally the album does not resemble *The Man Who Sold the Earth* or Bowie's post-*Hunky Dory* albums. The most notable exceptions are "Changes," with its clearly pop-oriented music and lyrics about generational conflicts, and "Queen Bitch," with its harder rock style and lyrics about drag queens and anonymous on-the-street sexual hookups. "Queen Bitch" is catchy, well rhymed, and is performed theatrically enough by Bowie that the song remains effective decades later better than most of the material on *Hunky Dory*. In fact, it is a glam rock classic and sets up the lyrical and musical style of Bowie's next two albums like nothing else on *Hunky Dory*. The lasting quality of the song is confirmed by its appearance in the soundtrack of the movie *The Life Aquatic,* over thirty years after its initial release.

The thing that is most striking about "Queen Bitch," however, runs beyond the lyrics and the music. Bowie's lyrics, music, and his vocal performance are about campiness. His mannered vocal work makes it clear that this song is made up of a couple of stereotypical external manifestations of gayness: camp and queenish cattiness. His vocal approach also helps to highlight the voyeuristic aspects of the lyrics. So, is "Queen Bitch" something that can be taken seriously as a so-called gay song? Consider the song "Daniel," which was written by two openly gay contemporaries of Bowie, Elton John and Bernie Taupin. The Elton John song—from about the same time period—is understated in lyrics, music, and performance. Yes, the character Daniel could literally be John's character's "brother," as he is identified in Taupin's lyrics, however, the bond between the two characters could be that of lovers just as easily. In fact, the song seems to make more sense as a piece about a broken non-sibling relationship than it does as a story about two siblings. To the extent that the listener hears "Daniel" as a song about a love relationship that has gone south and a character (Daniel) who harbors deep-seated emotional pain from an experience that happened years before (coming out of the closet, perhaps?), it is thoroughly sensitive and near universal: the feelings of the characters could be projected onto gays or straights. "Queen Bitch," though, is all about stereotypes. In the final analysis the difference between the two contemporaneous songs would seem to be that one is the work of a gay artist who is unwilling to identify himself as gay (Elton John would not profess his sexual orientation openly for another couple of years), while the other is by an artist who goes out of his way to scream, "Look at me, I'm gay." The irony is that, while Bowie's biographers—and eventually Bowie himself—would claim that he was a closet heterosexual,[4] and despite the reliance on stereotype, "Queen Bitch" is highly effective as a piece of pop music theater.

The final song on *Hunky Dory*, "The Bewlay Brothers," is a strange collection of disparate images that many David Bowie fans believe reflect the complexity of Bowie's mental, psychological, religious, and sexual state, both at the time, and from his youth.[5] Certainly, there are clues in the lyrics that suggest as much—including the fact that the title of the song was inspired by the name of a tobacconist shop located near Bowie's childhood home—however, he paints the images in such broad strokes that autobiographical specifics are difficult to discern.[6] More so than any other song on the album, the lyrics of "The Bewlay Brothers" are open to a wide variety of interpretations, mostly due to their highly impressionistic nature and also to the fact that they seem to appear in almost stream-of-consciousness order. Just as the fantasy-like images meander, so does the music of the verses. Bowie's musical material in the chorus sections is more concise and accessible. Throughout the song, he works in a psychedelic folk style, related to but much more distinctive than the pseudo-Donovan style Bowie had used earlier in his career. Curiously, the musical and lyrical sense of foreboding and emotional uncertainty raise the question of just how "hunky dory" things had been in David Bowie's life up through this time. Be that as it may, it is a piece that presents the listener with a wide palette of sounds and quite a lot of imagery to raise many questions and to encourage careful, active listening.

*Hunky Dory* found David Bowie bringing together many of the themes that he would continue to explore in his more popular work together on one album. These themes include isolation, the questioning of sexuality and gender roles, rejection, and the dark underside of human psychology and sociology. Musically, Bowie was still playing the role of a ping-pong ball: the folk psychedelia of *Man of Words, Man of Music,* had given way to the hard rock and heavy metal of *The Man Who Sold the World,* only to return along with a more accessible pop approach on *Hunky Dory.* What Bowie needed in order to breakout as a world-famous star was just a slightly more focused, fully integrated approach. That approach would come with his next album.

## THE RISE AND FALL OF ZIGGY STARDUST AND THE SPIDERS FROM MARS[7]

Anyone who has heard David Bowie's famous song "Ziggy Stardust" knows that "Ziggy played guitar." For those who have not heard the entire album *The Rise and Fall of Ziggy Stardust and the Spiders from Mars,* that might be just about as far as it goes. In fact, this package is a 1972 concept album that concerns the fictional character Ziggy Stardust, his band, the Spiders from Mars, and others who are directly involved with them, including groupies and more casual fans. There is not so much a coherent storyline as a wide-ranging series of snapshots of the life of and around the fictional band. If one, then, takes the title of the album too literally in defining the concept, the program seems to, as critics have duly noted, run somewhat thinly through the work.[8] However, if one defines the concept more broadly, as a hazy, impressionistic look at the entire rock and roll scene and lifestyle through and around Ziggy Stardust and the Spiders from Mars, it is a viable concept album, positioned somewhere between the looseness of the Beatles' *Sgt. Pepper's Lonely Hearts Club Band,* and more fully focused works such as the Who's *Tommy* or Marvin Gaye's *What's Going On.* It was the album that made David Bowie a star of major proportion in the United States. More importantly, it was the album that found Bowie creating a fully coherent, unified artist statement that fully integrated all of the stylistic voices with which he had experimented in the past. The androgynous glam and metal figure is here, as is Bowie's Anthony Newley figure, not to mention the folksinger, the consummate societal outsider, and the mainstream pop musician. What Bowie does here is to weave all of these voices and styles into one. In short, he becomes a man of contradictions, yet (irony of ironies) a man of a strange consistency. *The Rise and Fall of Ziggy Stardust and the Spiders from Mars* is also important purely from a musical standpoint. The album contains Bowie's fully integrated versions of a number of contemporary styles, and it anticipates styles such as punk rock, which would not become mainstream within pop music for nearly half a decade.

*Ziggy Stardust* opens with a minimalistic drum figure that bears resemblance to Carl Palmer's drum work in the fadeout of Emerson, Lake and Palmer's 1971 hit "Lucky Man."[9] Like the story of the "lucky man" of the Emerson, Lake and Palmer song, the story of Ziggy Stardust, his band, and the fans, groupies, and assorted hangers on turns out to be anything but a happy tale. That is about where the resemblance between the two songs ends, though. The song "Five Years," which begins *Ziggy Stardust,* effectively introduces the characters that presumably make up the Spiders from Mars. I say "effectively" because Bowie does not clearly identify them as members of the fictional band. Given the context with the album's programmatic concept, however, one can logically make the connection. Bowie presents apocalyptic images of a dying earth, street violence, public apathy, and personal alienation. In the context of the album and its fictional band, it is this dark, gloomy scene that seems to have driven the boys into music: music was the ticket out of the urban British environment. It is never clear, however, if the five years that Bowie's character and his mates "got" is time to live, jail time for some unspoken crime, or perhaps the duration of the Spiders' career. One unspoken thing that comes through clearly in the song is that the name of the band probably represents a desire to escape from the harsh realities of being an earthling.

The song "Five Years" is written in what even in 1972 would have been considered something of a retro style. His music resembles slow gospel-influenced late 1950s rock and roll more than just about anything his has ever written before or since, especially with its repeated diatonic chord progression that is a slight reworking of the old "Heart and Soul" I-vi-IV-V structure.[10] The gospel feel and use of short, simple, largely diatonic chord progressions was certainly in the air in the early 1970s. Several Carole King songs come to mind: "Way over Yonder" and "You've Got a Friend" from the 1970 album *Tapestry,* in particular. There is an even closer relationship to John Lennon's song "God," from the 1970 album *John Lennon/Plastic Ono Band.* The sonic resemblance to the Lennon song is especially interesting, considering that "God" deals with and was inspired in part by the breakup of the Beatles, while the Bowie album deals with the rise and fall of a fictional band. The use of a simple 1950s-derived harmonic progression was in the air in other musical styles in the 1970s as well: Jeff Lynne, chief composer of the Electric Light Orchestra (E.L.O.), wrote a number of hit songs that made generous use of the I-vi-IV-V progression. It is easy enough to hear the Bowie-E.L.O. relationship on this track. Incidentally, the retro feel on *Ziggy Stardust* is not limited to "Five Years." Bowie's incorporates elements of older pop and rock sounds several times throughout the album. Each time he does so, Bowie includes a little twist so that the songs never lose their 1970s feel and therefore never turn into purely nostalgia pieces.

The next track, "Soul Love" would seem to be a song from the Spiders from Mars. For one thing, it is a rare Bowie composition that actually uses the word, "love." In fact, the entire focus is on various positive and negative forms of love. Incidentally, not only were references to love rare in Bowie's work from the period; his later song "Be My Wife," from *Low*, is perhaps the only marriage proposal ever put forward in song that never once uses the word "love."

Bowie's arrangement on "Soul Love" also suggests that this is supposed to be one of the Spiders' "hits." The pop-jazz orchestration is very "un-Bowie" and Bowie's vocal approach finds him seemingly imitating the other David Jones, the Manchester-born member of the Monkees who was particularly well known for his middle-of-the-road pop performances. In addition, Bowie's lead vocal is double tracked on the first line of each phrase, which creates the effect of two singers performing. This suggests a band—rather than a solo—performance. It should also be noted that although Bowie's best saxophone work on record features him playing the larger saxes (tenor and baritone), "Soul Love" is perhaps his best recorded alto saxophone performance ever released commercially.

"Moonage Daydream," the next track on *Ziggy Stardust,* uses strong harmonic (a diatonically descending progression) and melodic hooks. Bowie's vocal melody and arrangement in the song's chorus sections also closely resemble Elton John's contemporary work (notably "Tiny Dancer"), although "Moonage Daydream" includes enough of a touch of heavy metal-style electric guitar and percussion in the verses and at the end of each statement of the chorus, so as to provide a bit of distance from John's music. Not only was the name of the fictional band, the Spiders from Mars, possibly related to the gloomy prognosis for the survival of Planet Earth introduced in "Five Years," it also provided the opportunity to include references to extraterrestrial life on several tracks, including this one. The lyrics of "Moonage Daydream," in contrast to the intuitive-sounding music, are a bit abstract—all well and good for a song from a fictional band, but something that makes the song one of least memorable of the album.

The next song, "Starman," features one of Bowie's strongest commercial melodic hooks in the chorus. The harmonic progression is just as intuitive-sounding as that of "Moonage Daydream," and in fact bears some resemblance in the verses to the earlier song. Since one of the hallmarks of the *Ziggy Stardust* album was the way in which Bowie captures a bunch of contemporary styles, it is worth noting that the instrumental work in the bridge between the chorus and following verses is closely related to the sound of the popular early 1970s Apple Records band Badfinger, both in content and in electric guitar tone color.

"Starman" is another song that references extraterrestrial life, seemingly the thing that defines the fictitious Ziggy Stardust and the Spiders from Mars. Here, the extraterrestrial, the Starman of the song's title, debates making an appearance to Earthlings, but decides against doing so as not to "blow our minds." Because of the fact that Bowie writes that the Starman had at one time given humans the order "not to blow it," the character takes on a God-like quality. It is the view of the creator as an extraterrestrial who visited Earth ages ago to start life, and now is keeping tabs on just how human life is progressing. Part of the beauty of Bowie's lyrics is that the Starman character can be taken literally (the alien space creature and creator) or as a metaphor for the rock star who once was an equal of members of his audience, but is now looked upon as a Messianic figure who can no longer hang with the crowd.

The Ron Davies song "It Ain't Easy" is the sole non-Bowie song on *Ziggy Stardust*. Bowie's albums of the period—*Hunky Dory, Ziggy Stardust,* and *Aladdin Sane*—each featured one well-chosen cover track that played an important structural role: this one on *Ziggy Stardust* and "Let's Spend the Night Together" on *Aladdin Sane* function more successfully than "Fill Your Heart" on *Hunky Dory*. The Davies song, while ultimately optimistic, suggests the development of a crack in the dream life of the rock star. The sense is that the singer is teetering on the edge and his rock-star lifestyle could ultimately end in disaster or in glory. The song sets up the darkness that emerges more and more as the album progresses.

Apparently, the fictional members of the "public" who counted themselves among the fans of Ziggy and the Spiders were not aware of the darkness that lurked beneath the surface, at least if the song "Lady Stardust" is any indication. This song is an anthem that extols the virtues of the androgynous Ziggy (the title character in this song) and the beauty of he and his band in concert—all of this from the viewpoint of a fan. With its moderate tempo, piano-based accompaniment, and strong pop hook, "Lady Stardust" finds itself in the same structural and stylistic ballpark as early and mid-1970s top-40 favorites by singer-pianists such as Elton John and Billy Joel.

The next song, "Star" also resembles the piano-based retro rock feel of Elton John, in particular the well-known songs "Crocodile Rock" and "Saturday Night's Alright for Fighting." Incidentally, these two Elton John songs became hits just after the release of the Bowie album. "Star" portrays a young man who has chosen to pursue the dream of becoming a rock and roll star, while all of his old school buddies have scattered off in various directions. The song fits the program of *Ziggy Stardust;* however, it falls in a curious place on the album: if Bowie's character is supposed to be a member of the Spiders from Mars, or even Ziggy Stardust himself, as would seem to be the case, the track should have been placed earlier on the album. In part because of the fact that the song seems chronologically out of place, and in part because it is perhaps the least substantial piece (lyrically and musically) on the album, "Star" is perhaps the weakest track on the album.

"Hang on to Yourself" is perhaps the closest David Bowie performance to suggest the work of his friend and fellow glam-rock star Marc Bolan. Significantly, Bowie's writing, the electric guitar playing of Mick Ronson, and Bowie and Ronson's arrangement all anticipate the musical sound of mid-to-late-1970s punk rock. In particular, British bands such as the Damned and the Sex Pistols come to mind, as does the American band the Ramones. "Hang on to Yourself," though has just enough of the glam ethos and just enough dynamic contrast that it does not sound like a prototypical punk rock song. The roots of the 1970s punk style, probably by way of Iggy Pop and the Stooges and other late-1960s Detroit-area bands such as the MC5, however, are certainly in evidence.

"Hang on to Yourself" portrays a male rock star who anticipates a sexual encounter with a well-known groupie. While Bowie's text makes it clear that his character's primary aim purely is physical satisfaction, this song does not exhibit the depth of Gerry Goffin and Carole King's "Star Collector," a 1967 song recorded by the Monkees, or the Rolling Stones' 1973 "Star Star." In those two songs, the rock stars exhibit a mix of desire and disdain for the women who give them near-anonymous physical pleasure; they are exposed as users of women. And, the Mick Jagger and Keith Richards composition "Star Star" brings out the sleaziness of rock star, groupie sex more effectively and more graphically than the Bowie song. Lyrically and musically, with its glam-rock concept and focus on sex for the sake of physical pleasure, "Star" also is at least a cousin of Marc Bolan's 1971 T. Rex hit "Bang a Gong (Get It On)." Again, however, the Bolan song brings out the irony of the peculiar mix of attraction and revulsion ("dirty sweet" is how Bolan describes the object of his sexual desire) a little more clearly than Bowie's "Hang on to Yourself."

Even though the song "Ziggy Stardust" works well conceptually as an independent composition (it does not require the context of this album in order to make sense), it serves an important purpose in giving the Ziggy Stardust album a conceptual focal point. Several of the album's songs deal more generically with the idea of rock stardom; this song puts it all into focus with the story of the fictional band Ziggy Stardust and the Spiders from Mars. By putting faces and a name on the characters Bowie not only provides stronger focus for the album, but also provides a reason for the sub theme of extraterrestrial life that marks a few of the album's early songs (e.g., the sub theme ties in with the band's name). This song's placement late on the album helps to tie the disparate songs that precede it together.

"Suffragette City," the album's penultimate song, is perhaps the second best-known song on the Ziggy Stardust album, second only to the title track itself. Ironically, it is one of the album's tracks that fit in less obviously with the programmatic theme; however, it remains one of the strongest straight-ahead rock songs that David Bowie has ever written and recorded. The exact relationship of all the characters is open to interpretation. The listener never learns, for example, what the exact nature of the relationship of Bowie's character and "Henry." It would seem that Henry and Bowie's character are roommates and that this is a classic case of one roommate trying to get rid of the other so that he can have sex with a girlfriend. Or, perhaps Henry just likes to hang with Bowie's character and this just is *not* the time for him to hang out. While Bowie's lyrics are not particularly tawdry or graphic, it is crystal clear that his character has just enjoyed a sexual encounter with a woman who apparently will be arriving back at his character's place. But, alas, Henry insists on hanging out. That is about as far as "Suffragette City" goes: it sets up a situation, but never resolves the conflict. Despite this open-endedness, it is a strong enough composition, arrangement, and vocal and instrumental performance by Bowie and his band that it could be about just anything and still be successful as a rock and roll song.

Although the song has a stronger sense of theatricality in Bowie's later *Ziggy Stardust* concert film, "Rock 'n' Roll Suicide" as a purely musical expression (absent the drama of Bowie's costumed and choreographed live performance) provides a strong end to the album. Here, Bowie addresses all the disillusioned young people who try to find some meaning for their lives through music, when family, peers, and everyone and everything else seems to let them down. Here the understanding rock star offers his hand to the forlorn young person in an effort to rescue them. At first glance the song might not seem to fit the program of *Ziggy Stardust,* especially given that the story might seem to be over once the listener hears the story of the fall of Ziggy two songs earlier. The focus of the song is on the disen-franchised disaffected youth (both singular and plural) that make(s) up the rock audience. The most obvious messages of the song are that despite their feelings to the contrary, the suicidal youth truly is "not alone," and that there are some heroes out there who really do care about helping teens make it through the rough times. The unspoken message—whether Bowie intended it or not—that comes from placing this song at the end of this particular album is that bands may come and go, but the audience for a music that speaks to their generation will remain. Viewed that way, "Rock 'n' Roll Suicide" brings perfect closure to Bowie's journey through the rock lifestyle and the rise and fall of one fictional band. Perhaps the mes-sage of *Ziggy Stardust* is that the music and audience's interaction with it is ultimately more important than any rock star or any band.

Like several of the songs on the album, "Rock 'n' Roll Suicide" uses a simple and long-standing chord progression, which effectively links the music of the early 1970s to the rock of the 1950s and early 1960s. Although the harmony is based largely on these early rock models, the song's overall struc-ture is more complex than most rock songs. It is not in a verse-verse-verse-verse form like a blues-based song, nor is it in the Tin Pan Alley A-A-B-A form. There are essentially two verses and then repetitions of a chorus. The interesting thing is that the "chorus," such as it is, is so closely related melodi-cally and harmonically to the verses that the effect is of an evolving variation form, something more likely to be found in a nineteenth-century art song or a twentieth-century musical theater song than a rock song per se. And, the idea of "Rock 'n' Roll Suicide" as a piece from a musical theater performance is not too far fetched. The minimalistic texture of acoustic guitar and Bowie's voice in an updated version of his "Anthony Newley" voice at the beginning of the song resembles cabaret music: the image of a male Edith Piaf (or maybe

Marlene Dietrich) in the rock era comes to mind. The texture builds over the course of the rest of the song, as does the intensity of Bowie's voice until it reaches a climax as he metaphorically stretches out his hand to the young person standing on the ledge about to jump. While there were bigger, longer, more elaborately arranged theatrical pieces later to come from artists ranging from Queen to Meat Loaf, and while there were several classics in the genre that had come from the pen of Jim Morrison of the Doors back in the late 1960s, "Rock 'n' Roll Suicide" is a highly effective example of the rock theater genre. It is not as big as "Paradise by the Dashboard Light" (Meat Loaf), "The Celebration of the Lizard" (the Doors), or "Bohemian Rhapsody" (Queen), but is packed with a strong musical and dramatic progression.

Although it certainly is in evidence on "Rock 'n' Roll Suicide," one of the sonic features that runs throughout the entire *Ziggy Stardust* album is David Bowie's acoustic rhythm guitar playing. Throughout his career, Bowie has been known primarily for his compositions and for his voice. Fans can hear his saxophone playing on many of his post-1960s albums, and Bowie's work as a pianist, synthesizer player and programmer, and occasional harmonica player typically come more to the fore than does his guitar playing.[11] Although the listener probably tends to be drawn more to Mick Ronson's lead guitar playing on *Ziggy Stardust,* it is one of the better albums at highlighting Bowie's rhythm guitar playing.

So, in the final analysis, what is it that makes *The Rise and Fall of Ziggy Stardust and the Spiders from Mars* stand out as the first great David Bowie album? Here, for the first time, Bowie built an entire album around a single, well-defined theme: the rock star. The success of the album has everything to do with how conceptual focus allowed David Bowie the freedom to include all of the musical styles, while never letting the songs meander from lyrical theme to lyrical theme. The focus can also be seen in Bowie's tightly structured poetry: song-by-song the lyrics are shorter and in a more predicable rhyme scheme than the songs of his previous three albums. The music, too, is more focused—full of melodic and harmonic hooks. The songs are progressive without *sounding* experimental, yet possess much more commercial possibility than the vast majority of the songs of Bowie's folk and heavy metal phases.

While *The Rise and Fall of Ziggy Stardust and the Spiders from Mars* may not be the first glam-rock album, a title sometimes given to T. Rex's *Electric Warrior* (1971), it is in some respects the quintessential glam-rock statement, filled with sex, sexual ambiguity, a tawdry sense of fashion, and driving rock music. Marc Bolan's poetry on *Electric Warrior* tended to meander somewhat like Bowie's did prior to *Ziggy Stardust. Ziggy Stardust,* on the other hand, has a much tighter focus, and its clear concept probably was what helped Bowie to be seen in the United States as the quintessential glam-rock star. The earlier psychedelic-folk incarnation of Bowie and the similarly wide-ranging impressionistic Bolan did not have what it truly took to stake a claim on the American youth audience, at least compared with the Bowie of the *Ziggy Stardust* album.

Although not a track on Bowie's *Ziggy Stardust* album, "John, I'm Only Dancing" is a Bowie song that dates from the same period, and was in fact released as the B-side of the U.K. release of the "Starman" single. It is easy to understand why the song was not included on the album: it does not fit the album's theme particularly well. "John, I'm Only Dancing," however, is an interesting song, especially in the context of Bowie's musical exploration of sexual orientation in his 1971–1973 work. And, yes, it is another one of these genre songs that leaves sexual orientation up to the interpretation of the listener. The title character John seems to have caught Bowie's character dancing with a woman to whom Bowie's character is attracted. Bowie's character tries to explain that, while he needs love, and is attracted to the woman, he is "only dancing." He, essentially, makes light of the relationship between himself and the woman. What is unclear is exactly why he feels that he has to explain away the situation to John. It would seem that either Bowie's character and John are lovers, or John and the woman with whom Bowie's character is dancing are lovers. The listener can interpret either meaning into the relationship, depending upon what he or she wants to hear. "John, I'm Only Dancing" raises interesting questions about sexual identity and stereotyping. Questions such as "What makes me think that Bowie's character is bisexual?" or, "Do I hear any stereotypes of supposedly gay mannerisms in Bowie's vocal style that lead me to believe that the character is bisexual?" as well as many other questions, can arise from deconstruction of one's reaction to an interpretation of the song. And, this is one of the great values of Bowie's work of the early 1970s—it forces everyone but the most casual of listeners to deal with identity questions (whether sexual or otherwise) both in the characters in the songs and in the listeners themselves. Even into the twenty-first century, Bowie continues to create lyrics that can be open to interpretation, which in turn encourages listeners to grapple with questions of identity.

The year 1972 had seen David Bowie breaking into the big time internationally. In addition to his own recordings of the year, he began working with other artists, including Lou Reed and Iggy Pop. Bowie also appeared as a guest saxophonist on the Mott the Hoople album *All the Young Dudes* (Columbia KC 31750), an album for which Bowie composed the title song.

## ALADDIN SANE

The year 1972 also included the recording of *Aladdin Sane*, an album that bears a 1973 copyright date. Although it represents Bowie's continuation of the *Ziggy Stardust* style and attention to the musical and lyrical themes of glam-rock, *Aladdin Sane* is somewhat more scattered than Bowie's previous album with regards to structure, sound, and style. There is a basic theme that ties at least part of the album together: the concept and definition of sanity. Though the concepts of the two albums are different, each deal with the concept of learning how to cope with difficulties. A fair number of the songs of *Aladdin Sane* deal with coping with one's psychological state; the songs of *Ziggy Stardust* deal with coping with stardom, coping with the realities of life for youths, and coping with professional jealousies, and so forth. Musically, too, the two albums are related, but with important foreground distinctions: Bowie's compositions on *Aladdin Sane* are not as conventionally pop-oriented as those of *Ziggy Stardust,* probably because the fictional Spiders from Mars band was in Bowie's conception of the nature of the group more pop-oriented than Bowie himself. The other reason for the relative lack of so-called pretty melodic and harmonic hooks was probably the fact that on *Aladdin Sane* Bowie is working with lyrics that are darker and more inwardly focused and analytical than those of *Ziggy Stardust.* As a result, *Aladdin Sane* is not as accessible, requires more careful listening, and ultimately is not as well remembered as its immediate predecessor.

Bowie's "Watch that Man" leads off the album. Unfortunately, the recording is marred by the fact that Bowie's vocals are somewhat covered in the mix.[12] This is not a problem, however, just with this one track: nearly every song on the album features a more obscure vocal setting than the songs of *The Rise and Fall of Ziggy Stardust and the Spiders from Mars.* With its hard rock style and obscure, impressionistic lyrics, "Watch that Man" fits right in with the glam style developed by Marc Bolan. There are also compositional, arrangement, and production ties with the contemporary rock songs of Elton John and the *Exile on Main Street* style of the Rolling Stones. So, "Watch that Man" sounds very much like what was in the air, rock music-wise, in the early 1970s. Unfortunately, the universality of the style, along with the lyrical and musical ties to the Bowie songs "John, I'm Only Dancing" and "Diamond Dogs," tends to make "Watch that Man" sound like a work in progress—it is not cutting edge in the way that some of Bowie's best songs are.

Bowie's play-on-words title song, "Aladdin Sane (1913–1938–197?)" (a lad insane), follows. It shares a spirit of impressionism and lyrical obscurity with "Watch that Man" and other songs on the album. The thing, though, that really makes it clear to the listener that Bowie really refers to "a lad insane," and not Aladdin Sane (as it is presented in the printed lyrics and song title), is the musical setting. Bowie's backing vocal arrangement and Mike Garson's avant-garde piano playing (which contains sharply dissonant virtuosic runs and arpeggios, as well as dissonant snippets of well-known tunes from George Gershwin and others) give the piece an otherworldly sound. The lyrics and musical setting speak of disconnection from reality and the alienation felt by the outsider, in this case the character Aladdin Sane. Incidentally, Mike Garson's piano work of "Aladdin Sane" and throughout the album is strongly reminiscent of the similarly over-the-top piano playing of Lincoln Mayorga on the 1967 Phil Ochs album *Pleasures of the Harbor* (an album with a related focus on alienation).

"Drive-In Saturday" continues the style of the songs Bowie wrote for his fictional Spiders from Mars band for his previous album. Here, we have music that seems at first to come straight out of the late 1950s doo-wop era, ironically matched to lyrics of obscurity, casual sex, lust for the alpha-male rock star, and a touch of kinkiness (not at all the kind of thing that one would actually have heard in a 1950s doo-wop song). This is the kind of deliberate mismatch of music and lyrics that Frank Zappa would use on numerous occasions in his own work to satirical effect. In Bowie's hands, though, a mismatch such as this is not really social satire; it seems meant more to force the listener to deal with inward assumptions and feelings. One of the more interesting aspects of the piece can be found in Bowie's musical writing, particularly in song structure. While each verse and the chorus maintain the rhythmic feel of 1950s pop, and start with melodic and harmonic material that would be not at all be out of place in an actual song from that era, the verses are extended beyond the conventional 8- or 16-measure length, and the harmony moves farther and farther a field from actual music of the 1950s. This allows the listener immediately to detect Bowie's musical reference, but also to understand that the song is really about twisting the music of the 1950s to fit the kinkier sexual culture of the 1970s. In short, Bowie tells us that the Saturday night drive-in culture of 1973 is quite different from that of 15 years before.

Not that the song exhibits much at all in the way of a retro feel, "Panic in Detroit" does, however, feature a variant on the famous "Bo Diddley" rhythm associated with the African-American R&B and rock pioneer Ellas Otha Bates McDaniel, better known as Bo Diddley. Again, Bowie's lyrics are impressionistic; however, the lyrics and the hard-rock quality of the music combine to create a disquieting atmosphere. Bowie hints at riots, violence, and a Detroit rock star associated with the harshness of life on the streets. Given Bowie's association with Iggy Pop, a native of Michigan who came to musical prominence in the Detroit area, as well as the city's notoriety as a hotbed of radical political activity in the late 1960s (race riots, White Panther leader John Sinclair, and the proto-leftist-punk rock of the MC5), "Panic in Detroit" seems like a swirling mix of all of these references and musical influences. In representing this mix, the lyrics add to the album's general theme of alienation. Here, the reference is to an alienation caused by political friction, the alienation between rock god and audience, and an alienation from the norms of society.

"Cracked Actor," too, speaks of one who just does not fit in with the social and sexual mores of conventional society. Bowie explores an almost emotionless, purely physical lust, with references to both conventional sexual intercourse and oral sex. Bowie also uses double entendres to mix drugs and insanity ("crack") and drugs and one-on-one violence ("smack"). Bowie's description of the woman[13] who his character has hired for sex, includes more direct references to drug addiction, including a description of her as a "porcupine," suggesting that she is full of needles. The seediness of the scene is not limited by any means to the prostitute: Bowie's character, a fifty-year-old has-been actor, clearly has been reduced to having to rely upon prostitutes for sex. He sets this tale of decadence to a hard, moderate-tempo shuffle beat that is supported by a harmonic progression that features dramatic, unexpected chromatic shifts in the instrumental introduction and in the verses. The music is as off-kilter as the two characters.

Bowie's fascination with old music-hall music comes to the fore in the song "Time." Buoyed by the virtuosic piano playing of Mike Garson and the powerful guitar work of Mick Ronson, Bowie rails against the onward march of time. Incidentally, Bowie would return to a focus on the onward march of time on his albums of the 1999–2003 period: *hours...*, *Heathen,* and *Reality*. Essentially, the song is a somewhat darker take on the same theme Bowie explored in the song "Changes." From the standpoint of its music, it is also one of the most conventional pop style songs on *Aladdin Sane*. On both this song, and on "The Prettiest Star," Bowie uses his best musical theater/ Anthony Newley-style voice. "The Prettiest Star," incidentally, is also backwards looking musically, resembling both the music of the British music hall and 1950s doo-wop pop music.

The Rolling Stones' 1967 hit "Let's Spend the Night Together" was a perfect choice for a cover song on *Aladdin Sane*. With glam-rock's focus on sex—especially as an act of physical pleasure—this Mick Jagger and Keith Richards composition provides Bowie with retro material that still manages to fit thematically into the glam rock reference point of the 1970s. Bowie adds a spoken tag to the song, which is disconcerting for a number of reasons. First, it changes a well-known song by one of the best-known bands of the rock era on the foreground level. More importantly, however, is the fact that this little piece of psychodrama acts to completely redefine the lust that is implied in Jagger and Richards's original song into something that is completely an act of political rebellion, rather than an act of love. Critics have not been particularly accepting of this track. Stephen Thomas Erlewine, an *All Music Guide Critic,* refers to Bowie's arrangement and performance as "clueless."[14] I believe that Erlewine and other critics who dismiss Bowie's take on the famous Rolling Stones song miss the point somewhat. If one deals with the track as an extension of the Ziggy Stardust, fictitious band performances of Bowie and company's previous album, or if one even just evaluates the Bowie arrangement and performance as a glam adaptation of "Let's Spend the Night Together," then the track makes a whole lot more sense. It is not a paean to the Rolling Stones. It is, however, an arrangement and performance that brings the almost purely physical lust of the original clearly into the realm of sex as physical pleasure. Bowie's spoken mini-drama at the end of the track also suggests that the couple's copulation can be seen as an act of defiance against the control of their parents. He adds a distinctive harder edge to the sexual politics of what the Rolling Stones had committed to back in the 1960s. By deconstructing such a well-known song and offering a single 1970s-oriented interpretation of the meaning of the text, Bowie takes a huge risk. He risks alienating listeners who hear the song differently; he also takes a chance by changing the song's musical setting from that of the Stones' original. The inclusion of "Let's Spend the Night Together," however, helps to set the stage for Bowie's next album, *Pin Ups,* which would consist entirely of covers of 1960s British rock songs updated to a glam-metal, early 1970s style.

Bowie's song "The Jean Genie" was first heard in its single release, before its appearance on *Aladdin Sane*. The title itself is a play on the name of the French writer and political activist Jean Genet. The title character of the Bowie song could be understood at least partially as a reflection of some aspects of Genet; however, the specter of Bowie's friend Iggy Pop looms large in some of the lyrical references. The title character, with his hair underwear and other queer (in the traditional, non-sexual-orientation meaning of the term) habits and traits, sounds like the ultimate outsider; he fits the amorphous theme of the album quite well.

Perhaps more important than the lyrics of "The Jean Genie" per se is Bowie's musical setting and performance. Considering the wide range (British music hall, heavy metal, pop, folk, psychedelic) of David Bowie's compositions and performances from the mid-1960s through 1972, the one area in which he had not established what we in the early twenty-first century might call street cred was British blues. This piece exudes the British blues spirit like no previous Bowie song. In part, this is due to the instrumental work of Bowie's band, but Bowie himself deserves a great deal of the credit for making "The Jean Genie" a powerful blues-rock piece. After all, he wrote it. In addition, though, Bowie contributes some fantastic (albeit somewhat background) blues harp (harmonica) that proves that his instrumental work went beyond blowing some rock tenor sax, playing rhythm guitar, and playing some generally chordal piano.

Perhaps one of the most interesting things about the last song on the album, "Lady Grinning Soul," is that it seems to anticipate the work that former Led Zeppelin vocalist Robert Plant would do in the early-1980s on his top-20 single "Big Log" and on the album *The Honeydrippers, Vol. 1* (Es Paranza 90220). In part, this is thanks to some of the connections between Bowie's singing and Plant's retro style on his Honeydrippers project. But, some of the credit goes to Mick Ronson's lead guitar work: his Spanish-style acoustic lead is the antecedent of Robbie Blunt's playing on Plant's "Big Log." The song also anticipates some of Bowie's later work. The style is very much in the same vein as his work on Dmitri Tiomkin and Ned Washington's "Wild Is the Wind" on *Station to Station* in 1976. At least one of Bowie's lyrical references—to driving "the Beetle car"—anticipates his twenty-first-century song "She'll Drive the Big Car," a track on Bowie's *Reality*. In the case of "Lady Grinning Soul," the Volkswagen Beetle seems to represent her cool, counterculture hipness. However, she is not so incessantly hip as to drive a Mini Cooper.

Musically, "Lady Grinning Soul" clearly hearkens back to the 1960s, and bears more than a passing resemblance musically to the Quincy Jones, Peter King, Don Black composition "On Days Like These," the opening title music for the 1969 British cult film *The Italian Job* (not to be confused with the early twentieth-century Hollywood "remake"). The opening upward melodic leap and subsequent stepwise descent also calls to mind the opening of Max Steiner's famous score for the movie *Gone With the Wind*. Bowie's song is haunting, both musically and lyrically. Perhaps more than any other song on *Aladdin Sane,* it is "Lady Grinning Soul" that relies on the virtuosic piano work of Mike Garson. Garson's arpeggios (broken chords), in particular, are so extreme that they bring Bowie's melody, harmony, lyrics, and vocalizing back from any move toward sentimentality. Garson adds that needed touch of irony—that needed question of whether or not Bowie is fully serious or is he putting the listener on. The overall effect of the song is perhaps open to more of a personal interpretation than most of the tracks on *Aladdin Sane,* particularly for men. I hear this as a song about that one woman who comes into a man's life and shows him sexually just what it is to feel like a man. It's that first sexual encounter that he recalls decades later. Whether this woman is the love of his life or not, she touches her companion in a way that no one else can. The music fits perfectly. In fact, in some respects, this is David Bowie's perfect marriage of lyrics, music, arrangement, and performance. Unfortunately, perhaps because the subject is somewhat outside the conventional wisdom of what a David Bowie song should be about, "Lady Grinning Soul" is not as widely known as it deserves to be. Fortunately, this song would not be a dead end for Bowie: the arrangement (in particular, his saxophone writing) would influence the *Diamond Dogs* and *Station to Station* albums, and the haunting mix of lyrics and music would reemerge on several later Bowie songs throughout the years—most recently on the 2002 album *Heathen*.

*Allmusic Guide*'s Stephen Thomas Erlewine gives *Aladdin Sane* four and a half (out of five) stars, and describes it as "stranger" and "lighter" than Bowie's *Ziggy Stardust* album.[15] In some respects, however, it is a darker album. It is also, in this writer's opinion, a considerably more difficult album for listeners to connect with, as it requires that they extend themselves further in order to identify with the vast range of characters—the characters of Ziggy Stardust are much easier to define, probably because they fall more into the realm of stereotypes. *Aladdin Sane* is an important album to listen to in order from beginning to end, for despite the alienation, insanity, and the darkness of the sexual situations of most of the album's songs, the final track, "Lady Grinning Soul" offers hope.

Fans of David Bowie—especially U.K. fans—are probably "well aware" (to use a phrase from Bowie's song "Changes") that Bowie made a number of appearances on the B.B.C. in the 1969–1972 period. These radio performances were issued in 2000 on the two-compact disc set *Bowie at the Beeb* (EMI 7243 528629 2 4). The album includes extensive program notes and follows Bowie through the period in which he became an international superstar. It is an album that hardcore David Bowie fans will want to own; however, it is a somewhat problematic collection. While the set spotlights Bowie's growth as a writer and performer, and provides a rare opportunity to hear him live in the radio studio, it ultimately tends to disappoint. It does so especially if one hears David Bowie as primarily—or almost solely—as a recording artist, and not a songwriter and not a singer. The famous arrangements aren't there; the multi-instrumentalist work of Bowie isn't there; and the generally careful presentation of Bowie's voice is not there.

## PIN UPS

David Bowie's final farewell to his Ziggy Stardust persona can be found in the album *Pin Ups*. While the persona per se is not really present here, Bowie performs with part of the Spiders from Mars band, although lead guitarist Mick Ronson and bass guitarist Trevor Bolder are joined by other studio musicians and luminaries such as guitarist Ron Wood (who would later become a member of the Rolling Stones), and Spiders drummer Mick "Woody" Woodmansey is absent.[16] This 1973 package includes songs that were among Bowie's favorites in the 1964–1967 period. Bowie's selections betray knowledge of some of the most progressive—if not underappreciated—work that was coming out of British bands in the period. Notably absent are Beatles and Rolling Stones songs. The Who and the Yardbirds (to name the two best-known bands represented) songs that Bowie includes are not the big pop hits (no, "My Generation" and "For Your Love" are not his choices), but are lesser-known releases. At the time of its release, *Pin Ups* seemed to confuse Bowie fans, especially his new American fans. The American fans, who were not familiar with his prefame work in the 1960s, knew of David Bowie as an androgynous glam-rock star who wrote all his own songs. The days of bands such as the Lower Third, the King Bees, and the Manish Boys covering the latest singles from the Yardbirds, the Who, the Merseys, and the Pretty Things were unknown to Bowie's new audience. Later critics have not given much in the way of approval to this album either: Critic Bruce Eder of *All Music Guide*, for example, gives *Pin Ups* only three of a possible five stars.[17] It is not an album without flaws. A few of the songs do not measure up particularly well to the originals: the Who's original recording of "Anyway, Anyhow, Anywhere" is so powerful and definitive that it would be very difficult for any cover to measure up, and a couple of the other tracks sound not quite as convincing as others.

Confusion at the time of its release and the later reaction of critics to *Pin Ups*, however, tends to relegate *Pin Ups* to second-class status among David Bowie albums. This sort of status does not give Bowie all of the credit that he deserves. For one thing, *Pin Ups* anticipates the work of other British singer-songwriter rock stars. For example, in *Rock 'n' Roll* (recorded between October 1973 and October 1974),[18] John Lennon covers songs by various artists whom he fondly recalled from his teen years, such as Chuck Berry, Little Richard, Buddy Holly, Ben E. King, and others. Later, Elvis Costello would cover American country songs on his 1981 album *Almost Blue* and would then cover R&B and pop songs with which he had grown up on the 1995 album *Kojak Variety*. David Bowie, unlike Lennon and Costello (each of whom took a more deliberately "retro" approach), put the oldies he chose into a thoroughly contemporary setting: the arrangements on *Pin Ups* exude the 1970s. A song such as the Yardbirds' "Shapes of Things," for example sounds as much like a "Spiders from Mars" song as a mid-1960s classic, due to the setting and Bowie's vocal style.

The importance of *Pin Ups* does not rest, however, solely on the fact that it anticipated the attention British rockers of generations would place on the music of their youth. Bowie and his associates' work on the Them (Van Morrison's 1960s band) song "Here Comes the Night" in the verses anticipates the sound of British post-punk new wave music of the late 1970s and early 1980s. All the listener need to do is to compare the rhythm style, instrumental setting, and Bowie's vocal approach to a song such as "Karma Chameleon" on Culture Club's 1983 album *Colour By Numbers* to hear the connection between Bowie's work and the music of a decade later.

The other feature of *Pin Ups* that is important is purely internal within Bowie's output. Whereas the album represents the last stand of Bowie's "Spiders from Mars" band, it also anticipates his brief move in the direction of American soul music. In his vocal work on the chorus sections of "Here Comes the Night," Bowie uses the wide vibrato and strong tone that characterize his work on the soul-oriented albums *Young Americans* and *Station to Station*. The arrangement on the Kinks song "See Emily Play" anticipates Bowie's avant-garde experimentations during his Berlin period in the late 1970s.

Aside from these marks of importance, *Pin Ups* serves as an effective bookends-type album: it gives Mick Ronson and the other members of Bowie's group a chance to just play, without any sort of artistic pretense; and it shows that Bowie's musical performance style is not tied to a particular lyrics-writing style. *Pin Ups* finds Bowie incorporating some of the vocal and arrangement styles that would mark his work between 1974 and 1977. And, to top it off, Bowie utilizes his saxophone a greater extent than he had ever done before, anticipating his work in the future.[19] The album is old and yet, it remains very new sounding.

# Of *Diamond Dogs* and Plastic Soul

Perhaps the ultimate question about David Bowie's career will be, "Was he a musical chameleon who seemingly adapted to current stylistic trends in progressive pop music with ease, or was he more of a musical visionary who committed sounds to vinyl months or even years before those sounds became mainstream?" Certainly, there were elements of both in his Ziggy Stardust period. The period framed by *Diamond Dogs* (1974) and *Station to Station* (1976), would find Bowie mostly exploring aspects of life in America and American music, particularly soul music.

## DIAMOND DOGS

After effectively exhausting and retiring the so-called Ziggy Stardust persona and effectively breaking from the musicians with whom he had collaborated during the Ziggy Stardust period, Bowie turned to a most intriguing project: a musical setting of George Orwell's *1984*. Unfortunately, Bowie could not get permission from the estate of the late author to use Orwell's material, so he had to change the project midstream. The resulting *Diamond Dogs* album mixed part of the storyline—or at least the feel—of the Orwell novel with elements of some of Beat poet William Burroughs's most famous works: *Junkie* and *Queer*. These works examined the dark side of drug abuse and sexuality. All in all, Bowie's *Diamond Dogs* is a look at the dark side of life that ends up not being as well-focused as *Ziggy Stardust* and *Aladdin Sane*. Some listeners may even sense that Bowie had basically played out the focus on darkness and alienation, as the themes seem a little tired on *Diamond Dogs*.

Despite the fact that the *Diamond Dogs* album was by necessity something of a bunt for David Bowie—due to the fact that he had to modify his original intent to create a musical setting of George Orwell's *1984*—the album contains several very good songs, two of which became famous: the title track and "Rebel Rebel." Another important feature of *Diamond Dogs* is it is the first project in which Bowie takes full control of writing, arranging, and producing; he is also the sole credited guitarist on the album (except on one track).

The album opens with "Future Legend," a spoken-word mini-drama supported by snippets of 1940s-era American pop music. Here, Bowie sets up the theme of the album as the decadence and seediness of modern urban life in a manner that follows in the tradition of the American Beat writers of the 1940s and 1950s, particularly Allen Ginsberg and William Burroughs. Like the Beats, Bowie places this decadent society in the United States. The setting deviates from Orwell's *1984,* the 1948 work on which *Diamond Dogs* is based, which is the work of a British writer commenting on post–World War II Europe. Bowie's monolog contains some free association and some of William Burroughs-esque cut-up technique. In Burroughs's *Naked Lunch,* and in some of his other writings, the Beat writer cut scenes out of the text and rearranged them in what would appear to the reader to be random order. The whole story would be there, but not in chronological order. To the contemporary student of pop culture not familiar with the exploration of random ordering that was in the air in the 1950s and 1960s in the work of Burroughs, composer John Cage, and others, the effect is akin to the seemingly wildly illogical cuts in the Quentin Tarrentino film *Pulp Fiction.* In the case of the Bowie album, if one hears *Diamond Dogs* as a song cycle focused on the decadence of contemporary urban life, the way in which it jumps around between specific subjects, with the somewhat strange reprises, resembles an adaptation of the Burroughs cut-up technique on an album-length structural level. For Bowie, this is not a revolutionary step, but an evolutionary step: his earlier album *The Rise and Fall of Ziggy Stardust and the Spiders from Mars* also suggests a loosely constructed narrative that has been shuffled and with some of the logical linkages snipped out.

The first track "Future Legend" makes a direct segue into "Diamond Dogs," a track that includes a faux live-audience ambience. The characters Bowie describes are meant to show that circus side-show freaks are really living among us. Bowie describes one of the characters as "Todd Browning's freak." Browning was the early twentieth-century filmmaker who cast actual circus freak show performers in the 1932 movie *Freaks.* The Browning film created a scandal at the time and was banned for several decades. Likewise, the characters of Orwell's *1984* are decadent social outcasts to the extent that they could be defined as freaks of their day. Bowie's freaks carry on in the tradition; however, his impressionistic lyrics in "Diamond Dogs" leave it to the listener to interpret just what they look like and just how they live to a greater extent than in the more pointed works of Browning and Orwell.

In contrast to the strangeness of the various "Diamond Dog" characters, Bowie's music in the song is conventional rock and roll, with clear phrase structure, extensive use of the fundamental tonic (I), subdominant (IV) and dominant (V) chords, along with a catchy pop-oriented melody. Bowie incorporates a fair amount of syncopation in the short phrases of the melody. This gives the music its snappy, disarming quality, which is at odds with the characters. And, it is this disconnection that tends to weaken the impact of some of the songs throughout the album. For, some of the music is just too pop oriented to convey a strong enough sense of the freakiness of the characters and the entire gestalt of Bowie's recreation of *1984*. The edge of Orwell (and Browning for that matter) just is not here. In fact, the art for the album cover itself is edgier than some of the songs, including "Diamond Dogs."

The come-on of the prostitute that forms the song "Sweet Thing" carries considerable more edge and dramatic focus, however, than "Diamond Dogs." She entices the listener with an invitation to "love in a doorway," and acknowledges (to herself) her inability to feel emotions—a common character trait of the freaks that frequent the entire *Diamond Dogs* album, The music of "Sweet Thing" is slow, ponderous, and ominous. Bowie includes playing sections of music backwards, distortion, and feedback in the electric guitars, and a somewhat unpredictable melody, all of which work together to enhance the depressing scene. Interestingly, Bowie's vocal harmony arrangement on the choruses, as well as his multi-tracked performance of the harmony parts, suggests American soul music. This is particularly noticeable in the close harmony of the arrangement and in Bowie's use of the exaggerated vibrato of soul and gospel music. In addition to being a track that is stronger than some in terms of its depiction of an urban world of emotionless existence, it is important as a sonic anticipation of Bowie's so-called plastic soul style of his next two albums. It is worth noting that Bowie's character uses the word *love* to mean emotionless, purely physical, cheap, and tawdry sex. This is especially interesting because Bowie's songs so infrequently use the word *love* in any context. In Bowie's post-modern world of the societal fringes, love—platonic or romantic—has no place. This is not true just on *Diamond Dogs,* but characterizes almost all of his output of the 1970s up through this album. Things would change somewhat as he entered his Plastic Soul and Berlin phases.

"Sweet Thing" makes a direct segue into the song "Candidate," a song that relates more closely to George Orwell's *1984* than most of the other songs on *Diamond Dogs*. In this song, the corrupt political candidate delivers his rap, and in the course of it he acknowledges his dishonesty. True to the spirit of *1984*, however, the candidate sounds secure that he will be elected no matter what evils he has done. The music retains the tempo and stylistic feel of "Sweet Thing," which—along with the immediate segue between the two songs—suggests that the politician who is willing to sell himself and his vote to the highest bidder is as much a prostitute as the woman who sells herself for cheap sex in an urban doorway. Bowie emphasizes this connection, just in case the listener had not gotten the point, by including a reprise of "Sweet Thing" following "Candidate."

One of David Bowie's best-known songs, "Rebel Rebel," follows. Here, Bowie uses a 1965–1966 style electric guitar riff (think of the Rolling Stones's "Satisfaction," the Beatles's "Day Tripper," or the Standells's "Dirty Water") to accompany his description of the subject of the song's title. The vocal melody consists of short repeated phrases, which are closely related to the guitar riff. The song is not quite so monothematic as, say, Bruce Springsteen's 1980s hit "Born in the U.S.A.," but it is in the same ballpark. The easily remembered riff is a double-edged sword for Bowie: on one hand, it provides a strong commercial hook for the song (which is certainly part of the reason that this remains one of Bowie's best-known works); however, it also tends to make the 1960s connection a little too strongly. The androgynous Rebel, with his or her Quaaludes, lust for men, and tackiness for the sake of rebellion, is very much a part of the pre-punk 1970s. To the extent that a song such as "Rebel Rebel" is supposed to represent Bowie's interpretation of Orwell's *1984,* a work that masks contemporary social commentary as futuristic fiction, the use of a musical style so closely influenced by music of the previous decade, does not make a great deal of conceptual sense. As a stand-alone song about a young person living on the extreme fringes of society, though, it works very well indeed.

Essentially, "Rebel Rebel" is David Bowie's take on the Marc Bolan/T. Rex song "Bang a Gong (Get It on)." Both songs present a strong commercial musical hook in a rock composition and performance and both display a prototypical glam-rock fascination with and lust for what can only be called sluttiness. When Bolan sings of a "dirty sweet little girl" that he loves and Bowie sings of a "hot tramp" that he loves, they are dealing with exactly the same subject, a love and lust for the kind of girl of whom probably neither Mrs. Bolan nor Mrs. Jones (Bowie's real name) would have approved. These two songs, of all the music that falls into the glam-rock genre, probably best illustrate this sexual fascination with so-called bad girls.

The ties to George Orwell and Todd Browning wear quite thin on the next track, "Rock 'n' Roll with Me," which Bowie cowrote with Warren Peace. This power ballad finds Bowie playing the role of rock star, who is in demand from "tens of thousands" of fans. The gist of the song is that Bowie's character finds fulfillment in performing on stage. It all seems like a theme better suited to *The Rise and Fall of Ziggy Stardust and the Spiders from Mars* than to the Orwellian urban landscape of *Diamond Dogs.* Some of the song's specific passing references in the lyrics—"lizards," in particular—also provide strong connections to Bowie's rock-star fantasy masterpiece. The music is not particularly distinctive, keeping within a top-40 power rock ballad format, and, unfortunately, Bowie's lead guitar playing is not nearly as seamlessly woven into the texture the way that the work of Bowie's Spiders from Mars lead guitarist, Mick Ronson, so often was.

Bowie returns to the Orwellian scene in "We Are the Dead." His rambling lyrics paint a dismal urban scene of filth, disease, and despair that can only be overcome by the pleasure of sex with the woman he addresses—a woman who is described as wearing "fuck-me pumps." The music of this nearly five-minute song wanders melodically and harmonically. Intentionally or not, the driftless feel of the music matches the lack of closure that the song's character seems to find in his daily life: he is alive, yet counts himself among the living dead, for whom nothing ever really changes at all. It is not Bowie's most lyrically or musically distinctive song, but within the context of the world he paints in this album, it fits. It is also one of the songs most closely tied to the work of William S. Burroughs with its graphic lust and unabashed exposure of the seedy side of urban life.

The song "1984" breaks with the slow, somewhat plodding nature of the previous two songs on *Diamond Dogs*. Supported by a Philadelphia Soul-style string arrangement by Tony Visconti, the song strikes an intriguing middle ground between early disco and the heavy metal style of Bowie's *The Man Who Sold the World*. Bowie's warning to avoid the "savage lure of 1984" is full of energy and drama. Had Bowie actually been able to mount a full musical theater adaptation of Orwell's *1984*, this song would have made an excellent introductory piece. It manages to define (despite, or perhaps because of the concise nature of the lyrics) the allure and danger of a world ruled by Big Brother, in which the populace is anesthetized by drugs and simulated sex. Used as the opening song of the adaptation of *1984*, it could have also be used at the end of the show to tie the whole theme together. But, that never was to be.

In the song "Big Brother," Bowie plays the role of a man who has been convinced that the Big Brother character of *1984* is a savior. It is a song of praise to the leader, and it is one of the most dramatic songs on *Diamond Dogs*. Bowie uses his voice to suggest both the emotionless living-dead feeling of his character at the beginning of the song, to the dramatic, emotion-filled cry for help directed at Big Brother in the song's chorus. He achieves this emotional range both through his writing (low register melodic material associated with the emotional impotence of the character versus high register material with dramatic upward leads as Big Brother is praised and begged for help) and through his singing technique, especially through the use of a wide expressive vibrato in the pleading and praising sections. Bowie's melodic writing in the pleading and praising sections goes beyond conventional pop song and moves squarely into the world of contemporary musical theater: the entire melody of these sections is jagged and not hook-focused like commercial pop songs and the upward leaps are difficult to sing.

*Diamond Dogs* concludes with the curiously titled "Chant of the Ever-Circling Skeletal Family." This hard rock chant feels as though it is constantly changing meter. However, the repetitive nature of the piece creates more of a sensation that each phrase is really one very long measure of music, with a meter that is impossible to determine, unless one consciously counts beats. The effect is similar to that of the long meters of Hindustani music, in which essentially one measure of music consists of a rhythmic pattern that might be notated as three or four measures of changing meters in Western music. This goes beyond the occasional quintuple meter songs or metrical changes of art rock bands such as King Crimson, or the metrical changes of some heavy metal bands, such as Black Sabbath. In this song, Bowie steps closer to the classical minimalist composers and the music of the Indian subcontinent. In the genre of pop music, he anticipates Talking Heads's exploration of African and eastern rhythms by in their 1977–1979 albums. In fact, the sense of deliberate strangeness, emotional detachment, and non-linear poetry that moves throughout *Diamond Dogs* are all found echoed in the Talking Heads' first three albums: *Talking Heads: 77; More Songs about Buildings and Food;* and *Fear of Music.* One of the main points of contrast between Bowie's work on *Diamond Dogs* and Talking Heads songwriter David Byrne's early work was that Bowie always sounds brutally serious, whereas Byrne (in his early work) displayed a very non-Bowie-esque sense of humor.

## *Young Americans*

One style that no one had probably associated in a significant way with David Bowie before *Young Americans* was American soul music.[1] Sure, there were hints of soul in a couple of the songs of *Diamond Dogs,* but what Bowie did in his version of *1984* was to adopt some of the musical trappings of soul, while assiduously avoiding the standard emotional content of African American soul music. As Bowie toured in the wake of his *Diamond Dogs* album, he began exploring soul more and more. His band included several American musicians who were versed in the form. Because Bowie had already displayed a proclivity to change styles drastically from album to album, perhaps it was only natural that he would tackle soul music next. In fitting with the more accessible nature of the music on *Young Americans,* Bowie also created easier-to-understand, mainstream characters and situations in his lyrics. In addition, the album is notable for Bowie's first explicit embrace of the style and songs of the Beatles.

The album begins with the title song, "Young Americans." Even at the start of the piece, it is clear that the musical style is completely different from those with which Bowie had been associated over the course of a decade in the recording industry. For one thing, the studio echo that producer Tony Visconti uses on David Sanborn's saxophone *obbligato* and featured solo that comes right before the song's middle eight section calls to mind the production work of Phil Spector on John Lennon's first post-Beatles recordings of the 1970s. And the ties to former Beatle John Lennon are not limited to Visconti's production on this song: Bowie also quotes both the music and lyrics of the Beatles' "A Day in the Life" ("I heard the news today, oh boy."). The gospel-style backing singers and the instrumental work of the accompanying

American musicians on the track also clearly place "Young Americans" apart from anything Bowie had recorded before in terms of musical composition, arrangement, and performance. The emotional detachment that Bowie exhibits as a singer on the track stands in contrast to the African American soul style, but this is entirely consistent with the so-called Plastic Soul style that Bowie created with this album. By adopting most aspects of soul, while maintaining a sense of detachment, Bowie does not come off as a white blue-eyed soul singer (in the manner of the Righteous Brothers, for example), or a white singer merely imitating the style of soul music. No, the effect on "Young Americans" is more that of a new hybrid style.

It is not just the music of "Young Americans" that marks this as a new-phase Bowie song. The characters, a young American couple, appear to be typical teens. They are not the shady figures living in the future or on the present-day fringes of society. This change about helps Bowie to deliver a powerful message. His tale of emotionless sex "behind the fridge" tells the listener that emotional impotence, sex as pleasure, sex as male domination, and sex as escape from whatever problems one experiences in life is not limited to those on the outside of mainstream society, or even on the fringes or borderlines of mainstream society. Rather, Bowie's tale demonstrates that animal-like carnal needs and desires can be found even in the homes of the middle class and upper class, no matter how vehemently polite society might deny the fact. Subsequent verses expose racism, discrimination against the poor, and the futility of life for the disenfranchised in U.S. society.

Another mark of the influence of American soul music on "Young Americans" is Bowie's use of clearly defined four-measure phrases. The harmony of the phrases of the verses are entirely conventional within the soul style. Bowie ends most of these phrases on the dominant (V) chord. This creates an unresolved feel, because the natural motion of the dominant chord is back to tonic (I), the chord built on the principal note of the key. This allows the phrases to flow from the end of one into the beginning of the next in a completely natural way. Bowie did not always use this kind of short, four-bar chord progression in his earlier work, especially in the somewhat meandering music of his psychedelic-folk period. Although this may be atypical of his previous work as a composer, he is not doing anything new in "Young Americans" with respect to popular soul music. What he shows here is a command of the style.

The lyrics of the next song, "Win," are more abstract, and as such are open to a variety of interpretations. Given the slow soulful style of the composition and performance, Bowie's character seems to be unable to connect with a potential lover. They seem to be somewhat conflicted and in a situation in which the potential lover needs to feel as though he or she is in control and the winner in the conflict. Like "Young Americans," "Win" finds Bowie treating melody in a fundamentally different way than he typically had on his previous several albums. He does not rely as heavily on short repeated phrases on his soul-style songs. "Win," in particular, is built with more of a natural and slightly longer-range rise and fall than Bowie's more rock-oriented songs. As a singer, Bowie tends to improvise melodic figurations more than on his more rock-oriented songs, which is perfectly in keeping with the soul style.

In so far as the song "Fascination" is largely the work of Luther Vandross—Bowie and Vandross co-authored the lyrics, but the music is completely the work of Vandross—discussion will focus on Bowie's performance. Bowie sings with a great deal of emotional display, but to his credit, the expressive vibrato never reverts to the exaggeration of his Anthony Newley style, and his expressive singing here finds him avoiding some of the intonation (tuning) inconsistencies of some of his more dramatic recordings of the past.

Bowie wrote both the words and music of "Right," the song that closes side one of *Young Americans*. This 4-minute, 13-second song, consists of a mere 12 lines of lyrics and simple chord progression of E minor followed by A major. It is a classic example of a groove piece. The basic feel, or groove, of the piece is what makes this music work. Although this may be common practice in soul music, it is quite an anomaly in the canon of David Bowie music, at least up to this point in his career. Bowie and the backing vocalists, with their improvisations, and the rhythm section and saxophonist David Sanborn, carry it off quite well. Bowie would return to harmonically simple groove pieces later in his career, particularly on the early 1990s album *Black Tie White Noise,* and on the song "Bring Me the Disco King," from the 2003 album, *Reality.*

The second side of *Young Americans* begins with "Somebody Up There Likes Me," a song that starts with an extended instrumental introduction. This introduction suggests the feel and chord progression of Stevie Wonder's 1967 hit "I Was Made to Love Her." In fact, this particular Bowie song would not be out of place within the Motown-style soul repertoire of the 1966–1968 period. One of the characteristics of songs such as Wonder's "I Was Made to Love Her" that stands out is that the rhythmic groove and the text of the title line are the most important—and the most memorable—parts of the song.[2] As such, this song stands perhaps in sharpest contrast to the best of what Bowie had written and recorded prior to *Young Americans.* In all of these previous songs, the imagery of Bowie's lyrics went well beyond the title line. Motown writers of the 1970s, too, had moved beyond the focus on the musical groove of a track such as "I Was Made to Love Her." Therefore, "Somebody Up There Likes Me" tends both to sound weak lyrically, as compared with much of Bowie's work on the past several albums, and dated, as an example of soul.

The next track on the album, "Across the Universe," rekindles the connections of *Young Americans* to John Lennon, which the reader might recall initially went back to the more extensive use of reverb on the vocal and drum tracks of the album's first cut. Bowie creates a very individualistic arrangement of this John Lennon and Paul McCartney composition, which first had first become widely known on the Beatle's 1970 album *Let It Be.*[3] Perhaps the most distinctive part of the recording is Bowie's vocal performance, filled as it is with drama, lots of vibrato, and a mannered, oh-so-very-British pronunciation. It stands in complete contrast to Lennon's understated performance on *Let It Be*. Given the impressionistic nature of the visual images Lennon's lyrics create,[4] Bowie's performance sounds over the top. Still, if this recording is taken as a groove piece—and it would be natural to perceive it that way, given the enormous length of the fade-out coda section—it works, in spite of the excessive expression. It would seem to be no accident that Bowie chose this particular Beatles song to cover, as the style of his lyrics is closer to Lennon's style in this song than in practically anything else—with the possible exception of some of the Beatles's psychedelic (and by this point somewhat dated sounding) songs.

"Can You Hear Me" is maybe the closest thing to a prototypical soulful love song that David Bowie has ever written in his four-decade career. And it is one of the most autobiographical-sounding songs he has ever written and recorded. The lyrics find him acknowledging that he has strayed from his lover numerous times out on the road, but that in his heart, she is still the woman he loves. The most impressive aspect of the recording, however, might just be Bowie's vocal work. Intentionally or not, he perfectly imitates American soul singer Al Green on the track. In doing so, Bowie proves himself to be one of the more underrated vocalists in pop music by virtue of his huge expressive and stylistic range. Bowie's music falls completely within the soul style. The melody is memorable; the harmony and arrangement are conventional, accessible, but very catchy. The long and short of "Can You Hear Me" is that it represents Bowie capturing African American soul music completely. Not only is this good soul music, but by giving such a heartfelt-sounding performance, Bowie reaches a higher level of autobiographical-sounding attachment than he allows in any of his post-Pye and Deram songs. This is because, whereas some of his psychedelic folk, heavy metal, and glam material may have been autobiographical, the characters Bowie created were so unconventional—extreme, really—that they seemed to be more fiction than fact. The specifics of the situation in "Can You Hear Me"—that of the roving rock star who cannot stay loyal to his soul mate—might be outside the experience of the vast majority of listeners, but the general theme is one that one hears about everyday. The so-called regular guy nature of Bowie's character is confirmed by the fact that Bowie does not paint him as a circus freak in the manner of the characters of *Diamond Dogs*, or in the more graphic descriptions of the unconventional sexual encounters of Weird, Gilley, and Ziggy Stardust, the caricature-like members of the Spiders from Mars.

The song "Fame" is credited to Bowie, John Lennon, and Carlos Alomar. From the standpoint of the lyrics, which focus on the downside of fame, it is interesting to consider that this was one of the last performances of Lennon before he retired from the music industry for five years. The lyrics capture the suspicion, emotional coldness, lack of privacy, tension, and attachment to things and wealth (as opposed to people) that come with pop-star fame. In short, the song argues that fame is not what it's cracked up to be. The minimalistic nature of the song's harmonic and rhythmic background suggest the sparse nature of early 1970s compositions by Lennon, such as "Cold Turkey" and "I Found Out." Here, the harmony is firmly grounded on the tonic (I). When the harmony finally moves to the subdominant (IV) chord the song takes on the aura of a sort of hyperextended blues progression, even though a complete blues harmonic progression never really occurs.

The song "Fame" is so well known from the radio airplay it has generated and from its extensive sales as a single—the single spent two weeks at No. 1 on the *Billboard* pop charts and remains Bowie's most commercially successful single ever—that it is easy to overlook its role on *Young Americans*. Following "Can You Hear You Me," a song that found Bowie acknowledging the difficulty a rock star can have with the sexual temptations of the road, "Fame" takes on added meaning as he (and co-writers Alomar and Lennon) once again explore the downside of fame in the pop music world. The two songs become a miniature suite. The problem is that this little suite of two songs does not seem to fit particularly well with the rest of the album conceptually. They really fit better with the story of Ziggy Stardust.

When one listens to *Young Americans* all the way through, it is easy to be struck by the fact that none of the eight tracks are particularly short. With the shortest cut, "Fame," timing out at 4 minutes and 12 seconds, these songs seem more expansive on the whole than those on Bowie's previous albums. Another striking feature—but not a positive one—is the way in which *Young Americans* does not exhibit the same sort of musical and conceptual coherence as Bowie's past several albums, or *Station to Station*, which would follow. The track "Across the Universe" stands pretty much by itself, and the two songs that follow it, "Can You Hear Me" and "Fame" fit together nicely, but seem not to fit in with the earlier songs. Perhaps the most positive feature of *Young Americans* is that it presents a more accessible David Bowie—"Fame" was his biggest-selling single ever, and "Young Americans" is still a staple of 1970s oldies radio—not only was he integrating soul into his musical mix, but he was also addressing issues of relationships and personal identities without the trappings of glam rock's focus on androgyny and unclear sexual orientation. In this regard, *Young Americans* was not an end to itself: Bowie's *Young Americans* work would better balance his fascination of more exotic characters with his observations about more widely universal characters better than any of his pre-*Young Americans* albums.

## STATION TO STATION

Considering the fact that the general perception of David Bowie is that he is a musical chameleon, prone to change musical style radically and at a moment's notice, *Station to Station* occupies a curious place in his output: it is a rare transitional album. On one hand, *Station to Station* continues the Plastic Soul of *Young Americans*, although it is a much stronger package. On the other hand, however, *Station to Station* finds Bowie experimenting sonically and in his formal structures in a way that anticipates his next three albums, those of the Berlin period. And, it represents Bowie's first clear musical exploration of spirituality, a subject to which he would return in the 1990s and early twenty-first century.

The opening of this 1976 album's first song and title track "Station to Station" features a rhythmically interesting riff that could be interpreted as three measures of 2/4 time followed by a measure of 4/4 time with internal syncopated accents, or as a measure of 4/4, a measure of 2/4, followed by a unit consisting of two measures of 3/8 and a measure of 2/8 time. No matter how one hears this metrical division, however, it is fundamentally, and fully intentionally unbalanced. In the case of "Station to Station," this lack of metrical balance within the 10-beat riff is a perfect match for the seeming confusion that the main characters feel in their lives as they travel randomly through life (metaphorically, from station to station), before they find true love. The use of an *ostinato* riff[5] with changing meters (or anything other than straight-ahead, continuous three or four beats per measure) is somewhat unusual in pop music, although it can be found in some heavy metal and hard rock songs—Led Zeppelin's 1975 song "Kashmir" immediately comes to mind. The instrumental texture and the relatively slow tempo of the opening section of "Station to Station," however, do not completely suggest Led Zeppelin-style metal. In fact, throughout the first section of the piece— "Station to Station" is built in two large sections: one moderately slow and one fast—there are hints of heavy metal, hard rock, soul, and the kind of Latin beat associated with the Drifters's famous 1964 calypso-style recording "Under the Boardwalk." In general, David Bowie's pre-*Station to Station* compositions tended not to integrate quite as rich a palette of styles as this one. And, despite the danger of a mix with this degree of eclecticism—the danger being that the song could end up sounding like a loosely constructed pastiche—here, it works because it is all so well integrated.

The richness of "Station to Station" as a recording does not end with Bowie's integration of several musical styles. There is the subtle compositional touch of the rhythm guitar in the calypso-like places in which Bowie's lyrics describe "the return of the Thin White Duke" echoing the rhythm of a train on tracks, which is heard at the beginning of the recording. It is an example, in a manner, of life becoming art. And there is the fact that "Station to Station" consists of two large musically contrasting sections, which are held together by means of the lyrical references to Bowie's character unexpectedly falling in love.

Bowie's lyrics in "Station to Station" are interesting even apart from the music of the song. By attributing the love that his character comes to recognize as the work of the Thin White Duke, who throws "darts in lovers' eyes," Bowie—for about the first memorable time in one of his songs—acknowledges that some entity or higher force beyond the two people immediately involved might play a role in the establishment of the couple's relationship. Although there is nothing about Bowie's lyrics to suggest that this mysterious Thin

White Duke is any sort of spiritual figure, his power, which transcends the power of the humans he affects, fits in with some of the other more spiritually based, higher-power references in other songs on *Station to Station.* Bowie provides sharp contrasts in some of his other imagery in the song "Station to Station." The magic of the love that develops between the couple is enhanced by the image of them moving about like trains changing at random stations. That they finally meet and recognize each other as soul mates is depicted as truly magical in the song. Some of the other images, particularly that of the "European cannon" are strange. Love as the "European cannon?" Perhaps the reference is to the romanticism associated with nations such as Italy and France. Perhaps romantic love is so strong as to literally blow one away as a cannon would. Or, is the European cannon of love meant to contrast with the darts of love thrown by the Thin White Duke? Is this meant to be an unflattering appraisal of the level of romanticism of Britain (darts) compared with that of the European continent (a cannon)? Or, is the reference really meant to be to the word *canon?* In any case, this particular image is so divorced from the rest of the song that it cannot help but raise questions—most obviously, "Just what did David Bowie mean by that?" But, this is the genius of a song such as "Station to Station": some of the images are (to use the colloquial phrase) no-brainers, whereas others force the listener to pay closer attention and ponder the possible meanings. This is what is really behind the art of David Bowie as a lyricist: he forces the listener think about the meaning of the songs, as well as the listener's own inner thoughts and feelings to an extent that is rare in pop music.

The title track is followed by "Golden Years," the best-known track on the album. "Golden Years" is representative of the type of love song that Bowie was writing in the mid- to late-1970s: love songs in which the word *love* is notably absent. As Bowie's character assures his lover that he will always protect her and that the future will be brighter, he offers a brief one-line prayer that God save her soul, thus continuing the theme of spirituality and religion on *Station to Station.* Incidentally, one of the more vivid images that Bowie offers of a bright future is that of his lover riding in a limousine "twenty foot long." Although it may be purely a coincidence, it is worth noting that the limousine into which the character will step one day is exactly twice the length of that famous iconic of British motoring frugality of the time, the Austin/Morris Mini.

Musically, "Golden Years" continues the soulful feeling of most of the songs of *Young Americans,* with just a little touch of doo-wop mixed in. The song features a melody largely built in short phrases, which, by giving the listener smaller chunks of material, tends to make the melody easy to remember.

Easily the most obviously spiritually oriented song Bowie would write and record for years, "Word on a Wing," is essentially a prayer and ruminations on the impact of that prayer. In the first two verses of the song, it is unclear just who it is that walked into Bowie's life: it could be a lover, or someone or something else. Eventually, it becomes clear that it is God, in whatever way Bowie's character would define God. The "word on a wing" of the song's title is Bowie's prayer that he finds a way to fit into God's "scheme of things." The song's ties to the music of American rock and roll pioneer Roy Orbison are evident from Bowie's wide vocal range, expressive vibrato, and the rhythmic figure in the drums in the chorus that comes right out of Orbison's hit "Oh, Pretty Woman."

"TVC15" ties in with the lyrical theme of spirituality and religion that runs throughout this album, and it contains subtle musical connections to three of the album's other songs. Bowie's character sings the praises of his high-tech "TVC one five," while also disclosing that he has lost his lover because of this piece of technological dream equipment. Interestingly, it seems that she was swallowed up by this piece of holographic entertainment technology. As strange as it sounds, this lends a nice sci-fi touch to the song, and it fits right in with the film in which Bowie was starring at the time, Nicholas Roeg's *The Man Who Fell to Earth*. Perhaps not coincidentally, Bowie's character in the film, who came to Earth disguised as a human being, finds his relationship with his human lover disintegrating when he becomes engrossed in watching an entire wall of televisions simultaneously. In the song, Bowie's character prays that he and lover will once again be together, although he concludes that the only way that will happen is if he jumps into the TVC15.

The music of "TVC15" strongly suggests a pseudo-late-1950s style: in the same ballpark as the light-hearted pseudo-1950s music of the American group Sha-Na-Na, which was popular in the 1970s. Despite the resurgence of interest in the style of 1950s rock and roll in the mid-1970s, it should come as no surprise that "TVC15" did not break into the pop top 40 when released as a single: conceptually, the lyrics are just too challenging and strange, and musically it is too different from what Bowie fans would ordinarily expect from their hero. The song does, however, contain a few decidedly non-1950s-style features, including a rhythmic stumble that suggest changing meters, which happens in the repeated fade-out section. This metrical ambiguity provides a direct musical link to the metrical complexities of the song "Station to Station." During the run-out section the electric guitar texture moves toward a hard rock (late-1970s style) tone color. This softens the 1950s musical references and effectively brings Bowie back to a more familiar musical milieu.

The instrumental accompaniment groove of the song "Stay" suggests the merger of hard rock and blue-eyed funk (a harder version of the Plastic Soul of *Young Americans*). The verses feature a narrow melodic range, which suggests heightened speech. The complex rhythms of the chorus are matched by a wide, disjunctive melody. The tortuous, difficult-to-sing melodic intervals and unpredictable rhythms underscore the desperation that Bowie's character feels as he begs his lover to stay. His character is a conflicted man: he has wanted to ask his lover to stay in the past, but now seems to believe that if she leaves this time, it may be the last time. This realization seems to force his hand: he has to verbally acknowledge his need for her. Both the musical approach and the lyrical theme of desperation anticipate some of the songs on "*Heroes,*" especially on "Joe the Lion," as well as some of his less conventional songs on his albums of the late 1990s and early twenty-first century.

"Wild Is the Wind" is one of the best examples of the romanticism that pervaded Bowie's work in the Plastic Soul and Berlin phases of his career. The irony is that it is the one song on his albums of the period that he did not write or cowrite. In fact, this collaboration of noted film composer Dmitri Tiomkin (1894–1979) and lyricist Ned Washington was the title song for a 1957 Western starring Anthony Quinn. The best-known earlier versions of the song were those of Johnny Mathis (1957) and Nina Simone (1966). The version of "Wild Is the Wind" on *Station to Station* might be the best performance David Bowie has ever given on a cover song. Bowie sings with an intangible quality that suggests that his character is deeply touched emotionally by the woman to whom he sings, but is also somewhat strangely detached. The effect is that of a man who addresses someone who is no longer a part of his life as if she is still right next to him. It is as if he is in denial about his loss. Ned Washington's lyrics taken as words on a page do not necessarily require this reading, but there is an underlying sadness that Bowie conveys that adds this layer of depth to the song. Curiously, Bowie's expressive singing, his wide pitch range, and expressive vibrato once again call to mind the soaring vocals of Roy Orbison, who was known for his near-operatic rock vocal style on recordings such as "Only the Lonely," "Oh, Pretty Woman," and other hits. Compared with the earlier versions by Johnny Mathis and Nina Simone, Bowie's version of "Wild Is the Wind" is expansive. The Mathis recording, for example, clocks in at well under half the length of Bowie's recording. The Mathis version features a flexible metrical feel in both the easy listening-style string accompaniment and in his vocal line. In Bowie's rock ballad version, some of the lines that move quickly (in almost speech rhythm) in the Mathis version are stretched out considerably. Bowie's version is also thoroughly contemporary sounding, owing to the treatment of the vocal track and the guitar-based accompaniment by producers Bowie and Harry Maslin. Bowie must also be given his due as a coproducer of "Wild Is the Wind" for the overall shape of the arrangement. There are a few classic slow Bowie recordings that exhibit an unusually high degree of care given to arrangement, orchestration, overall dynamic shaping, such that the entire song becomes a true compositional whole. The song "Heroes," which Bowie also co-produced, is one such perfect arrangement, production, performance, and mix, and "Wild Is the Wind" is another notable example. The long and short of "Wild Is the Wind" is that, although Bowie did not write the song, it is the perfect match of material and singer, all supported by perfect arrangement and production.

So, what is it that makes *Station to Station* hang together as a song cycle to a greater extent than an album such as *Young Americans*? After all, there are touches of heavy metal, 1950s doo-wop, religiosity, and a religiously zealous addiction to futuristic technology. Despite what might seem like a mixed bag of influences and foreground lyrical themes, Bowie includes enough subtle lyrical and musical connections from song to song, making *Station to Station* considerably stronger as a whole than *Young Americans*. Insofar as his early solo albums appealed to what might be termed a boutique audience (small, but nearly rabid in their support), and that the Berlin albums presented more challenges to listeners, and that *Young Americans* lacked some thematic and musical connections that could have been developed, *Station to Station* stands as one of Bowie's most important, and most structurally coherent and broadly accessible, albums of the 1970s.

# Berlin

In a situation that resembles something from one of David Bowie's more bizarre songs about societal outcasts, a man gave the crowd a Nazi salute, stepped on a plane, and spent the next several years holed up in a recording studio in West Berlin trying to kick a cocaine habit. The thing is, this is not the story out of one of Bowie's songs: it is essentially the true story of Bowie's own life during the 1976–1979 period. While Bowie was not necessarily holed up in a West Berlin studio, he did spend a great deal of time in the city during the period, and the music he made there, including the albums *Low*, *"Heroes"*, and *Lodger*, reflected the aesthetics of his new, but temporary, home and the musicians with whom he worked, primarily the avant-garde rock keyboardist, composer, and producer Brian Eno. By the time Bowie left Berlin, he had explored post-punk new wave, ambient music, the electronic avant-garde. Along with exploring new styles of music, Bowie continued to incorporate the styles he had used on *Station to Station*, the last record he recorded before his move to Berlin.

## *Low*

While David Bowie's previous album, *Station to Station*, hinted at some of the new directions in which he would be moving, it really did only provide hints of what was to come. The 1977 album *Low* found Bowie, working in collaboration primarily with Brian Eno, exploring electronic and ambient music, paring down his lyrics to what at times seems like a haiku-like minimalism, and writing and recording instrumental compositions to an extent unheralded in any of his previous albums. It may seem surprising, then, that despite the eclecticism, the strangeness, brevity, and sparseness of the lyrics, not to mention Bowie's use of dissonance and experimentations with structure, there are some beautiful melodies on *Low*. In addition, it should be noted that this is the first David Bowie album on which there are clear connections with respect to motivic structure from song to song.[1]

Unusual even by today's pop standards, *Low* begins with an instrumental: "Speed of Life." When dealing with pop singer-songwriters, one usually expects songs, that is, compositions with singing. When one hears an instrumental composition produced by someone such as David Bowie, who is so closely linked with songs, the suspicion can arise that the piece is an outtake (a song for which the lyrics just were not good enough) or instrumental backing track that is missing the vocals. Although it is not the best example on *Low*, "Speed of Life" sounds as though it is meant to be an instrumental piece. There are more instrumentation and tone color changes from phrase to phrase than is customary in an instrumental backing track for a song. Still, Bowie's experience as almost exclusively a composer of songs comes through on "Speed of Life": the sections resemble the verse, chorus, and middle-eight sections of pop song form more than the larger sections that one might expect to hear in a more classically oriented instrumental composition. Interestingly, it is the only instrumental composition on the album to rely on song structure: the instrumentals at the end of *Low* owe a much greater debt of gratitude to the freer forms of minimalist classical composition. Despite its structural kinship to pop songs, however, "Speed of Life" finds Bowie using musical contrast to a greater extent than in most of his songs. Not only does the tone color and instrumentation change from section to section, each section has its unique melodic shapes, almost like the contrasting themes found in classical compositions.

A collaborative composition of Bowie and his band mates for *Low*, Dennis Davis and George Murray, "Breaking Glass" clocks in at just under two minutes. Here, Bowie's character warns someone (the exact nature of the relationship between the two is unclear) that he has broken glass in her room and thrown something "awful" on the floor. Clearly, this is a completely dysfunctional couple of characters. The poem is short—six lines altogether—and the musical setting, too, seems very brief. To the extent that *Low* is a theme album with various snapshots of what it means to feel emotionally and psychologically low and the various causes of one feeling low, the song works. As a standalone piece, though, it seems underdeveloped. One of the notable positive features of the song is the high degree of musical contrast between sections, a factor that links the song to "Speed of Life" and some of the later compositions on the album.

Bowie's "What in the World" is the first hint on *Low* of the punk/new wave style of British bands such as the Stranglers. Insofar as the song "Be My Wife" is even more representative of the style—and specifically the sound of the Stranglers—I will discuss this aspect of *Low* later. Suffice it to say that the musical setting of the tale of the "little girl with grey eyes,"[2] who shuns crowds and stays in her room (of whom Bowie's character is both afraid and desirous), uses the instrumentation of post-punk new wave, as well as the style's high energy and fast tempo. More interesting than the ties to the foreground manifestations of the then-popular style is Bowie's melodic writing, which is not necessarily dependant upon rhythmic or instrumentation style. The melody of the verses moves back and forth below, through, and above the tonic pitch. This motion around the piece's central pitch helps to make the key center clear in the listener's mind. It is in these sections that Bowie describes the girl's eye color and psychological state. The start of the chorus, in which Bowie continues to deal with the girl's psychological state (she stays in her room), maintains a fairly narrow melodic range, low in Bowie's vocal range. The second part of the chorus, in which Bowie details his desire for the girl, however, is entirely different. In this section, the melody is far wider in range, includes more rhythmic diversity, in a generally higher range, and in a more unpredictable phrase structure. The contrast in melodic treatment serves to heighten the differences between the two characters, as well as Bowie's character's conflicted feelings. The song goes by rather quickly (it is less than two-and-a-half minutes long), and there is not a whole lot of repetition in it, so it is possible to miss the fact that the material that is focused on the female character herself and that which is focused on Bowie's reactions to her are so sharply different. The song deserves careful listening for these subtleties; however, its brevity also suggests a lack of development. It is a brief vignette of an eerie codependent relationship.

The spirit of lyrical and musical romanticism that began in earnest with Bowie's *Young Americans*, returns in *Low*'s next track, "Sound and Vision." This G major song is largely built on a repeated I (G major), ii (A minor), V (D major), I (G major) chord progression. Ending so many of the phrases on the tonic (I) chord gives the song a near classical harmonic feel, since blues and many rock songs tend to end several phrases away from the tonic. The rhythmic and stylistic feel, however, is far from classical in nature: the song as a whole feels more like an easygoing hybrid of soul and pop. The character describes the pale room in which he lives each day "waiting for the gift of sound and vision." It sounds suspiciously like the chronicle of a man who has moved into an unfamiliar room to recover from chemical dependency and to recover his artistic muse. In other words, it sounds about as clearly autobiographical as any song David Bowie had written up to that time.

The next song, "Always Crashing in the Same Car," is also in the key of G major and is also built upon an easily recognizable, short harmonic pattern. In this case, Bowie uses a variant on the "Heart and Soul" chord progression (I-vi-IV-V). Unlike the "Heart and Soul" progression, in which each phrase ends open (on the V chord, away from the tonic chord), Bowie's progression, I (G major), vi (E minor), bVII (F major), I (G major), has a feeling of closure at the end of each phrase. The motion from G major to E minor sounds typical of 1950s doo-wop music, but the upward motion of a half-step from E minor to F major gives the progression a decidedly 1970s twist.

Incidentally, Paul McCartney had incorporated a similar progression in his 1975 composition "Call Me Back Again," on the Wings's album *Venus and Mars* (Capitol 11419). Bowie's use of short, relatively simple progressions, as well as the use of the same very obvious key area (G major) links "Always Crashing in the Same Car" with its predecessor, "Sound and Vision." Like the withdrawn character of "Sound and Vision," Bowie portrays a character that seems to be living outside himself in "Always Crashing in the Same Car." In this song, the cruising around and around the hotel garage and crashing over and over "in the same car" seems to be a metaphor for living the same nightmare over and over each day. The specifics might not be the same, but just as with the character of "Sound and Vision," the character in "Always Crashing in the Same Car" feels disconnected from "normal" day-to-day life. In "Always Crashing in the Same Car," Bowie, aided by his co-producer Tony Visconti and the easily discernable electronic contributions of Brian Eno, creates a soundscape on an otherworldly nature. All of this bathes the relatively slow tune in a wash of strange electronic sounds, all of which suggest the boiling test tubes, Theremins, and Tesla coils of 1950s science fiction films. The slow tempo of the song and the electronic wash sharply contrast with the lyrics, which describe the rapid darting back and forth of the eyes of Bowie's character and his car (driving around in a parking garage) "touching close to ninety-four." This sharp contrast accentuates the otherworldly nature of the song. Incidentally, Bowie would explore the theme of the inevitable repeating patterns (and not necessarily good patterns) in other later songs, notably "Modern Love," from the 1983 album *Let's Dance.*

Writer Jerry Stahl presents a different explanation of "Always Crashing in the Same Car." Stahl describes an interview he conducted with Bowie at the Peninsula Hotel in Beverly Hills in which the two discussed the song. Bowie's explanation to Stahl was that, in a fit of depression during his stay in Berlin, he actually did drive his car around a hotel parking garage at speeds approaching ninety miles per hour, hoping to commit suicide by crashing into a post. The suicide attempt was a failure; instead of crashing his car, Bowie crashed (fell asleep) in his car.[3]

We might consider the musical style, the electronic effects, and the contrast between the lyrical and musical styles foreground elements of the composition: features that are on the surface and can be experienced in a short time span. The background structure of "Always Crashing in the Same Car" is interesting also. The song is written in a strophic form (several verses with different text, but the same music) with instrumental interludes, as opposed to a more traditional pop song structure with verses and repetitions of a chorus. Structurally, then, it is just a little closer to the nineteenth- and early twentieth-century art songs than most pop material of the late 1970s. The instrumental interludes present the listener with a somewhat more vague sense of tonality than the vocal sections. The music changes key, but Bowie's use of F major, G major, and A minor chords makes it unclear to the listener if the sonic focal point or goal is supposed to be C major (which is never heard) or A minor (which is reached, but which sounds like a deceptive cadence). The slightly unsettled nature of this motion to A minor fits in with the entire unsettling scenario that Bowie's lyrics set up. "Always Crashing in the Same Car" stands as a particularly strong, although not necessarily well-known, example of Bowie's work in exploring alienation and disconnection from the conventional concept of a so-called normal daily life.

David Bowie might not have created heavy metal; he might not have invented glam rock; he may not have invented punk; in fact, he might not have truly *invented* a whole lot of styles. But, what Bowie did was to have anticipated trends and, whenever musical change was in the air, to integrate the new styles into his own composite style. Generally he has done so in such a timely manner that his stylistic shifts rarely are perceived as mere cashing in. Incidentally, this attribute of Bowie has continued into the twenty-first century. As far as *Low* is concerned, "Be My Wife," fits perfectly into a style perhaps best exemplified by the British band the Stranglers. From the electronic Farfisa organ tone color, to the sound compression of Visconti and Bowie's production, the virtuosity of the bass guitar playing of George Murray, and the intensity of the entire musical *gestalt*, the song exudes the postpunk new-wave feel of such albums as the Stranglers *No More Heroes* (A&M Records SP 1659, 1977) and *Rattus Norvegicus* (A&M Records SP 4846, 1977). Bowie may not have invented this post-punk style, but on this track he fully integrates it into his complex personal style. And, the reader should note that Bowie's *Low* was a product of the same time period as *No More Heroes* and *Rattus Norvegicus;* it is an example of what was in the air in new British music and not a latecomer's cash-in on a trend. It is an easy-to-remember song, since the melodic material is distinctive and is built in short phrases. Bowie provides contrast between the verses, in which he expresses his loneliness and lack of roots ("I've left every place"), and the chorus, which contains the actual proposal. The verses feature higher-range, descending melodic phrases, with faster, syncopated rhythms, while the chorus is comparatively relaxed and almost static, with a lower-range, and longer note values. The instrumental accompaniment also reflects this contrast in intensity levels. All of this suggests the extent to which the marriage of the two characters will serve to alleviate the intense feelings of loneliness and alienation.

"Be My Wife" is one of Bowie's most intriguing songs, both from the standpoint of the emotional background of this proposal of marriage and from the standpoint of how Bowie manipulates the structure of his poem in the musical setting. Somehow, he manages to propose marriage without ever using the word *love*. His character clearly does not fit into conventional society: despite the fact that he has "lived all over the word," he has "left every place." The character's need for a wife stems from loneliness, not from a deep, abiding love for someone. By setting up the situation in this way, Bowie forces the listener to deal with the question: just how much is love based on giving, and how much of it is based on satisfying an inner need to circumvent loneliness? Or, more pointedly, to what extent is love self-serving? As he is so often wont to do in his songs, Bowie does not provide an answer; he forces the listener to grapple with the issue.

The structure of the lyrics of "Be My Wife" is basically verse, chorus, verse, chorus, fade out. Unlike a conventional pop song, the verses of "Be My Wife" are exactly the same. Bowie treats the two identical verses very differently, however, in terms of his text setting. The four lines of the first verse are set to four, two-measure musical phrases in succession: pretty much standard operating procedure in a pop song. In the second verse, though, Bowie inserts a two-measure instrumental interlude between each line. Since the text is exactly the same as in the initial verse, listeners can anticipate the next line during the interlude. It is a simple technique applied to a simple song structure; however, Bowie uses it to near perfection, thereby giving "Be My Wife" a poignancy and sense of sonic expansion that makes the overall piece much more interesting and significant than the sum of its parts.

"A New Career in a New Town" signals Bowie's entrance into the world of ambient music. This style, which was developed and defined by Eno in the 1970s owes a significant debt of gratitude to the French composer Erik Satie (1866–1925). In some of his compositions of the late nineteenth and early twentieth centuries, Satie wrote in what he called "furniture music" style. This music was designed not to draw attention to itself, but rather to be a background part of the environment. Likewise, Brian Eno's electronic music version served a similar function. The ambient style Bowie uses on "A New Career in a New Town," repetitive ambient music with a beat, is still around in the pop culture of the early twenty-first century: a television commercial for Audi automobiles that received widespread airplay in 2006 incorporates very similar music. The main feature of this composition that distinguishes it from full-fledged ambient background music is that it is built in two main sections. The first includes the floating electronic wash of ambient music, but the second section is more of a straight-ahead rock instrumental. The second section is more directional harmonically, too. The piece alternates between the two styles: ambient and rock. At slightly less than three minutes in length, it seems short and a bit lacking in development to really focus the listener's attention. As a piece of Satie-like "furniture music," it is not entirely successful, because the contrast between the sections tends to snap the listener's ears to attention at the sectional changes. Perhaps the most telling thing about the piece is the title itself: by turning to instrumental music, especially the hazy musical impressionism of ambient music, David Bowie did indeed seem to be embarking on a new career in a new town. However, the sudden snaps between ambient and rock suggest that he is not entirely content to leave his old career behind.

The next track, "Warszawa," is a collaboration of Bowie and Eno. Of all the pieces on the album that follow "Be My Wife," this one shows the most obvious structural craft. The opening four minutes and five seconds of the piece is strictly instrumental. After a brief modulatory passage, the piece features Bowie singing a chant-like melody. The astute listener may pick up on the fact that the various melodic themes are related by means of rhythmic motives. There is also a sense of ongoing development of the melodic figures with the subtle changes from section to section. In five years this track would find its way into the soundtrack of the motion picture *Christiane F.*, a look at the underworld of prostitution in 1970s Berlin. It is a slow-paced, very eerie-sounding, stark composition, and is very consistent with regards to presentation of mood. Interestingly, despite its impressiveness as a largely electronic composition, it does not fit the album as well as some of the other instrumental pieces, largely because its length (almost six-and-a-half minutes) overbalances the much shorter rock-oriented songs of the first half of *Low*.

Bowie's "Art Decade" is purely an instrumental piece. Here, Bowie establishes a moderately slow background *ostinato* over which he writes tonally vague material. Because of his use of dynamics, subtle balance changes, and background noises, there is both a sense of the stasis of minimalist compositions and a feeling of progression toward the ends of the larger-scale sections. It is a well-crafted piece with a melody that is both accessible and experimental sounding—perhaps an ideal for a composer bridging the gap between pop and classical minimalism. Incidentally, every time I hear this piece I am reminded of the instrumentals on the Beach Boys's *Pet Sounds* album (perhaps it is because of Bowie's use of electronic sleigh bells) and the debt of gratitude ambient composers of the 1970s and 1980s owe to Brian Wilson.

Bowie's "Weeping Wall" moves even closer to the minimalism of composers such as Philip Glass, whose *ostinato*-based music was very much in vogue at the time.[4] Bowie sets up *ostinato* figures in the synthesized mallet percussion parts. He then places a short melodic phrase in other electronic tone colors over the top of the *ostinato*. He presents this melodic phrase in a variety of ranges, tonalities, and tone colors. Taken as a stand-alone electronic composition, it is interesting, although certainly conservative by the standards of academic composers of electronic music. Compared with the *ostinato*-based minimalism of composers such as Terry Riley, Philip Glass, and Steve Reich (each of whom comes at minimalism from a classical and world music perspective), composers who have bridged the gap between classical and pop, "Weeping Wall" does not fare so well. The music of Riley, Glass, and Reich generally has more levels of rhythmic activity and therefore more cross rhythms for the listener to enjoy. This is one feature that makes minimalism particularly appealing. Bowie's piece, although interesting as an ambient composition, does not hold up under repeated listenings as do the works of the classical minimalists. It is, however, a composition that suggests that had Bowie developed his material just a little more, he could have mastered the genre. It also shows that Bowie had a keen sense of large-scale structure in his instrumental work of the period, but was not composing on the scale of the classical minimalists. Instead of further pursuing the genre and perhaps working his way closer to Riley, Glass, and Reich, Bowie instead found those elements of minimalism that most appealed to him and integrated them into his later compositions, as his expressive needs made it appropriate.

*Low* concludes with "Subterraneans," a largely instrumental piece in which Bowie focuses on creating a very slow, impressionistic electronic wash of sound. This gentle electronic wash of sound continues throughout the five-and-a-half-minute piece, but is all that is heard for well over the first half of the composition. Eventually, Bowie sings a short abstract poem in multi-tracked harmony with himself. The few recognizable words take on the same characteristics of the other, more abstract syllables: they are sounds with musical (as opposed to narrative) meaning. Bowie's use of the saxophone to humanize the piece deserves applause; however, his tendency to slide up close—but never quite all the way up—to pitch does not wear particularly well: whereas Bowie's use of flexible intonation adds expression, his tendency towards flatness detracts somewhat from a slow piece such as "Subterraneans."

One of the interesting features of Bowie's saxophone arranging and playing, particularly during his Berlin period, is his approach to voicing the accompaniment multi-tracked saxophone ensemble. In sharp contrast to big band jazz, which usually features one or two alto saxophones as part of the sax section, Bowie has concentrated solely on the larger instruments of the family: the tenor and baritone saxes. In addition, he generally has avoided the extreme upper range of the instruments. This gives his sax section writing (when he is the sole player on a given track) a depth of tone rare in recordings of the period. Curiously, the closest precedent to Bowie's low saxophone voicings in British pop music are some of the 1960s recordings of the Dave Clark Five, in which the multi-tracked tenor and baritone saxophones of Dennis Payton feature the same kind of low range chordal voicings that Bowie would later use. In fact, some of the instrumental recordings of the Dave Clark Five, most notably the first instrumental number in their mid-1960s cult movie *Having a Wild Weekend,* sound as though they could have been a model for Bowie's writing in the mid-1970s and beyond.

When placing Bowie's *Low* in context, it is important to keep in mind that the album's focus on instrumental music precedes the so-called classical compositions of artists such as Billy Joel and Paul McCartney by years. Chronologically, the closest such mixture of songs and instrumental pieces is Stevie Wonder's 1979 film soundtrack double-album *Journey Through the Secret Life of Plants.* Wonder's compositions share with Bowie's *Low* the use of repetitive techniques of minimalism, impressionistic lyrics (although of a much sunnier mood than those of *Low*), as well as that background nature known as ambient.

As a listener, I have to admit that I enjoy listening both to the individual songs of *Low* as well as to the entire album. The thing is, it is difficult to explain why. By all rights, this album should be a disaster: there are strong elements of British post-punk new wave, but nowhere near a complete album's worth, and there are strong elements of the almost diametrically opposed ambient style, but, again, no album-length commitment to the style. In short, musically it is Kraftwerk meets Philip Glass meets the Stranglers meets Eno meets Paul McCartney's Rockestra.[5] The psychological states that Bowie explores through the album's characters are, frankly, disturbing. Somehow, though, through a mix of focus on detachment, repressed emotions, and self-centeredness, it all works as a whole, despite the extremely wide range of musical styles.

While Bowie's previous album, *Station to Station,* included 6 lengthy songs, *Low* includes 11 short pieces. There is a restlessness that runs throughout—the fairly short poems, the relatively short (at least in the context of *Young Americans* and *Station to Station*) songs and instrumental pieces (only "Warszawa" and "Subterraneans" exceed five minutes in length) seem to dart back and forth like the character's eyes in "Always Crashing in the Same Car." It's a sort of "there's so much to do and so little time in which to do it" album. As a whole package, *Low* is not even particularly long; it lasts less than 39 minutes. Of course, it was a product of the pre-CD era, but even by the standards of the late 1970s, it is not a particularly long album. *Low,* however, is a crucial album in David Bowie's musical development. The seeming fascination that he has with the sundry possibilities presented by electronica on the second half of the album would serve him well: he continues to incorporate technology in his recordings into the twenty-first century.[6]

Incidentally, one completely non-scientific indication that an artist has become an iconic part of pop culture is when other artists parody them. In the case of David Bowie's *Low,* this parody—not of the music, nor of the man, but of the album title itself—came from the British pub-rock singer-songwriter-guitarist Nick Lowe. Lowe titled his 1977 EP *Bowi* (Stiff Records SABAM, 1977). At the time, he was widely quoted as saying that if Bowie would use his name (Lowe) and drop the final letter for an album title (*Low*), he would take Bowie's name and drop the final letter for the title of his EP.[7]

This era of Bowie's career was quite productive, not only in terms of his own recordings, *Low,* "*Heroes,*" and *Lodger,* but also in terms of his outside work. Principal among Bowie's other projects was his work on Iggy Pop's comeback album, *The Idiot.* Bowie helped Pop to form his first post-Stooges band, cowrote all the songs on the album, and produced it. Although I will not detail the eight collaborative compositions on the album here—because they are meant as Iggy Pop vehicles, and not David Bowie vehicles—it is important to note that one of the songs, "China Girl," would later appear on Bowie's *Let's Dance* album.

## "*HEROES*"[8]

Bowie's 1977 album "*Heroes*" continues the overall feel of *Low*—that is, a mixture of songs that largely focuses on social outcasts and experimental instrumental pieces.[9] Generally, though, it is a more accessible package, mostly because it contained one mega-hit song ("Heroes"), and because the instrumental pieces feature more acoustic instruments and fewer hazy, impressionistic washes of ambient sound. Still, there is a darkness that pervades "*Heroes,*" which is part of what makes this album both fascinating and challenging. The cover art, which shows Bowie in stark black and white in a highly stylized, almost kabuki-like gesture (dressed in leathers), hints at the stark contrasts that the songs and instrumental pieces present. This becomes the overarching theme of "*Heroes.*"

The album's first song, "Beauty and the Beast" bears a superficial resemblance to the title track of Bowie's *Station to Station*. This can be heard especially well in the opening accompaniment figures. Once Bowie's vocal melody begins, though, the resemblance to "Station to Station" is forgotten. This is a particularly interesting melody in terms of Bowie's use of short motivic figures to construct a longer-range melody. Although it is a generalization, Bowie typically writes melodies that feature a high degree of melodic contrast between the verse and chorus sections. "Beauty and the Beast" contains contrast between the sections, but there is one phrase in the chorus that clearly is based on the opening melodic motive of the verse. This gives the piece a greater feeling of structural integrity than would be provided by a lack of motivic sharing from verse to chorus.

"Beauty and the Beast" is one of those David Bowie songs with lyrics that can leave the listener scratching his or her head and wondering just what they mean. Bowie establishes a basic of feeling of evil in the air through his impressionistic and non-linear lyrics. Bowie's references allow the listener to read the Beauty and the Beast characters two possible ways. Either they are two entities, or perhaps, two sides of a single entity. In either case, the fact remains that the dark side—which Bowie paints as unavoidable—rules the situation he constructs. The listener must keep in mind that Bowie has created images based on the good-evil dialectic throughout his career: it is not unique to "Beauty and the Beast." However, it is interesting to consider the possible influence of Berlin on Bowie at this point in his career. Certainly, the East Berlin-West Berlin, Communism-Democracy dialectics fit conveniently in the listener's possible understanding of the song.

The second track on "*Heroes,*" the song "Joe the Lion," paints the picture of a man—the title character—who morphs from one personality type to another after "a couple of drinks." Joe the Lion is emboldened by drink. In so far as David Bowie has turned time and time again to depicting various social outcasts who fit in *only* within their own subculture, this character is somewhat atypical. Joe seems to fit in with the regulars at the local bar, at least after he has enjoyed his drinks. There is nothing to suggest, however, that he cannot fit into the world at large when he is fully sober. His almost Jekyll and Hyde personality represents a concrete manifestation of the rather more abstract feel of the song "Beauty and the Beast." It is with "Joe the Lion" that the theme of the entire album revolving around the good-evil, Jekyll-Hyde dialectic starts to become clear. It is not always as easy to hear as in these two songs, but there clearly is always a sort of black and white contrast lurking below the surface throughout "*Heroes.*"

Bowie's music for "Joe the Lion" is closely connected to his work on *Station to Station* and *Low*. In particular, he uses ample dissonance in the harmonies and harsh electric guitar timbre, but balances this with tuneful melodic hooks. He also balances the avant-garde tendencies and thick texture of the introduction and verses with a middle eight that features a thinner texture and rounder tone colors, both in Bowie's voice and in the instrumental accompaniment. One of the more interesting features of the song from a musical standpoint is Bowie's use of an easy-to-remember, three-note descending stepwise figure in the lead guitar in sharp contrast to the meandering, *sprechstimme*-like melody of the vocal line.[10] All in all, Bowie balances his avant-garde and pop sensibilities throughout the album, sometimes falling more clearly on one side of the fence than the other. In the case of "Joe the Lion," the balance favors the avant-garde. This makes the song's middle-eight section stand out in fairly stark relief. The more avant-garde nature of "Joe the Lion" also makes the track that follows seem even more accessible, since it falls more squarely on the other side of the musical fence.

The album's title track is easily the best-known song on "*Heroes.*" In a 2004 issue, *Rolling Stone* magazine placed "Heroes" at No. 46 on its list of the 500 greatest songs of all time.[11] In order fully to appreciate the song, the listener must keep in mind that the song was a product of the end of the Cold War, when today's Germany was still divided into East Germany and West Germany, and the infamous Berlin Wall was still standing. During his extended stay in Berlin, Bowie happened to see a couple rendezvous near the wall and kiss. The song "Heroes," represents his view of what could be behind the couple's rendezvous, and its symbolic defiance of the political state of Europe at the time. And like "Beauty and the Beast" and "Joe the Lion," "Heroes" has at its core a conflict between two opposing forces. In this case the dialectic is formed by the sense of separation caused by the Berlin Wall, on one hand, and the couple's dedication to each other, on the other.

The text of "Heroes" is written from the viewpoint of the male member of the couple and stresses first the unity of the couple (verse one), then their unconditional love and acceptance of each other (verse two). After those first two verses the concept of being heroes seems only to mean that they will be unconditionally supportive of each other; at this point there is no other, political, message. The instrumental interlude that follows features a synthesized-sounding solo that more than anything else suggests Keith Emerson's Moog synthesizer solo in Emerson, Lake and Palmer's "Lucky Man," that band's famous 1970 song of chivalry. The third verse finds Bowie's character moving away from the naïve clarity of the song's opening and wishing that his lover could "swim, like dolphins can swim." This lyrical shift, and the fact that it has instrumental interludes on either side of it, gives the listener a sense of a long transition and perhaps a more significant shift in the nature of the story. The fourth verse, which Bowie sings an octave higher and in a near scream, is a restatement of the first. In the song's next verse, Bowie's character recalls the couple standing and kissing by "the Wall," in open defiance of the bullets flying overhead. At this instant, it becomes clear that the character's love can overcome anything. And, at this point the meaning of his desire to see his beloved able "to swim like dolphins can swim," takes on a hidden political meaning. Dolphins swim as they wish; they are free. Bowie's character's lover does not enjoy that degree of freedom. It is clear that the heroism described at the end of each verse—"we can be heroes"—goes well beyond anything the listener might have anticipated at the start of the piece. Bowie's narrative technique, in which he presents a fairly generic picture at the start and then sharply and quickly focuses the scene and its meaning in at the conclusion, works exceptionally well.

The other obvious strength of "Heroes" is that the song is so full of vocal melody and accompaniment hooks that it is a great example of contemporary pop music. This is balanced by the early 1970s progressive-rock nature of the synthesizer interlude and the avant-garde tone color manipulations of Eno. One might reasonably assume that a song with a near-ideal mix of pop and avant-garde sensibilities and a storyline that reflects the times could not help but be a commercial success as a single release. Curiously, Bowie's highest-ranked song on *Rolling Stone*'s list of the 500 greatest songs of all time did not even make it into the *Billboard* Pop Top 40. Why? The answer might at least in part lie in the way in which the single version was chopped up to make it fit commercial radio. The single version omits the first two verses, thereby degrading the entire pacing of the song and the tension that Bowie's album version creates by sharply contrasting the deliberately vapid sentimentality of the first two verses with the emotional defiance of the Cold War battle lines at the song's conclusion. The song does not make as much sense, nor have nearly as much impact, if it starts with the reference to dolphins swimming. The long and the short of it is that the artistic integrity of an exceptionally strong pop song was severely compromised in an attempt to place the record on more radio playlists. It seems curious that this happened, because the full album version weighs in at just over six minutes, shorter than a number of highly successful singles of the rock era (The Beatles' "Hey Jude," for example).

The next song on "*Heroes*," "Sons of the Silent Age," is one of those Bowie songs that probably raise more questions than answers. For example, the listener never learns definitively just who these men are, the ones with "blank looks and no books." These characters could be members of just about any marginalized group. They could be citizens of East Berlin or East Germany, those faceless victims of Communism whose access to literature ("books") was inhibited by a repressive regime. In so far as "*Heroes*" is a product of Bowie's stay in Berlin, this would seem to be a workable interpretation, but it is by no means a necessary interpretation: he does not give the listener enough clues to nail down the identity of the characters in any definitive way. The fleeting reference to the sons of the silent age listening to "tracks by Sam Therapy and King Dice" raises the specter of a fictional rock band on the order of Ziggy Stardust and the Spiders from Mars. The chorus, on the other hand, sounds like a lover's plea for forgiveness after some transgression, but it does not necessarily directly relate to the verses. But then again, Bowie has used the technique of juxtaposing seemingly contradictory or seemingly unrelated images in numerous songs. He has also used the technique of placing abstract or highly impressionistic images right next to concrete images in numerous songs before "*Heroes*" and since. As he customarily does when he presents highly contrasting lyrical images, Bowie also writes highly contrasting music: the verses use speech-like rhythms and a low part of Bowie's vocal range, while the chorus is more pop song like and in a higher range.

Even more than its predecessors on "*Heroes*," "Blackout" is a mood piece replete with disconnected images. The mood is that of desperation, and Bowie plays it out in both his words (written in free verse) and his music. Significantly, co-producers Bowie and Tony Visconti treat Bowie's vocal lines with more than a little artificial reverberation. This renders some of the lyrics nearly incomprehensible (although they are printed on the album's inner sleeve), and really leaves the listener with only impressions of the atmosphere surrounding Bowie's character's desperation. The song is harrowing, and easily the least accessible piece on the album. In that regard, it sets the stage for the challenging experimental songs of Bowie's next album, *Lodger.*

After five songs, Bowie turns to instrumental compositions for the next four tracks. The first, "V-2 Schneider," is the closest of these instrumentals to pop song structure and feel. Once the tonality is established, approximately 20 seconds into the piece, a groove is established. Following that, Bowie basically alternates between an R&B-style saxophone section (Bowie multi-tracked) figure and a melody performed by electronically processed voice that uses the approximate spoken rhythm of the phrase "V-2 Schneider." Since the piece has a clear tonal center, uses conventional symmetrical phrase structure, and contains melodic hooks, it the one part of the four-composition instrumental suite to most closely resemble pop music. Because of this nature, it provides a nice transition into the more experimental instrumental pieces that follow.

Bowie's "Sense of Doubt" is an entirely synthesizer-based composition. It begins with a dramatic, ominous, low-register descending four-note figure, C-B-B flat-A. This helps to establish the key of A minor as the tonal center. Ultimately, there are hints of major tonality, but the vast majority of the nearly four-minute composition maintains the minor, slightly ominous feel. The slow pace of the piece, as well as its minimalistic, static feel paints it as an example of the Eno-inspired ambient music Bowie had first included on the second half of *Low.* The pacing, however, is better in "Sense of Doubt" than in the electronic pieces of *Low.* Most importantly, Bowie takes his time developing the material and allows for more stasis than in his earlier electronic compositions. Here, he sounds more like a composer of electronic ambient music and less like a pop song composer experimenting in ambient music.

Bowie certainly is not best known as a multi-instrumentalist. In fact, aside from *Diamond Dogs,* on which he is the only credited guitarist, and on the recordings throughout his career on which he plays saxophone, Bowie's instrumental contributions are easy to overlook. Such is not the case on the

Bowie and Eno collaboration "Moss Garden." Here Bowie performs on *koto*. The solo passages he performs on this Japanese stringed instrument are consistent with the faux-Asian atmosphere of the piece. Bowie and Eno develop their material to an even lesser extent than on the Bowie-penned "Sense of Doubt." "Moss Garden" becomes, then, truly an ambient composition that captures a Zen-like state of being. Because it is the only such instrumental piece on the album—all of the others contain more thematic contrast and are more clearly sectionalized works—it seems not to fit quite as well. However, Bowie and Eno deserve credit for sticking to their guns and maintaining that Zen-like state of being, since it is entirely consistent within a certain style of Asian music.

"Neuköln," another collaboration of Bowie and Eno, features a slow-moving ambient texture with a melody based on a three-note descending motive. What really sets the piece apart from the electronic compositions of *Low* is Bowie's tenor saxophone improvisation. Bowie plays the instrument with the intensity of the American avant-garde saxophonist John Zorn and members of the Dutch avant-garde school of saxophone playing, and his playing combines elements of avant-garde jazz, blues, with a couple of passing references to a Middle-Eastern musical scale. The Middle Eastern reference effectively connects this piece with the song "The Secret Life of Arabia." In fact, it is Bowie's careful use of transitions ("V-2 Schneider" to link the opening songs with the experimental instrumental pieces, and the Middle-Eastern scale material to link the last of the instrumental compositions to "The Secret Life of Arabia") that gives *"Heroes"* a much more thoroughly integrated, composite sound and progression than *Low*.

The last piece on the album, "The Secret Life of Arabia," is another mood piece. Here, writers Bowie, Eno, and Carlos Alomar combine faux Middle-Eastern music with funk. There are even a few rhythmic references to the early Bowie song "Golden Years," probably the best-known song on *Station to Station*. This is most evident in the background hand-clapping part (a two-measure pattern, with claps on beats two and four in the first measure, and on two, the and of three, and on four in the second measure). The lyrics suggest images or impressions from watching a film with an Arab theme. Since the other vocal compositions on *"Heroes"* feature contrast between opposing forces as their theme, "The Secret Life of Arabia" seems a little out of place. The song also does not fit in with the explicit and implicit German references in songs such as "Heroes" and "Sons of the Silent Age." In fact, thematically and musically "The Secret Life of Arabia" would have been a better fit on Bowie's next album, *Lodger*. And, to the extent that listeners today hear the song as a prelude to the around-the-world references on *Lodger*, it serves as a suitable segue between the two albums.

It is convenient to group *Low*, *"Heroes,"* and *Lodger* together since the three albums all come from Bowie's Berlin period. *Low* and *"Heroes,"* because of Bowie's inclusion of a mix of songs and instrumental compositions, are most closely related; however, *"Heroes"* feels a little more thoroughly integrated. This is because there are more vocal pieces than purely instrumental pieces, and because Bowie begins and ends the album with songs. More importantly, however, the transitions from style to style and linkage of the instrumentals "Sense of Doubt," "Moss Garden," and "Neuköln" (the three pieces flow from one to the next with no complete sonic break) give the listener the distinct feeling that *"Heroes"* was composed and meant to be experienced as a unified whole.

Incidentally, in addition to his work as a singer-songwriter on his own solo albums and as a cowriter and performer with Iggy Pop, David Bowie was involved in other projects in the late 1970s, sometimes surprising ones. Perhaps the most unexpected was his 1978 narration of Sergei Prokofiev's *Peter and the Wolf* for the RCA recording of the piece made by the Philadelphia Orchestra, under the baton of Eugene Ormandy (RCA Red Seal ARL1–2743).

## LODGER

While it may not be entirely appropriate to label David Bowie as "rock's chameleon" as numerous commentators have done, it is true that he rarely rests on past successes and is always willing to take artistic chances. In particular, Bowie has undertaken major, album-length projects that go beyond collections of songs to the level of challenging concept albums. The most challenging of these—*Diamond Dogs, Lodger,* and *Outside*—did not achieve the critical success or the commercial success of Bowie's other albums. *Lodger,* one of these challenging concept albums, basically revolves around the subject of sanity and insanity, with a look at political oppression (based on society's views of insanity) mixed in. It is truly one of Bowie's strangest mixes in that there are (depending on how one interprets the lyrics and the visual images presented in the album) visual and lyrical references to psychological experiments in Nazi Germany, World War II and Cold War political intrigue, and drag queens set to thoroughly late-1970s-style music.[12] Because of some of the lyrical and musical connections of the songs, *Lodger* seems like an integrated whole. There are even hints that there may be some sort of storyline behind the collection. Insofar as the prototypical rock opera, such as the Who's *Tommy,* is linear in construction—that is, the storyline is developed through the songs—then *Lodger* is not a rock opera in the traditional sense. This is because what storyline might exist in *Lodger* is nonlinear. In fact, *Lodger* is so nonlinear that it would be next to impossible for the listener to even tell that the songs relate to the same story. It is as if David Bowie took a page from the book of the mid-twentieth-century compositional techniques of the aeleatoric (incorporating chance and randomness) composer and philosopher John Cage and Beat writer William Burroughs and cut up the story into little pieces, scattered them, and then reassembled the whole thing in random order. It tends to confound the listener, but, then, that is probably just what Bowie had in mind. With a theme that revolves around senseless political oppression and insanity, the structure matches the material. The music also carries a significant challenge. Every song comes right out of the techno new wave style that was in vogue at the time. Bowie certainly captures the style; however, a single hearing of his 1980 song "Fashion," which includes hints of some of the same kinds of lyrical themes and some of the musical style of the songs of *Lodger*, reveals just what makes *Lodger* such a challenge. "Fashion" contains in the first verse more obvious commercial musical hooks—in both the vocal melody and in the instrumental parts—than the entire *Lodger* album. Musically, *Lodger* is unrelenting; beauty is de-emphasized in the melodic lines, and just sounds mechanical. Again, though, this mechanical sound fits the concept behind the album. Perhaps the ultimate story of *Lodger* is that it found Bowie taking some of the more progressive elements of *Low* and *"Heroes"* and putting a more narrow, laser-like focus on them. The coda to the story of *Lodger*, the album, is that Bowie's next album, *Scary Monsters (And Super Creeps)* (1980) took the themes of *Lodger* and combined them with a better-balanced approach to mood, and more sensitivity to melodic beauty and interest. In short, of all of Bowie's albums from the late 1970s and early 1980s, *Lodger* is by far the most lyrically and musically challenging. In some respects, it is the most musically progressive, and for that reason may have been the most influential on other musicians, and is probably the one Bowie album of the period that most clearly illustrates the influence of his contemporaries on him. As far as the general public goes, though, it was not given the same degree of attention as the albums on either side of it. Today, however, some critics have reassessed *Lodger* and acknowledge it as one of Bowie's better efforts. *All Music Guide* reviewer Stephen Thomas Erlewine, for example, gives the album four-and-a-half out of 5 possible stars.[13] And even more to the point, an online article in *Stylus* magazine states that, "it is perhaps the great lost Bowie album, with not a single dud to be found in the ten songs and maybe the finest second half of any of his efforts."[14]

The album's opening song, "Fantastic Voyage," exhibits more conventional commercial potential than any other piece in the collection, at least musically. This collaboration between Bowie and Eno deals with the topics of depression and the need to treat those suffering from mental illness with dignity. Added to this mix is a little bit of absurdist anti-war commentary. All of this, however, is set to retro-style music that sounds like a late 1970s take on the rhythmic, harmonic, and melodic feel of late 1950s and early 1960s pop. It is the same sort of approach that probably is better known through John Lennon's 1980 song "(Just Like) Starting Over," or (nearly a decade later) several songs on Roy Orbison's album *Mystery Girl*. On "Fantastic Voyage," however, Bowie creates an intriguing sense of disconnection between the pleasant, familiar sounding, easily understandable, almost lush musical setting, and the disturbing images of missiles flying through the air, and people trying to "live with somebody's depression."

Although David Bowie incorporated traditional rhyme schemes in most of his songs of the 1960s, he increasingly used freer poetic structures in his work of the 1970s. Certainly, the song "Fantastic Voyage" is not unique in this respect; however, this song and some of the other songs on *Lodger* are unusual in that Bowie uses fairly standard rock musical structures in setting his free verse poetry. This creates a truly interesting tension between verse and setting. Given the fact that "Fantastic Voyage" is the most musically accessible and musically conservative piece on the album, the tension is especially great here. The thing is, it works beautifully in giving a strong poignancy to Bowie's lamenting having to "live with somebody's depression," the over-the-top pleas for destruction by means of missiles, and the gentle assertion that the lives of the mentally ill are "valuable too."

The non-linear nature of *Lodger* and Bowie's challenging juxtapositions and contradictions come to the fore as "Fantastic Voyage" gives way to the high energy, avant-garde near-rap of "African Night Flight." As *Stylus* magazine points out, this song "(and later 'DJ') shows that Bowie and Talking Heads were paying attention to each other."[15] Actually, there are even some relationships between Talking Heads's "Life During Wartime" and Bowie's "Fantastic Voyage." In considering, then, several of the songs on *Lodger,* the listener must keep in mind the nature and the source of the ties between David Bowie and the Talking Heads's David Byrne. Both artists were influenced and were working at the time with producer, keyboardist, composer, and electronic manipulation specialist Brian Eno. Eno is the real link between Bowie and Byrne, and Eno's influence on Bowie's writing on *Lodger* is not limited to the 6 (out of 10) songs on the album on which Eno and Bowie collaborated as writers.

The music of "African Night Flight," which is one of the Bowie-Eno collaborations, is aggressive and somewhat vague as far as key center. In addition to singing convoluted, difficult-to-perform melodies double-tracked in octaves with himself, Bowie also performs a thoroughly British version of rap. His accent and references to various African scenes in his rap suggests that he is portraying the prototypical Great White Hunter. The entire piece resembles a high-speed chase through Africa. This song, probably better than just about anything recording David Bowie has ever made, shows off his skill as a vocalist who can compose and perform extremely difficult melodies. Bowie may not possess the most classically beautiful voice in pop music of the past forty years, but his multi-tracked performance of this disjunctive melody of "African Night Flight" exhibits a vocal technique that is very rare in rock music.

Bowie's solo composition "Move On" also includes references to Africa, as well as to Cyprus, Russia, and Kyoto, Japan. His character moves from one place to another and bids farewell to someone who he "can't forget," despite the fact that he will soon be moving again. Here, the music is more in keeping with conventional British rock, evoking the style of the Who in the mid-1960s. The listener familiar with late-1970s British bands that were influenced by the Who—the Jam, in particular—will also hear close relationships between "Move On" and the work of Bowie's late-1970s contemporaries. The harmonic progressions, strummed chords that approximate Pete Townshend's power chords, and short phrases in the vocal line all combine to suggest the Who and its followers. Bowie uses a free rhyme scheme in the lyrics of "Move On." In this regard the song is closer to the work of the Jam's Paul Weller than to the work of the Who's Townshend. The lack of a memorable chorus lyrical hook and the unpredictability of the verses make the lyrics difficult to follow. They, like the character Bowie portrays in the song, meander all over the place. Although this may not make for the most pleasant listening experience, the lyrical style fits the character well.

The instrumental introduction and the rhythm guitar, bass, percussion rhythm section of the album's next track, "Yassasin (Turkish for: Long Live)," sounds suspiciously like the instrumental accompaniment on the earlier song "Fame." Once the Middle-Eastern scales of the synthesizer and violin melody lines enter, however, the music takes the listener (and the main character of Bowie's loosely structured drama) to Turkey. Taken by itself, out of the context of other Middle Eastern-influenced British rock of the 1970s, the song succeeds as a character piece. The metrical shifts in the repeated statements of the phrase "look at this" are especially intriguing and catchy. Unfortunately, however, the Middle-Eastern milieu invites comparison with Led Zeppelin's grandiose production "Kashmir," from the 1975 album *Physical Graffiti*. Compared with the John Bonham, Jimmy Page, and Robert Plant composition "Kashmir," "Yassassin" seems thin in texture: it becomes a vignette instead of the grand statement the Led Zeppelin song delivers. There are, though, many interesting features of the piece. One of the most interesting background features is the hint of Jamaican ska and rock steady rhythm in the accompaniment. The unison male backing chorus parts also suggest the 1970s version of ska, which was very much in the air at the time with popular contributions to the genre by bands such as the Specials. Once again, Bowie's poetry is free with respect to rhyme. However, because there is enough direct repetition that the listener periodically hears something familiar, it is easier for the listener to follow this song than "Move On."

"Red Sails" suggests the punk rock and British new wave that was still very much au courant in 1979. This Bowie-Eno collaboration also features an electric guitar–based texture that is reminiscent of Bowie's flirtations with heavy metal in the early 1970s. The lyrics suggest a trip aboard a ship; however, like so much of *Lodger,* the lyrics are decidedly non-linear and provide disconnected impressions of the trip, rather than a conventional time-line based description of the trip. There are hints of the music of the infamous punk band the Sex Pistols in Bowie's presentation of the text "The hinterland, the hinterland" near the conclusion of the song—one can almost hear Johnny Rotten screaming out "Anarchy for the U.K."

Most of the songs of *Lodger* include such unconventional poetry (at least for pop songs) that they are always interesting, thought provoking, and challenging. The song "D.J.," however, is one of the most interesting due to the depth into which Bowie probes the psychology of personal identity and the psychology of one person's control over another. The DJ in the song's title is portrayed by Bowie in the first person, and becomes the vehicle through which Bowie deals with the subjects of the psychology of identity and control.

Collaborators Bowie, Eno, and Carlos Alomar set up the themes of identity and control in the song's opening. Here, Bowie's character states that he is at home, has lost his job, and is suffering from an incurable illness. His "girl" is "out there" dancing, somewhere. Bowie's character then becomes a dance club DJ, who (to paraphrase) is what he plays. It is as if the man waiting at home imagines himself in the role of a DJ. In his imagination, he becomes the music he plays, and he takes delight in the control that he exerts over the crowd—and not, coincidentally, over the woman who left him at home. The disconnection between the character both exercising puppet master-like control over the dancers at a club while also being unemployed and home-bound, suggests that the only way he is ever going to feel in control of his life is to imagine being a DJ. There is also a slight nagging feeling that perhaps he is delusional, a control freak. or both. As such, "D.J." fits in with *Lodger*'s overarching themes of mental illness and political control.

Musically, "D.J." is another of *Lodger*'s thoroughly contemporary sounding songs, in this case a near sibling of the Talking Heads song "Life During Wartime." Musically, both "D.J." and the Talking Heads's song share a similar hook-laden accompaniment, and a chorus melody based on short, phrases related by motive. Both songs also deal with characters that really are not in control of their situation, even though they try desperately to present themselves as having the appearance of being in control.

Bowie and Eno collaborated on the song "Look Back in Anger." In the song, an angel appears to a man and then invites the human to go along with him. Although the lyrics are not explicit about this point, it would appear that angel is present to welcome the man to his death. The angel tells the man to "look back in anger" until he comes with him. Although the music is very minimal from the standpoint of harmonic change, the melody of the verses is dramatic and the sing-along part of the chorus ("Waiting so long") is quite catchy. The catchiness of this phrase suggests that the man has been so angry either with life or in life that he is ready to find release in death. The man notes that the angel seems to be sane, which suggests that perhaps he is looking to the angel for the go ahead to end his life. Bowie and Eno really provide nothing more than a hint, though, that the man might even be considering suicide. However, the listener must keep in mind that "Look Back in Anger" exists within the overall context of *Lodger,* with its array of mentally ill characters. In this context, even a small hint of the man's contemplation of suicide is probably enough that more than one listener would hear this facet of the song's meaning.

Bowie has dealt either explicitly or implicitly with the concept of identity on every one of his albums. In a way, his work in this area suggests an amateur fascination with and application of the science of psychology. Interestingly, the writer whose technique perhaps most obviously influenced Bowie, William S. Burroughs, also expressed a fascination with psychology.[16] The song "Boys Keep Swinging," a collaboration of Bowie and Eno, might not be the most psychologically probing selection on *Lodger;* however, it does deal with the concept of identity, specifically gender identity. Bowie and Eno present several stereotypes of handsome boys: other boys will "check [them] out"; girls will be interested in them; they can "wear a uniform" (and not have to fear dying); and they will "get [their] share." The song is all about the good life, the unlimited possibility that is felt by typical young men. Given the nature of the other characters that inhabit the soundscape of *Lodger,* however, "Boys Keep Swinging" is a song that is full of irony. And, this is one of the features that marks this album as a standout among Bowie's output of the period. There were no hit singles on *Lodger;* there were no songs that were reissued on the single-disc greatest hits RCA Victor albums. The songs on the album, and "Boys Keep Swinging" in particular, really take on deeper, more significant meaning within the context of the album than they otherwise might. Out of context, "Boys Keep Swinging" says that boys will "always work it out"; however, in the context of the rest of *Lodger,* the song suggests that all the stereotypical easy and glorious expectations of boyhood and young manhood are nothing more than a cruel illusion. For example, the text of the song presents the stereotype that it is manly to feel militaristic. What happens if a boy does not feel that way? What are the implications for his sense of masculinity? Likewise, the text presents the stereotype that all males need to do to "work it out" is to just keep trying. The implication here is that masculinity can only be achieved through self-reliance; it is not masculine to ask for help. What happens when trying and trying on one's own does not yield success? Does one dare to risk one's masculinity by seeking help, or must a truly masculine man accept increasing levels of frustration until they boil over? Although the song's presence within the context of the album as a whole encourages these questions to be raised, the consequences of society's unrealistic stereotyping of so-called correct masculine traits is not addressed directly within the song itself. The next piece on *Lodger,* however, gives the listener a concrete example of how one man deals with frustration.

"Repetition" suggests at least in part Bowie's work of the late 1960s. The melody is based on a short, simple motive—it is basically a monothematic song. This is a technique Bowie used in that brief period between his more pop-oriented material of 1965–1967 and his heavy metal (*The Man Who Sold the World*) period. The characters are John, a man who is "bigger than you," and his wife. Apparently, John could have married Anne, a woman "in a blue silk blouse," but did not. John is a systematic physical abuser of his wife, who he accuses of not being able to cook, and who apparently has played a role in his having to drive an old Chevrolet instead of a Cadillac. What is perhaps just as interesting as what Bowie tells us is what he leaves to the listener's imagination. It seems fairly likely that this really is a tale of a man who got a woman, with whom he was not in love, pregnant, married her, and now abuses her for depriving him of what he thinks he deserved. It is a disturbing scenario. Bowie makes the scene more disturbing by counterpointing Anne's blue silk blouse with the long-sleeve blouse John's wife must wear in order to hide her bruises. Coming as it does immediately after "Boys Keep Swinging," "Repetition" becomes one very specific, literal and concrete manifestation of the idea of "swinging"; in this case it means a husband throwing punches at his wife. And this is significant, for as disjunct as some of the characterizations, situations, and music of the first half of *Lodger* are, the last three songs are thematically and musically linked. In the case of "Boys Keep Swinging" and "Repetition," the linkage comes when the wonderful bright future promised to boys is broken. Because John feels that his dreams were never realized, he feels frustrated and powerless, and his reaction is to lash out with physical violence.

The album's last song, "Red Money," retains the monothematic feel of "Repetition." This provides a stylistic link between the songs, even though there is not much of a lyrical link between the two songs. The listener will tend to hear the musical link between "Repetition" and "Red Money" because of the fact that these two songs are closer in melodic style and structure than any of the pairs of songs on *Lodger*. Bowie's exaggerated vocal delivery and the monothematic nature of the music resembles some of the contemporary work of Talking Heads. Of course, Bowie had used an exaggerated delivery in his Anthony Newley-influenced work of the 1960s and at times throughout the 1970s. Clearly, he influenced David Byrne of Talking Heads, but Bowie's use of post-punk minimalism and his style of vocal delivery suggest that the influence was at least in part a two-way street.

All in all, *Lodger* is a decidedly short album. It largely went unappreciated at the time of its release, especially as it followed *Low* and "*Heroes*," both of which attracted considerably more commercial and critical attention. *Lodger* is a challenging album even though it consists entirely of songs (unlike *Low* and "*Heroes*," which were divided between songs and experimental instrumentals). These songs, though, find Bowie suggesting the difficult-to-follow cut-up techniques of William S. Burroughs and free verse writing, with almost entirely non-rhyming lyrics. Although the song styles and structures might be in keeping with what was au courant at the time, the lyrics make *Lodger* more difficult to make sense of than anything else that was on the album charts in 1979 and 1980. Today, the album has grown in stature, not at the expense, however, of Bowie's other Berlin-era work. *Lodger* was recorded in Switzerland, an officially politically neutral country, which makes Bowie's political musings on *Lodger* just that much more intriguing. The move to studios in Switzerland also make *Lodger* a transition from the musical and lyrical references to Germany (the avant-garde instrumentals and the images from Cold War–era West and East Berlin) to Bowie's work at the start of the 1980s.

One of the most unusual, yet perhaps substantial endorsements of the artistic merit of David Bowie's work during his Berlin period came from the American minimalist composer Philip Glass. Glass based his 1992 "*Low*" *Symphony* on the pieces "Subterraneans" and "Warszawa" from Bowie's *Low* album. Glass also incorporated the 1991 Bowie-Eno song "Some Are" in his symphony. Four years later, Glass wrote his "*Heroes*" *Symphony*, which is based on five Bowie and Bowie-Eno songs from the "*Heroes*" era. Famed choreographer Twyla Tharp developed a ballet for her company based on the "*Heroes*" *Symphony*. Both Glass compositions have been recorded commercially and are available on compact disc.

After years of work in the British recording industry, Bowie made his worldwide break-through as part of the early 1970s glam rock movement. Here, he performs during his Ziggy Stardust period, 1973. Copyright Chris Walter (www.photofeatures.com).

The return of the Thin White Duke: Bowie performing at Wembley at the time of his *Station to Station* album, 1976. Copyright Chris Walter (www.photofeatures.com).

Bowie in concert at Earls Court near the end of his Berlin period, 1978. Copyright Chris Walter (www.photofeatures.com).

The epitome of "Fashion": Bowie performing in the United States at the height of his popularity in 1983. Copyright Chris Walter (www.photofeatures.com).

Although the 1990s were a period of intense experimentation with jazz, industrial, and electronic jungle music for Bowie, here he performs on twelve-string acoustic guitar, 1997. Copyright Chris Walter (www.photofeatures.com).

A member of the Rock and Roll Hall of Fame and winner of a number of prestigious awards, here Bowie receives a 1999 Radio Music Award. Copyright Chris Walter (www.photo features.com).

# To the Dance Club and Down

The 1980s was a decade of extreme contrasts for David Bowie. On one hand, the years 1982 and 1983 found him dominating record charts and radio airwaves to a greater extent than ever before or since. This was also the time period in which he acted in the films *The Hunger* and *Merry Christmas, Mr. Lawrence*; he recorded the theme song for the film *Cat People;* and he recorded the hit song "Under Pressure" with the band Queen. By the middle of the decade, however, his music became less distinctive and both his output and popularity faded. There were a few other recordings, but the by the late 1980s Bowie's biggest contributions to pop culture were as an actor; he portrayed Pontius Pilate in the controversial 1988 Martin Scorsese film *The Last Temptation of Christ.*

## SCARY MONSTERS (AND SUPER CREEPS)

Bowie's first post-Berlin album, *Scary Monsters (And Super Creeps)* (1980), found him retaining some of the sonic elements of *Low,* "*Heroes,*" and *Lodger,* while moving even closer to the then-popular new wave style of bands such as Talking Heads, Blondie, and Television. This is a more accessible album than any of the three Berlin-era collections, principally because it is a collection of songs (as opposed to an eclectic mixture of songs and experimental instrumental compositions), and because it does not focus on an esoteric storyline (as had *Lodger*), and because Bowie turned to more mainstream lyrical structures (more equal-length phrases and verses, and more rhymes). The accessibility of *Scary Monsters* was enhanced by Bowie's incorporation of contemporary dance rhythms in some of the songs. This accessibility forms an ideal counterpoint to the sometimes-bizarre characters and situations that can be found in Bowie's lyrics on the album.

*Scary Monsters* begins with the track "It's No Game (Part 1)." Although this song is not the title cut, it establishes the overarching premise of the album very well. In fact, the song is one of Bowie's best non-title track cuts to establish an album theme. Bowie's lyrics include a Japanese rap—delivered by Michi Hirota—which the liner notes do not translate. The English-language lyrics sung by Bowie establish the overall theme of scary events, some political, some sociological, some psychological. At the end of each statement of the chorus, he screams "It's no game," to drive the point home. Even though Bowie's collaborator over his previous three albums, Brian Eno, is not present on *Scary Monsters,* there are some Eno-influenced avant-garde touches. On this first song, the avant-garde sound is provided for the most part by guitarist Robert Fripp, and in Bowie's melodic and harmonic writing. Of particular note are the repeated tritones (pitches that are three whole-steps apart; C to F-sharp, for example) in Fripp's guitar solo. This figure resembles a demonic European-style ambulance siren. The piece ends dramatically with Fripp playing a nearly atonal (without a key center) repeated guitar figure and Bowie screaming "Shut up" twice.

Just as he had done on *Lodger,* Bowie juxtaposes highly contrasting musical styles on *Scary Monsters.* His song "Up the Hill Backwards" suggests a stylized version of the popular, gentle Quiet Storm form of late twentieth-century R&B. In sharp contrast to the disjointed melody, touches of atonality, sonic overload and distortion, and impressionistic lyrics of "It's No Game (Part 1)," here the key center is clearly established, the chorus melody consists of short, predictable, easy-to-sing phrases within a small pitch range, and the phrase structure is that a conventional pop music. The "kicker," as it were, comes from Bowie's lyrics, which speak of desperation and all sorts of personal travails. The mix of music that invites the listener to sing along in the chorus (in which Bowie offers the assurance that "it'll be alright"), with the vivid impressions of utter desperation in the verses (in which he creates the image of trying to push the weight of the world "up the hill backwards") is an example of Bowie in fine ironic form. The imagery of desperation is so extreme that the listener is left wondering if the hopefulness of the chorus is real or just a cruel illusion. That is Bowie's genius: that he is able so consistently to create musical and lyrical conflicts in his compositions that force listeners to grapple with their own experiences and emotions. In short, Bowie is at his best when he raises the questions and forces the listener to find the answers. He accomplishes just that in "Up the Hill Backwards."

The next track, "Scary Monsters (And Super Creeps)," falls roughly in the category of punk rock, bearing some resemblance to elements of bands such as the Stranglers, the Sex Pistols, and the Damned. Compared with the so-called true British punk bands of the late 1970s, though, Bowie's composition is more consistently tuneful, with memorable pop melodic hooks. The out-of-key avant-garde meanderings in Fripp's guitar solos also exhibit more technique and more purposeful motion away from the backing harmonies than what the listener would have found in the so-called real punk music of the general period: Fripp's dissonance is studied dissonance. The song is very up-to-date in the early 1980s, both in terms of the music and the theme of seeing people as "scary monsters and super creeps," or in other words, seeing people as being (in general) monstrous and lacking civility in relationships. The combination of high energy with a pop twist and the focus on the macabre all around us anticipates Rod Temperton's well-known 1982 composition "Thriller," the centerpiece of Michael Jackson's enormously successful album of the same name. "Scary Monsters (And Super Creeps)" might not be the best-remembered song on this album, but it certainly is a Bowie track worth knowing.

"Ashes to Ashes" in part deconstructs the David Bowie mystique, as well as offering one possible assessment of his work between the time he took the pop music world by storm with the song "Space Oddity" and when he confounded fans with *Lodger*. Here Bowie declares that Major Tom, the star of is song "Space Oddity," is a junkie, "strung out on heaven's high, hitting an all time low." Another important lyrical reference to Major Tom's role in the David Bowie mystique comes in the song's fade. Here, Bowie sings that his "mama said" that in order to "get things done," one had best "not mess with Major Tom." These two references seem to suggest that Bowie was aware that his life was ruled by his achievement of world-wide fame on the strength of "Space Oddity" ("strung out on heaven's high"), and that perhaps some of the low level of acceptance some of his latest work received was possibly a result of his having grown musically and lyrically too far away from his work of the early 1970s: he had, in effect, messed with Major Tom. The reference to "ashes to ashes" in the song's title and chorus suggests that Bowie was, in effect, fully prepared to bury (or cremate) the past. Whether that meant burying Major Tom (his pop side) or burying his challenging focus on the avant-garde remained to be seen. Ironically, by the mid-1980s Bowie's emphasis on nearly anonymous dance music would further "mess with Major Tom," and would represent some of the lyrically weakest work of his career.

There are also some noteworthy things happening instrumentally on "Ashes to Ashes." In particular, George Murray's incorporation of funk-style string snaps suggests the return (at least in part) of Bowie to the Plastic Soul style of *Young Americans* and *Station to Station*. "Ashes to Ashes" is in many respects the most popish, accessible song musically on *Scary Monsters*—or in fact, on any of his albums in years. Despite the song's tuneful accessibility and the popish nature of the instrumental work, Bowie incorporates a number of sophisticated structural features that make "Ashes to Ashes" stand out. In particular, Bowie handles the structure of the verses in an unusual way. Unlike most pop songs in which the verse consists of several related phrases, "Ashes to Ashes" features an unusually high degree of contrast from phrase to phrase. The effect is that the verse consists of several unrelated sections, rather than related phrases. Bowie delineates these by means of key changes, large register changes in the vocal melody, and contrasting singing styles. The sectional nature of the music of the verses allows Bowie to shift poetic voice and focus easily from section to section. It is a perfect alignment of musical and text structure.

Whenever I hear "Fashion," I always come away from it thinking that this is the best David Byrne song that David Byrne never wrote. It has all the wry social commentary and irony, the seeming glorification of the trivial, and the danceable, commercial musical hooks of the best songs chief Talking Head Byrne ever wrote; however, it is fully the product of the Bowie, not Byrne. "Fashion" has the tune, beat, and hooks to make it a successful early 1980s dance track. It might not have been a top-40 pop hit on the *Billboard* charts, but it captures the dance club spirit of the time. Curiously, Bowie's lyrics are open to several contradictory interpretations. On one hand, the overall gestalt of the song (music and lyrics, especially the oft-repeated word *fashion*) seems to celebrate popular fashion trends. Upon careful study of the lyrics, however, there is plenty to suggest that Bowie considers both those who suppress fashion trends *and* those who demand strict adherence to those same trends, as sort of fashion fascists, the "goon squad" in Bowie's lyrics.

"Teenage Wildlife" clearly shares an instrumental lick in common with "Clowntime Is Over, No. 2," from the Elvis Costello and the Attractions's album *Get Happy!!,* which just so happened to be a product of the same year. On the Costello recording, organist Steve Nieve plays the lick, whereas on the Bowie song, the lick is heard in the lead guitar. Interestingly, both of these instrumental figures are related by motive (although maybe not very obviously) to the lead guitar hook in Bruce Springsteen's classic 1975 song "Born to Run." The other notable texture-related feature of "Teenage Wildlife" that is interesting to note is the steady repeated eighth-note rhythm guitar and bass line. This was very much in keeping with the new wave style of the day, and is probably best known through songs such as the Cars' 1981 hit "Shake It Up" and the 1983 Police classic "Every Breath You Take." Bowie's use of this sound speaks to how in 1980, even as an over-30-year-old songwriter, Bowie was abreast of the current style. In this song, Bowie also takes many dramatic chances with his vocal delivery. For one thing, the melody is complicated—although thoroughly accessible—with a wide range. Even more notably, however, are the dramatic stylistic touches that Bowie incorporates into his singing: from a howl, to what resembles a stylized imitation of Mick Jagger's pouting lip presentation, to touches of a sob in places. Yes, there is overacting here; however, somehow it works because there is that unquantifiable real feel to the passion Bowie expresses as a singer. The overall premise of the song, the establishment of teenage identity and a rock and roll lifestyle, calls to mind Bowie's "Rock 'n' Roll Suicide," a track from the 1972 album *The Rise and Fall of Ziggy Stardust and the Spiders from Mars.* Despite his age, 33, Bowie could still both observe the problems of teens and empathize with them. It helps considerably that the musical style sounded thoroughly contemporary. "Teenage Wildlife" is a strong and unjustly overlooked Bowie track.

"Scream Like a Baby" is one of the most disturbing and provocative songs on *Scary Monsters*. Here, Bowie portrays a presumably gay character that was involved sexually with a character named Sam. Both characters seem to have been institutionalized: apparently (although Bowie does not make a clearly definitive statement) in a mental institution. Bowie's lyrics state that Sam "jumped into the furnace," which in the context of the song implies that the character committed suicide. Bowie's music for "Scream Like a Baby" does not conveniently fit any single genre like some of the other *Scary Monster* tracks. This makes the piece stand out, particularly from the new wave and dance songs on the album. The wide-ranging melody to which Bowie sets the text "But I remember Sam 'cause he was just like me" is haunting and memorable.

In addition to the aforementioned Elvis Costello, Tom Verlaine was one of the most critically acclaimed of the songwriters of the late 1970s new wave. David Bowie has covered so few songs by other writers throughout his career that it is important to give attention to his choice of, and style of presentation of, covers. *Scary Monsters* contains Verlaine's "Kingdom Come." Verlaine uses the image of breaking rocks (suggesting a chain gang deployed from a prison every day to do hard labor) as a metaphor for finding and realizing one's personal identity in the face of personal and societal rejection. Lyrically, this sounds like something right out of the David Bowie songbook, for Bowie had been dealing with the general subject of personal identity at least since 1970. Musically, however, "Kingdom Come" has too many melodic and harmonic ties to introspective folk music to sound much like a David Bowie composition. It is the kind of song that could be at its best when the music and lyrics are allowed to speak to the listener in the purest possible way, so that the individual listener could apply the imagery to her or his own life. The problem is that Bowie adds too much dramatic interpretation, especially as the song progresses. The result is that the listener gets one interpretation of the inner feelings that Verlaine's piece suggests: Bowie's highly stylized interpretation. The listener's ability to project the music and lyrics into his or her own life is diminished by means of Bowie's overacting. A more balanced approach, such as that taken by Bowie on the song "Wild Is the Wind" on *Station to Station,* or even a completely cool, detached, Paul Simon-esque approach probably would have resulted in a stronger reading of the Verlaine composition.

The reader might recall that at the very beginning of his recording career David Bowie was part of the mod movement. Musically and thematically he moved in the same general circles as the Who. Bowie and the Who's Pete Townshend continued to explore some of the same issues in their later songs—especially the concept of identity—but they tended to grow apart both musically and lyrically. Actually, that probably could not be helped, especially given Bowie's inclination to attack and incorporate nearly every contemporary musical style he encountered.[1] "Because You're Young" actually brings Bowie and Townshend together on the same recording. The composition is in fact Bowie's, even though it comes about as close to any pop song of the era to an adult version of the Who's "My Generation." In "Because You're Young" Bowie portrays a character not unlike himself: someone perhaps in their thirties who observes a teenaged girl about to throw her life away on someone she meets on a chance encounter. The implication—although not clear—is that he may have been involved in a similar chance encounter years ago and doesn't wish to see the girl make the same mistake. Like the classic tragic clown Pierrot, Bowie feels sad for the girl, but continues to dance his life away—the only escape he can find from the scars of the past. The sound of the track is thoroughly late-1970s new wave. That fact makes for one of David Bowie's double-edged swords (or, in this case, a triple-edged sword). On one hand, "Because You're Young" easily fits in with the prevailing rock style of its era; however, because that style is so thoroughly based on the sound of the Farfisa organ, it finds Pete Townshend playing a nearly anonymous role (he could be any studio guitarist, so indistinctive is his contribution); and the contemporary nature of the style does not fit well with the concept of an older adult addressing a teen. In other words, Bowie's rhetorical voice in this context would have benefited from a so-called older-sounding music.

The final song on *Scary Monsters*, "It's No Game (Part 2)," recaps the album's opener, although some of Bowie's imagery—particularly that of children around the world putting "camel shit on the wall"—perhaps is even more disturbing than the more general apocalyptic imagery of "It's No Game (Part 1)." Although a reference such as this might be interpreted as politically and socially insensitive in today's post-9/11 world, what Bowie seems to be trying to do is to point out the squalid living conditions in the Middle East. Unfortunately, the reference does not wear well in the twenty-first century.

The thematic undercurrents on this album are nearly as dark as those of *Lodger;* however, *Scary Monsters* is considerably more accessible. For one thing, Bowie uses (at least in a few songs) more conventional pop musical structures and more conventional rhyme schemes in his lyrics than he had been utilizing for several years. Bowie also manages to maintain a consistent theme throughout the album, without using the cut-up techniques of he used on *Lodger. Scary Monsters* represents an important accomplishment for Bowie: it is a near-perfect balance of his pop and experimental sides. Curiously, though, it is also a transitional album in that it basically sums up Bowie's career up to 1980, while simultaneously anticipating his move toward even more mainstream sound throughout the 1980s. In short, it is one of David Bowie's most important and consistent albums.

The time period between *Scary Monsters* and *Let's Dance* found Bowie active on several fronts. In 1982, Bowie's recording of the song "Cat People (Putting out Fire)," which he co-wrote with disco pioneer Giorgio Moroder, was the theme song for the movie *Cat People.* That same year, he also recorded "Under Pressure" with the band Queen. The recording was issued as a single and on the Queen album *Hot Space* (Elecktra E1 60128). Music from Bowie's Berlin period was used in the soundtrack for the film *Christiane F.*, the tale of a girl caught in the trap of prostitution in Berlin's Zoo Station.

## LET'S DANCE

David Bowie's 1983 album *Let's Dance* was his most successful album ever from a commercial standpoint, and it included three hugely successful dance hits: "Modern Love," "China Girl," and "Let's Dance," each of which made it into *Billboard* magazine's pop top 40: a record for a David Bowie album. Because of the way in which the release of these singles was stretched out, parts of *Let's Dance* continued to enjoy airplay on top-40 radio for months and months throughout 1983. Why this sudden, dramatic commercial success? Even though Bowie had long ago put aside writing conventional-sounding lyrics in conventional forms, about conventional subjects and mainstream characters—basically abandoning conventional pop-rock structures and subjects as early as his early twenties—*Let's Dance* found him turning toward mainstream dance music and somewhat more conventional lyrical references. In short, while *Scary Monsters* hinted at this move, *Let's Dance* found Bowie losing some of what had made him unique throughout the 1970s. The man who had made his mark in the music industry as a singer-songwriter portraying the outsider and social outcast had moved closer to the center, and the center had moved just a little closer to Bowie.

For *Let's Dance*, Bowie engaged the services of Nile Rodgers, guitarist with the disco group Chic,[2] as coproducer for *Let's Dance*. While Rodgers helped to bring popular dance beats to the album, these are balanced by the appearance of blues-rock guitarist Stevie Ray Vaughan. Vaughan brings a blues edge to the recording, minus the avant-garde solos of Bowie's previous lead guitarist, Robert Fripp. Vaughan also plays in a style that is completely different from other Bowie lead guitarists, such as Mick Ronson and Carlos Alomar. Stevie Ray Vaughan had not yet become an international superstar when he recorded on *Let's Dance*, but his work on "Let's Dance," "Without You," and "China Girl," in particular, hint at not only his technical brilliance, but his ability to use space effectively: he knows when to play and when to leave brief silences.

The liner notes of *Let's Dance* credit coproducers Bowie and Nile Rodgers with the album's horn arrangements. Certainly, the overall texture of the horn arrangements, with their emphasis on the lower saxophones (tenor and baritone) call to mind Bowie's albums of the early 1970s. The main difference is that on those recordings of a decade before and during the late 1970s Berlin period, Bowie played all the multi-tracked saxophone parts himself. On *Let's Dance*, Bowie and Rodgers incorporate a small brass and saxophone ensemble. In fact, Bowie does as little instrumentally on this album as on any album he ever made—this is not necessarily a good thing, despite any inferences that might be drawn from album sales figures. Sure, the horn playing generally is more polished and consistently in tune, but an element of personality is missing in the slickness.

The album begins with "Modern Love," a song that is filled with musical and lyrical hooks—it is instantly recognizable and practically invites the listener to sing along. That is, it practically invites the listener to sing along with parts of the song. Some of the lyrics seem to be clearer than others, but it is mostly individual lines of the chorus that stand out in the sing-along department; lines such as "gets me to the church on time," and a few others from the verses, such as "I never wave bye-bye." Upon careful analysis, though, the chorus is really almost a developed series of free-association references that ultimately find conflict between "modern love" and "god and man." Bowie's lyrics of the chorus seem to be the self-psychoanalysis of someone who is trying very hard to come to grips with his true feelings about love and (especially) commitment in a marriage. It seems the story of a man who is torn between the easy freedom of "modern love" (possibly what drove him in his youth) and commitment. Interestingly, Bowie creates a vicious circle in the chorus such that he, or rather the character he portrays, can never resolve his inner conflict. This, plus the calculated obscurity of the verses, represents Bowie's more or less traditional approach to lyrics: leave it up to the listeners to ask questions and grapple with their own conclusions. There is, to be sure, a touch of poetic brilliance at the beginning of the first verse. Here, Bowie's character tells the listener that he finds life to be unchanging and entirely predictable with the simple statement, "I caught a paperboy, but things don't really change." In other words, the front-page headlines, and everything else in the news has all been seen before. The significant thing is that he expresses this observation in such an unconventional way. He links the paperboy with the character's observation about the nature of the daily news (and, presumably his everyday life as well) and not the paper itself. It matters not whether or not David Bowie was the first person to make this observation by merely implying the paper (John Lennon's "I read the news today, oh boy" implies the same thing); what matters is that the line sounds as though it is a casual statement from one person to another, yet it is an entirely unusual way of framing the statement.

The clarity of the instrumentation of "Modern Love"—including the electronic keyboards—call to mind other artists of the 1980s, such as Culture Club,[3] Orchestral Manoeuvres in the Dark, and the Human League. The voicings of the horn arrangement, though, are vintage Bowie, and the use of baritone saxophone (played by Steve Elson) as the improvising solo instrument, also suggests Bowie's earlier recordings. Bowie's coproducer Nile Rodgers brings contemporary dance rhythms, as well as a contemporary approach to recording the drum track, to the table. The sound is so contemporary and the melody is so tuneful, with its short motivically related phrases, that the music and the setting and production pull the listener's attention away from the subtleties of the lyrics. Or, perhaps another way to look at the song is that the subtleties of Bowie's psychodrama go beyond the kind of trivial stuff that sometimes finds its way into the lyrics of dance tracks.

Over the years, Bowie had been associated in one way or another with the American rocker Iggy Pop. The two co-wrote the song "China Girl" for Pop's 1977 comeback album *The Idiot.* As the second song on Bowie's *Let's Dance,* however, it seems also to be perfectly at home. In fact, Bowie's crooning style on this recording represents some of his most effective vocal work on *Let's Dance.* The song's lyrics find Bowie's character expressing his love and desire for his "little China Girl," without actually including the word "love" anywhere in the text. While I have dealt with this curious idiosyncrasy of Bowie's typical approach to love songs, it is worth noting the presence of his technique in "China Girl." There are several little lyrical references that also take this interracial love song well beyond the level of the mundane. There is one section in which Bowie sings in a higher register than anywhere else in the song. Here, he tells of stumbling "into town just like a sacred cow," and of the swastikas that form visions in his head. On one hand, the references seems to be something of a mixed metaphor: his lover apparently is Chinese, but the sacred cow and the Hindu good luck symbol, the swastika, both suggest the Indian subcontinent: not exactly the same place. On the other hand, when paired with the references of his "plans for everyone" that follow, the "visions of swastikas" suggest the fascism of Nazi Germany. In this reading, the character is so completely set in his master plan that he is a self-recognized fascist. Regardless of how the listener reads the swastikas within the context of a song about a Chinese woman, mixed metaphor or oblivious-to-the-needs-of-everybody-else fascism, the references create intriguing images and questions in the mind of the listener. Bowie and Pop resolve the character's stubbornness in a most distinctive way: the China Girl of the song's title simply tells Bowie's character, "just you shut your mouth," to which she adds a prolonged "shhhh." The quiet way in which Bowie sings her command makes it clear that he, being like putty in her hands, complies.

Bowie and Iggy Pop set their text about a man whose love for his "little China Girl" makes his innate stubbornness magically melt away to music that features a fairly short, simple chord progression with a descending bass line that ends each time on the dominant (the fifth note of the scale). The repeating succession of harmonically open-sounding phrases create the same effect as the more classically oriented minimalism of Philip Glass and other minimalistic composers of the same era: that the music could go on forever. Combined with the lyrics and Bowie's almost-resigned vocal style as he tells of his lover's order to shut his mouth, the listener is left with the feeling that his character's devotion to his "little China Girl" is so intense that she will forever hold sway over his tendency to insist on his own way. It comes, then, as something of an aural shock when the hypnotic chord progression is broken at the end of "China Girl" by a reprise of the song's faux-Asian introduction.

The astute listener—especially the listener who is familiar with Asian philosophies and musical traditions—may even find a subtle sophistication in Bowie and Pop's "China Girl" that is unusual in western pop music. The repeated, open-ended chord progression upon which the song is based creates something of a feeling of musical stasis for the listener. The instrumental background becomes a state of being. This is in keeping with the concepts of Eastern aesthetics and in some respects it contradicts the Western desire for goal-oriented melodic and harmonic motion. Bowie, Pop, and Bowie's coproducer and arranger Nile Rodgers point out the cultural conflict between the white male character and the Asian female character by juxtaposing the introduction and run-out of the song with the feeling of musical stasis that pervades the bulk of the composition.

The next song, the album's title track "Let's Dance," was another of the album's big pop hits. Bowie's character invites his partner to dance, painting the dance as part of their ritual of courtship. This particular invitation to the dance seems to be coming at a critical juncture of the relationship. Bowie's character expresses his love and the feeling (in entirely more interesting and poetic words than these) that the upcoming dance will prove to him whether or not this relationship will be for the long-term. I base this interpretation of the song in part on Bowie's use of the adjective "serious" to describe the moonlight in which the couple will dance.[4] It is interesting for the listener to consider just how different "Let's Dance" is in its thematic focus from Bowie's overtly dance-oriented song, "Fashion," on *Scary Monsters*. In the earlier song, Bowie used the notion of popular dance to reflect the kinds of more general cultural and political differences that can be reflected in different nations' pop cultures. Here, he treats dance much more conventionally: it is solely part of the mating and courtship ritual.

The music of "Let's Dance" reflects the popular dance music of the day. Bowie clearly delineates the musical phrase structure. He also clearly delineates the verses and the chorus by means of contrasting melodic and harmonic material. The melodic phrases are memorable and the instrumental hooks are easy to identify. In short, it is squarely aimed at the pop audience that, before 1983, had not entirely embraced Bowie's lyrical and musical experimentations.

Given the popularity and the strength of the first three tracks on *Let's Dance*, it is easy to overlook the album's fourth song, "Without You." Of all of Bowie's work of the 1970s and early 1980s this is the one song that most suggests an obvious extension of his work of the 1960s—it as though Bowie completely bypassed metal, glam, and the Berlin-era experimentation. The tunefulness suggests late 1960s pop, and the lyrical references are clear man-woman relationship focused, sans any hint of seedy street characters, transvestites, mental illness, political repression, or any other of Bowie's decidedly non-pop subjects and characters of the years before he became a star. Still, though, the piece is not an entirely conventional pop song. Bowie's lyrics are in non-rhyming narrative form. They read almost like the text of a letter, or a heart-felt declaration of love, in which it is admitted that the loved one means literally everything in the world to the speaker. I say "almost" because Bowie does repeat some of the lines—the structure of the music practically requires that of him—however, the avoidance of rhymes renders the text more real, and less artificial than stereotypical "moon in June" pop song rhymes.

The album's next song "Ricochet" just does not seem to fit on *Let's Dance*. Bowie's stark lyrics about the plight of the poor and the powerless seem more the stuff of *Lodger* or *Scary Monsters*. The whole composition, too, with its spoken segments suggests the song "Scary Monsters (And Super Creeps)," with a touch of heavy metal and progressive rock effects. Part of this mix includes a compound meter, Jamaican-influenced background that continues throughout the song. The danger of including one song that just seems so different than everything else on an album, particularly when that song sounds so similar to material on an artist's previous album, is that it can come off to the fan as an outtake that some how just did not pass muster the first time around. In short, it can sound like filler. That is what happens with "Ricochet." Here was Bowie, a singer-songwriter who almost exclusively had recorded only his own material, literally on the cusp of the compact disc era, releasing an album that contained a cover of someone else's song ("Criminal World"), a cover of one of his earlier compositions intended for another performer ("China Girl"), an already released movie theme song, and a song that sounded suspiciously like an outtake from his previous album all in a package that weighed in at under 40 minutes. And, to top it off, it had come not exactly right on the heels of his previous release. While this situation could not undo the strength of the first half of *Let's Dance*, it portends the possibility that perhaps Bowie was at a critical artistic juncture at this point in his career. Admittedly, it probably is hard to get all of that from one seemingly out-of-place song. However, "Ricochet" does, I would argue, play a significant role in the uneasy feeling that *Let's Dance* might be simultaneously catching David Bowie at the height of mass appeal, but slipping artistically.

The glam-rock duo (and later a more full-sized band) Metro first released their song "Criminal World" back in 1977. The fact that the song deals with the seedy side of life probably explains its appeal to Bowie, an artist who focused on the unconventional, the bizarre, and the social fringe for so much of his career. The arrangement is classic 1980s new wave, with a sonic clarity, the use of over-layered riffs. The keyboard and electric guitar tone colors, too, represent exactly the kind of sound that was very much in the air in 1983. The one element that stands out from the new wave bands of the time is Stevie Ray Vaughan's bluesy guitar solo. Compared with some of Bowie's other cover recordings, "Criminal World" is vocally understated, much to Bowie's credit.

Bowie and famed disco pioneer Giorgio Moroder collaborated on the song "Cat People (Putting out Fire)" for the film *Cat People*. The overriding concept behind the lyrics—someone caught up so deeply in troubles that he has to resort to "putting out fire with gasoline"—is a classic Bowie image. The song works well within the concept of the movie, but is not the most memorable Bowie song. In particular, although the music is catchy, it is not the kind of thing that stays with the listener for a long period of time—certainly not like "Let's Dance," "China Girl," and "Modern Love."

*Let's Dance* concludes with the solo Bowie composition "Shake It." Bowie portrays a character that escapes from the meaninglessness of his life through dancing at a club. It is not the most profound lyrical concept that one can find in the Bowie canon, however, since this album seems to be aimed at greater accessibility, this song fits right in: it does not require a whole lot of analysis or self-reflection on the part of the listener. Even the first couple of lines of Bowie's lyrics rely on cliché (a boat adrift on the ocean) and, in fact, quote almost word for word from Brian Wilson's song "Until I Die," from the late-1960s Beach Boys album *Surf's Up*. Bowie, however, includes some sexual innuendo that is completely absent from the Wilson song. And, whereas Wilson expresses the belief that he will remain apart from mainstream society until he dies, Bowie's character can at least find solace at the dance club. Bowie's synthesizer-based music relies on short, *ostinato*-like harmonic patterns with a strong dance-based (of course) rhythmic groove. The melody is simple and not particularly memorable.

In hindsight, *Let's Dance* was something of a double-edged sword among David Bowie's albums. It represented the pinnacle of his commercial success; however, through its more conventional lyrical forms and themes, as well as its accessible dance music, it placed Bowie in somewhat unfamiliar territory as an artist: he was now one of many people doing approximately the same sort of thing. For an artist who had built his entire career up to this point on the premise of being—or at least portraying characters who were—outside the mainstream to become part of the mainstream would prove to be a decidedly negative career move. Despite the problems posed by Bowie's new approach, the first four songs on the album really are quite strong, both within Bowie's entire output and in the world of early 1980s pop in which they were born.

## TONIGHT

The year 1984 found David Bowie moving more into the musical mainstream with the album *Tonight*. While the album includes some of Bowie's customary explorations of personal identity—both in his lyrics and in those of his collaborators, and the songwriters whose work he covers on the album—the emphasis on reggae, ska, R&B, contemporary dance music, and other non-threatening (and certainly non-groundbreaking) musical styles, and the full, lush orchestrations make it seem as though the once ageless Bowie had become a middle-aged pop musician. There is far too much of an anonymous, slick quality about this album for it to stand in the company of *Low, "Heroes," The Rise and Fall of Ziggy Stardust and the Spiders from Mars, Scary Monsters,* and some of Bowie's better post-*Tonight* albums. The mood changes are extreme and inconsistent from song to song, which gives *Tonight* the feel of a collection of individual songs that just happen to appear on the same album. Although the album sold well, critics did not think highly of *Tonight*, with *All Music Guide*'s Stephen Thomas Erlewine pretty much summing up the critical reaction. Erlewine writes, "the record stands as one of the weakest albums Bowie ever recorded."[5] He gives *Tonight* two out of a possible five stars.[6]

The first track "Loving the Alien" features a promising chorus hook; however, the music of the verses does not stand out as memorable. Bowie's music fits within the Plastic Soul style he pioneered a decade earlier; however, this is music that more closely resembles the mellow Quiet Storm brand of R&B and not the more soulful brand. Arif Mardin's string and synthesizer arrangement helps to render the music so mellow that some of the edge inherent in Bowie's lyrics is lost. The lyrics themselves contain a number of references that ring eerily true in the early twenty-first century. In particular, the references to "Palestine a modern problem" and "Terror in a best laid plan" seem to pertain to the post-9/11 world perhaps even better than to the world of 1984.

The second song on *Tonight* is a cover of Iggy Pop and James Williamson's 1979 song "Don't Look Down," the album's first foray into the world of Jamaican-influenced music. The horn arrangements and general rhythmic feel suggest a combination of 1970s reggae and ska. In light of Pop's well-documented personal problems of the 1970s, the lyrics of this song (as printed on this album's inner sleeve) are poignant. The musical arrangement and Bowie's performance are so emotionally cool and slow-groove-oriented that much of the potential for poignancy is lost.

The album's next cover, Brian Wilson and Tony Asher's well-known "God Only Knows," is more successful. Although Bowie overacts somewhat—lapsing a bit too much into his long-dormant Anthony Newly voice—he conveys the vulnerability of the character Wilson and Asher constructed. Interestingly, although Wilson conveyed this vulnerability through the use of high-pitched falsetto singing in the Beach Boys's 1966 release of the song, Bowie makes good use of the lower end of his vocal range.

The mood of vulnerability initiated by "God Only Knows" is abruptly broken by Bowie and Pop's collaboration "Tonight," the song that closes off side one. On the surface, the basic premise of the song is that tonight "everything will be alright." The easygoing Jamaican-influenced music supports this surface reading. In the background, however, there is a hint that perhaps the reason that "everything will be alright" is that the character Bowie portrays is to die that very evening. This is a subtle subtext, suggested only by references to a love that will last "till I die" and the observation that tonight Bowie's character will see his lover "in the sky." The problem is that the listener can be so seduced with the slow groove of the beat and the poker-faced delivery that the darker subtext is too easy to miss. Another weakness of the song is that guest co-lead vocalist Tina Turner is relegated to a subservient, studio-singer role, thus underutilizing her talent.

Side two of *Tonight* begins with one of Bowie and Pop's collaborations from the late 1970s, "Neighborhood Threat." This story conjures up images of junkies shooting up in dank alleys and lost youth who cannot fit into conventional society. Appropriately, this is a hard-rocking song. However, the production and Carlos Alomar's guitar solos are missing the seventies edge that would have given even stronger support to the song's mood. But, then, that is characteristic of much of the entire album: it is unquestionably a product of mid-eighties pop style.

Following "Neighborhood Threat" is the solo Bowie composition "Blue Jean," which, with its decidedly mid-1960s lyrical and musical aesthetic actually works, despite the fact that it is the most conventionally pop song David Bowie had written and recorded since his pre-fame days. It is catchy, but lyrically insubstantial and the kind of song that is popular for a short period and then disappears into relative obscurity, despite some initial record sales. The reason? There is nothing to make it stand out from other good pop of the era. Likewise, Bowie and Pop's "Tumble and Twirl" is a snappy dance number that contains a few rhythmic references and horn arrangement references to world pop, but it just doesn't say a whole lot.

One of the most commercially successful songwriting duos of the late 1950s and early 1960s, Jerry Leiber and Mike Stoller provided hit songs for a wide variety of artists. Bowie's cover of Leiber and Stoller's "I Keep Forgettin'" is one of the better tracks on *Tonight*. Here, Bowie takes a step beyond the Plastic Soul of *Young Americans* and shows that he can turn in a well-tuned and soulful rock and roll performance. It is a performance that exposes Bowie's roots and range as a rock singer; he turns in a super performance by balancing emotional and rock vocal technique. The problem is that the song is so un-Bowie-like, yet possibly the strongest track on the album. For that to be the case on a cover for a singer-songwriter as closely associated with writing original, thought-provoking, unconventional material is a double-edged sword of the most cutting kind. As much as "I Keep Forgettin'" shows off Bowie's technique as a rock singer, the song's prominence on *Tonight* suggests that Bowie's songwriting work had suffered a precipitous decline.

Despite its shortcomings, *Tonight* ends on a high note with Bowie, Pop, and Alomar's "Dancing with the Big Boys." The lyrics deal with societal problems, such as environmental degradation, political repression, and personal alienation. Compared with the lyrics of most of Bowie's solo compositions that deal with similar topics, however, those of "Dancing with the Big Boys" are less pointed. The music is pleasant, fast-paced, danceable rock. Since the melodic phrases have such a small pitch range, and since the short harmonic pattern is also fairly minimalistic, the musical success of "Dancing with the Big Boys" is based largely on the fact that it establishes an effective groove. That is fine, but Bowie's best work has established a strong groove, with melodic, harmonic, and rhythmic hooks, and a better match of lyrics and music.

Unfortunately, Bowie took an undeniable step toward conventional pop with *Tonight*. This move may have led to strong album sales, but it made Bowie less distinctive, both musically and lyrically. The relative large number of cover songs and collaborative compositions added to this dilution of the Bowie mystique. To Bowie's credit, several of the songs find him turning in strong vocal performances; however, he contributed very little to the album instrumentally. As I mentioned at the beginning of the discussion of *Tonight*, the critic Stephen Thomas Erlewine considers this one of Bowie's weakest albums.[7] I would tend to disagree, if only to brand *Tonight* clearly Bowie's weakest album.

## NEVER LET ME DOWN

To Bowie's credit, he took time between *Tonight* and his next album, and he returned to crafting an album based primarily on his own solo compositions. The resulting package, *Never Let Me Down*, may not rank among Bowie's greatest albums, however, it finds him achieving a better balance between working on pop songs and challenging songs, and it provides a truly interesting link between his Berlin albums and his work of the late twentieth century and the early twenty-first century. In short, *Never Let Me Down* might not include Bowie's best-known songs, but it represents an important move back toward artistic relevance.

The song "Day-In Day-Out" leads off the album. There is an element of Dolly Parton's smash 1980–1981 hit "9 to 5" in this story of a poor young woman who struggles "day-in and day-out" to earn a living. In contrast to the lead character of Parton's song, the lead character of the Bowie opus is a recent immigrant to the United States. Whereas Parton's "9 to 5" is sung from the viewpoint of a working-class character, Bowie clearly is observing the situation from the outside. The high energy R&B style of the song steps well beyond the emotional coolness of Bowie's mid-1970s Plastic Soul; in "Day-In Day-Out" he sings with more passion than in the first generation of his R&B work. The track is danceable, like the material of *Let's Dance* and *Tonight,* but it generally is more to the point than some of the songs of *Let's Dance,* and reveals more social and musical significance than most of the songs of *Tonight*. The song is not as well known as any of the first three tracks on *Let's Dance,* but it is almost as strong. The casual listener who does not own *Never Let Me Down* would do well to seek out this track as an example of Bowie's strength in the R&B genre.

"Time Will Crawl" tends to fall into the category of apocalyptic, the-end-of-the-millennium-is-coming songs that seemed to emerge just before and in the Orwellian year 1984. Prince's "1999" is the best-known example. In terms of the structure of *Never Let Me Down*, "Time Will Crawl" plays a very important role. Bowie's text is impressionistic, and almost stream-of-consciousness in the way in which it paints a mood of pre-millennial malaise and his melodic writing comes close to being monothematic (there is a distinct and calculated lack of melodic contrast from phrase to phrase). This makes the more direct observations of "Day-In Day-Out" and the lovely contrasting melodic material and highly personal-sounding vulnerability of the lyrics of "Never Let Me Down" stand out in sharp relief. This high degree of contrast serves all the songs well; however, "Time Will Crawl" is not one of the stronger, or most memorable, tracks on the album.

The next song, "Beat of Your Drum," captures the techno style of the era, and also exhibits some of the sexual attitude of punk rock. Bowie's chromatic harmonic changes and use of synthesizers anticipates some of his work of the twentieth-first century, especially on the album *Heathen*. Peter Frampton's lead guitar solo is relatively short, but strong in the tradition of Bowie's previous lead guitarists Ronson, Fripp, and Alomar, and Lenny Pickett's saxophone solo calls to mind the spirit of abandonment of Bowie's own work on the instrument. The hook-laden chorus resembles some of the simple and thoroughly memorable work of Bruce Springsteen of the era, such as "Glory Days" and "Born in the U.S.A." It is a strong-enough album track, but does not exude a clearly defined Bowie character like his best work—in other words, any strong rock singer of the era could record the song convincingly. Although this clearly is a tribute to Bowie's songwriting craftsmanship, it also points to the fact that his lyrics were becoming more mainstream and relying less on the stories of quirky—but thoroughly fascinating—characters.

Although I would tend to disagree with the overall assessment of *Never Let Me Down* by *All Music Guide*'s Stephen Thomas Erlewine, who gives the album only two out of a possible five stars,[8] I would agree with his assessment of "Never Let Me Down" as one of David Bowie's most underrated songs.[9] Here, Bowie pays tribute to one of his most important songwriting influences, John Lennon. Unlike Lennon's friend and former bandmate Paul McCartney, who in "Tug of War" grappled with the complex relationship he shared with Lennon, and unlike Lennon's former bandmate George Harrison, who in "All Those Years Ago" documented Lennon's vision and the way in which some of Lennon's work (musically and otherwise) was misunderstood both by close associates and the public at large, co-writers Bowie and Carlos Alomar provide a song that is thoroughly in the mold, both musically and lyrically, of Lennon's work. It is not about John Lennon. Instead, "Never Let Me Down" resembles, more than anything else, a logical extension of Lennon's work just before the time he was murdered. In fact, the style and arrangement of "Never Let Me Down," along with Bowie's eerily Lennon-like vocals, fits with both Lennon and Yoko Ono's *Double Fantasy* (the last release of Lennon's life) and Lennon's posthumous 1983 album *Milk and Honey*. It is not just that David Bowie proves himself to be possibly the greatest Lennon imitator ever—there is even some of Lennon's son Julian Lennon's vocal tone color in Bowie's voice, too—his compositional approach is thoroughly in the mold of Lennon. In particular, Bowie contrasts phrase lengths in the songs sections—a technique that Lennon employed on more than one occasional. Even more Lennon-esque, however, is Bowie's use of clear chromatic (moving by half-steps) vocals leading in the inner notes of the chords in the accompaniment. The listener can find this in numerous Lennon songs; however, Lennon's last great single "(Just Like) Starting Over" might be the best example, since the rhythmic style and the style of the arrangement and record production is also so closely captured by Bowie. Bowie's lyrics capture the vulnerability that pervades much of Lennon's best work as a lyricist. This stands out quite starkly, because Bowie's lyrics usually come from the viewpoint of characters who are a lot of things, but rarely vulnerable in the manner of Lennon's characters. And, Bowie's harmonica playing eerily calls to mind Lennon's instrumental work on such early Beatles's songs as "Love Me Do." All in all, this song, perhaps more than any other song David Bowie has written and recorded, proves his skill as a pop craftsman.

The album's fifth song, "Zeroes," once again finds lead guitarist Peter Frampton coming to the fore. Bowie's writing suggests a popish vision of 1970s art rock, with sophisticated chromatic harmonies, experimental instrumentation (faux Indian sitar and percussion pervades the song), and a full arrangement. Bowie also hints at his famous Ziggy Stardust and the Spiders from Mars period in his references to a fictional band; in this case, the Zeroes. There are a few curious lyrical references in the song, notably Bowie's references to driving around in a "little red Corvette." Although the line goes by very quickly, a listener familiar with the big hits of the era cannot help but recall the 1983 Prince hit "Little Red Corvette." "Zeroes" is a strong album track, but like "Beat of Your Drum," is just a little too close to other good pop of the era to stand out as distinctive. In fact, in listening to *Never Let Me Down*, I suspect that this album was meant to showcase Bowie's ability to write and perform thoroughly contemporary sounding, but not necessarily very challenging, pop. Given the strength of "Zeroes" and the other songs on *Never Let Me Down* that resemble what other popular artists of the day were doing, I would suspect that any of these compositions could have been recorded to good effect by a number of top performers of the day. If one did not know that Bowie composed these songs, one might reasonably assume that they came from the pen of a young, hot, songwriter keen on establishing himself or herself with very au courant-sounding—yet thoroughly commercial—material. The danger with Bowie writing and recording material like this—material that is so different in rhetorical voice from his earlier, famous songs of the 1970s—is that he effectively moves himself from a class of performers who pretty much stand alone into a class in which he is lumped together with a bunch of competitors.

The track "Glass Spider," more than anything else, finds Bowie revisiting the fantasy world of his very brief psychedelic folk and heavy metal periods. It is a gross oversimplification of the general category into which this song falls, but it is something of a 1980s version of Donovan's "Atlantis." Bowie narrates the fantastic story of a "glass-like spider" that spins webs of multi-level floors. The electronic music that accompanies the story represents a combination of Bowie's Berlin work with his early heavy metal compositions. Since *Never Let Me Down* is not exactly a concept or theme album, "Glass Spider" works out fine; however, it is stronger on its own than on the album since both the rhetorical and the musical schemes are so different from any of the other songs on the album. The song should also put to rest any suspicions that guitarist Frampton was just a pretty face who sang "I'm in You" and "Show Me the Way": he could play.

"Shining Star (Making My Love)" finds Bowie revisiting some of the tragic, fringe characters of his early 1970s songs in the verses and in the mid-song rap. This he balances with a bright sunny chorus that sounds like the brightest declaration of love from the sunniest 1960s Smoky Robinson Motown track. Although Bowie incorporates texture, harmonic, and melodic contrasts to delineate these sections, the overall musical feel of the piece leans heavily in the direction of brightness. It is not as effective as Bowie's best songs that explore irony as a structural component. The musical setting is so bright that the dark images of Hitler, Sinn Fein, bloody fingers, and scabs lose much of their impact.

The song "New York's in Love" is an effective dance track that doesn't really say much. Although slightly anonymous dance music is not Bowie's forte, *Never Let Me Down* coproducers David Bowie and David Richards make this song an effective, rocking piece, from the musical arrangement and production standpoints. The lyrics get lost in the mix, but it is not a significant loss. The next song, "'87 and Cry," is more effective, but is not an essential Bowie track for the casual fan. It is a rocking groove piece that contains references to the political and social situation in Bowie's native United Kingdom.

*Never Let Me Down* concludes with Iggy Pop's "Bang Bang." This song, both as an abstract concept and in coproducers Bowie and Richards' arrangement, resembles the work of David Byrne, with its disconnected lyrical images, and short, distinctive melodic phrases, and snappy, danceable rhythms.

*Never Let Me Down* was a stronger album than its predecessor, *Tonight*. Although it did not reach the commercial heights of *Let's Dance*, the album tackled the prevailing pop styles of the day to good effect. In writing and recording music that is so closely in touch with the conventional pop of the time, Bowie continued his trend of the first half of the 1980s to move towards pop music with mass appeal away from more experimental music, populated by fringe characters. The main problem with this is that *Never Let Me Down* represents good 1980s pop. And, why might that be a problem? The conventional stereotype of 1980s pop is that it represents a sort of musical dead zone between the edge and innovation and relevancy of punk rock (the 1970s) and the grunge and alternative styles which would emerge in the future (the late 1980s through the 1990s). This music might be catchy, well crafted, and danceable, but it is less intellectually and artistically substantial than other forms of popular music of the rock era. The question that the album raises is, would Bowie continue the trend or return to his modus operandi of the 1970s and make an unexpected stylistic shift?

## IN THE WAKE OF POP SUCCESS

The answer to the question posed at the end of the previous discussion of *Never Let Me Down* would have to wait for several years. After his unprecedented pop success in 1983 and 1984, Bowie turned increasingly to acting and providing the occasional song to film soundtracks.[10] Despite the fact that his appearance represented a supporting role, he received star billing for his acting in the Nagisa Oshima film *Merry Christmas, Mr. Lawrence*. He also appeared in *The Hunger* and *Yellowbeard*, and in 1985 he provided songs for the films *The Falcon and the Snowman, Hero,* and *Boy Meets Girl*. In 1986, Bowie starred in the film *Labyrinth*, and he both appeared in and provided music for the film *Absolute Beginners*. Perhaps his most widely viewed film performance on the 1980s was his role as Pontius Pilate in Martin Scorsese's *The Last Temptation of Christ* in 1988. These film appearances over a six-year period suggest the extent to which David Bowie had become firmly ensconced as a general pop culture (as opposed to a strictly musical) icon. Even though Bowie returned to music at the end of the 1980s, he has continued to make cameo and co-starring roles in television programs and films.

# Tin Machine: 1989–1992

Although David Bowie had followed his pop successes of the early- and mid-1980s with a focus on acting, he was and has always been primarily a musician. In fact, it would seem reasonable to speculate that much of the success he has had as an actor largely can be attributed to the fact that he has been such an iconic figure in pop music. It was probably no surprise then when, in 1989, he returned to the music world. What surprised critics and his fans alike was that his return to the recording industry was not as a solo act, but as a member of a band: Tin Machine. Tin Machine recorded just two studio albums and one live album; however, the band forms a most interesting part of the David Bowie legacy. Tin Machine explored alternative and grunge before the styles were even widely known to exist.[1] It was a noble experiment for Bowie, and the band found him collaborating as a writer, producer, and performer with one musician in particular—Reeves Gabrels—with whom he would continue to work to the end of the millennium. Ultimately, though, Tin Machine was a band without an audience: Bowie's fans did not readily accept it, and the new alternative and grunge styles had yet to gain a wide international audience. Although the band proved that Bowie was once again catching the latest wave in musical style and anticipating what would eventually be quite popular, this time he was just a little too much ahead of his time.

## TIN MACHINE

The direction David Bowie's musical career had been taking in the first half of the 1980s dramatically shifted at the end of the decade in a most unexpected way: Bowie formed a band. Tin Machine had a checkered career—with one very good (but lyrically gloomy) studio album, one pretty good (but sonically challenging) studio album, and one ineffective live album can be. The band's first album, the self-titled *Tin Machine,* was not greeted with unanimous critical and popular appeal, but was a solid rock effort that found some of the 1970s edge returning to Bowie's music and lyrics. The album exhibits clear connections with Bowie's punkish Berlin-period music, as well as with his early 1970s heavy metal music, while more importantly anticipating the sonic and lyrical style of mid-1990s grunge and alternative rock.

Tin Machine consisted of Bowie on guitar and vocals, Gabrels on lead guitar, Hunt Sales on drums and vocals, and Tony Sales on bass guitar and vocals. The Sales brothers, incidentally, are the sons of American comedian Soupy Sales. These four musicians were joined on *Tin Machine* by guitarist and organist Kevin Armstrong. The band Tin Machine did not last beyond two studio albums; however, Bowie continued to collaborate with guitarist, composer, and producer Gabrels until the end of the twentieth century.

The album begins with Bowie's "Heaven's in Here," a number in which lead singer Bowie finds heaven in sex. The lyrics, however, are not as important or as interesting as the music. During the sung portion of the piece, the pace is moderate and the overall timbre and volume tend toward the relaxed. This is perhaps the mellowest part of any song on the album. At the conclusion of the last iteration of the chorus, the music breaks into a faster paced rock jam, complete with unusual and unpredictable metrical changes.

Bowie, Gabrels, and the Sales brothers collaborated on the song "Tin Machine." Again, the impressionistic lyrics do not make as much of an impact as on Bowie's best solo albums. However, the general sense of malaise that is painted—with such cheery images as a "mindless maggot glare" and the Earth as a "psycho-time-bomb planet"—certainly fits the fast paced, distorted, hard rock feel of the music. It is worth noting that both of the first two songs on *Tin Machine* include religious references that are twisted well beyond the spiritual ("heaven lies between your marble thighs" in the first song, and "preachers and their past" in the second song). "Tin Machine" itself is an apocalyptic nightmare that seems to be a completely pessimistic chronicle of and reaction to a dying species (homo sapiens) on a dying planet. Rarely in his previous work had Bowie included religious references in his lyrics. There are more to be found on this album, and not pleasant ones. The song "Tin Machine," then, with its apocalyptic imagery, defines the overall theme of the end of the world (on several levels), which pervades this album.

All four band members also collaborated in writing the song "Prisoner of Love." The album's sense of general malaise continues with Bowie's character smelling "the sickness sown in the city" and expressing a sense of desperation over the love he feels for the person to whom he sings. The syncopations in Hunt Sales's drumming in the chorus suggest the percussion approach of mid-1990s alternative rock drummers. The piece is tuneful and powerful.

Bowie's "Crack City" is based on a rocking guitar riff that recalls the Troggs's "Wild Thing," except that Bowie's riff is even one step more minimalistic than that of the Troggs's famous 1960s anthem. Bowie paints an ugly picture of Crack City, a locale frequented by drug addicts, who are "a bunch of assholes with buttholes for their brains." Gabrels's powerful, somewhat atonal guitar solo comes right out of the evilest sounding heavy metal performance the listener can imagine. The song is gloomy and dark, but as such fits right into *Tin Machine*'s overall gestalt. The number of incomplete profanities in the printed lyrics in the compact disc booklet in "Crack City," "I Can't Read," and a couple of other songs illustrates the way in which Bowie uses language of the street to an extent on *Tin Machine* that far exceeds anything he had done previously in his solo work. This use of vulgar vernacular works in "Crack City," but sounds silly in Bowie and Gabrels's "I Can't Read" ("I can't read shit anymore" is repeated in the chorus several times). It just sounds too artificially street to be convincing. "I Can't Read," however, is an interesting track if for nothing else than the deliberately out-of-tune guitars and singing.

The hard rock song "Under the God," a composition by Bowie alone, continues the theme of urban malaise. Here, however, Bowie describes such things as white, neo-Nazi skinheads beating black kids with baseball bats. The title line, "Under the God," suggests that the skinheads believe that God is on their side, and yet despite the presence of this God, urban violence and poverty exist. The implicit question is, "if God exists why does he do nothing to stop senseless violence?"

The next track, the Bowie and Gabrels's collaboration "Amazing" is a somewhat innocent love song. It really does not offer a whole lot, except for just over three minutes of relief from the sonic and lyrical intensity of the rest of *Tin Machine*. "Amazing" is an effective power ballad taken out of context; however, the lyrics are too mainstream to sound much like anything that Bowie had written since he became famous in the early 1970s. The song points out—just in case the listener had somehow missed the fact—that Tin Machine is really a band and not a disguised David Bowie solo vehicle.

Tin Machine's version of John Lennon's "Working Class Hero" owes little to the style of Lennon's 1970 original. Bowie's band presents a hard rock version of the song that is thoroughly in keeping with the rock of the time period. Gabrels's distorted solos and Bowie's powerful vocals capture the anger of Lennon's text. In fact, compared with Bowie's somewhat uneven covers of the past, "Working Class Hero" stands out by virtue of its stylistic integrity and ability to stand toe to toe with the original. It seems clear that Bowie was making a very real effort to work in a band context, especially in the context of some of his earlier work, when he tended to let his vocal per-formance dominate over other aspects of a song.

The next song, Bowie and Gabrels's "Bus Stop"—not to be confused with the early 1960s classic of the same name by the Hollies—owes a debt of gratitude to the power pop of British artists of a decade earlier such as Elvis

Costello, Nick Lowe, and (with a slightly harder edge) the Jam. The brief (less than two minutes) song finds Bowie portraying a young man "at odds with the Bible," who, nevertheless, does not "pretend that faith never works." This song offers an optimism not found in the song "Under the God," in which God is noticeably absent when it comes to solving the world's problems. Musically, too, "Bus Stop" with its resemblance to 1970s post-punk new wave, sounds more optimistic than the other fast-paced songs of social commentary on the album.

Bowie's solo composition "Pretty Thing" is not particularly significant. In fact, to my mind, it is the most dispensable song on *Tin Machine*. Tin Machine cannot be faulted too much, though, for putting some filler on the album. Unlike Bowie's pre-Tin Machine solo albums, the latest of which were produced very early in the CD era, Tin Machine is very much of product of the CD era. This means that 40 or 45 minutes of music was just not going to be acceptable. That the band's debut album weighs in at nearly 57 minutes that includes as much strong material as it does is a testament to the validity of Tin Machine as a strong forward-looking rock band.

Bowie collaborated with the Sales brothers in the writing of "Video Crime." Whereas this is not the most substantial song of David Bowie's career, it provides a vehicle for Hunt Sales's solid drumming and Gabrels's virtuosic guitar work. "Video Crime" concerns television coverage of various criminals, including mass murderer Ted Bundy. It exposes society's fascination with crimes of extreme violence.

Bowie and Kevin Armstrong's "Run" is another track that does not rank with Bowie's best; however, it is a solid album cut for a new band. It is a successful alternative rock style love song. The Sales brothers and Bowie wrote "Sacrifice Yourself." This is an effect piece, which for the most part showcases Gabrels and his electric guitar skills. Bowie's "Baby Can Dance" is also a band feature. The lyrics do not have a whole lot to say. The moves between slow meter and a double-time feel, as well as Gabrels's slightly atonal guitar work, really defines the piece.

*Tin Machine* took David Bowie fans by surprise, and some never did seem to warm up to the fact that their hero was now part of a reasonably democratic band. Anticipating grunge and alternative rock of the 1990s, the album features loud guitar rock, with a sonic edge and a general sense of malaise behind the lyrics. As interesting as it might be in retrospect that Tin Machine (the band) was as forward-looking as it was, the unfortunate commercial fact is that it the album is fairly unrelenting and generally is aimed at an audience that was not necessarily Bowie's substantial solo audience. A number of the songs, especially "Baby Can Dance," "Sacrifice Yourself," and "Run" do not feature lyrics that are as insightful or interesting as a whole bunch of songs from Bowie's earlier solo career. The long and the short of the album *Tin Machine* is that it is a solid effort for a new band that was exploring a style that would be popular in a few years; however, it finds Bowie turning his back on some of the best aspects of his solo writing: especially the tuneful melodic style he had incorporated even in his more rock-oriented compositions, and the quirky, but ever-memorable characters that populated his earlier songs. In between Tin Machine's two studio albums, a remix of Bowie's famous song "Fame" was used in the popular film *Pretty Woman*. This remix, entitled "Fame 90," incorporates some of the DJ techniques of early hip-hop with contrasts to the hard, alternative rock style Tin Machine material, and serves as a testament to the staying power of Bowie's 1970s compositions.

## TIN MACHINE II

Tin Machine's 1991 sophomore album finds Bowie, Gabrels, and the Sales brothers turning to more conventional-sounding hard rock styles and forms than what they had featured on the band's debut album. In fact, the songs are more generally tuneful, less incessantly gloomy, more accessible, and more closely related to Bowie's pre-Tin Machine solo material than anything on *Tin Machine*. As with any artistic change, however, this could be a double-edged sword: on the one hand, Tin Machine takes on musical aspects of Bowie's well-known solo work; however, on the other hand, Tin Machine loses some its own identity. The band sounds less ground-breaking and more mainstream than it did on its first album. That being said, there are several tracks on *Tin Machine II* that are highly underrated and deserve to be much better known.

The Bowie-Gabrels collaboration "Baby Universal" leads off the album. Bowie's impressionistic lyrics (Bowie wrote the lyrics; he and Gabrels collaborated on the music) come from the voice of a space alien. Beyond that, however, it is difficult to make sense of just what Bowie is trying to say. The music maintains a hard rock feel, but it is not particularly memorable rhythmically, melodically, harmonically, or in the area of the electronic effects that pervade the track.

"One Shot," with lyrics by Bowie and music by all four Tin Machine members, is a more conventional and memorable piece musically. Gabrels's experimental and highly virtuosic guitar solo style is at the forefront; however, the piece is interesting and memorable enough melodically that it is far more than just a technical showpiece for the guitarist. Bowie's lyrics deal with the end of a love relationship. He starkly recounts that, "one shot put her away," which forces the listener to speculate about his meaning. Does he literally mean a gunshot, or something less sinister? He skillfully avoids providing enough information for a definitive interpretation to result.

"You Belong in Rock & Roll," with music by Bowie and Gabrels, and lyrics by Bowie, recalls Bowie's work with his so-called Spiders from Mars band. The theme of the rock and roll lifestyle is not as fully developed as it is in the songs of *The Rise and Fall of Ziggy Stardust and the Spiders from Mars*, but it is consistent with the songs of that earlier era. Also returning is Bowie's use of distinctive popish easy-to-remember melodic hooks. The title line, in particular, is set to one of those simple tunes that invites singing along. The instrumental setting is subdued and invites comparison with T. Rex's work of the early 1970s. Bowie's saxophone playing on this track is a nice addition to the Tin Machine sonic palette.

The next track, "Amlapura," also features lyrics by Bowie and music by Bowie and Gabrels. It also represents a return of sorts to Bowie's solo work of the past, particularly his folk-rock period; the song would have fit nicely on the 1969 album *Man of Words, Man of Music*. The somewhat meandering melody and impressionistic lyrics all recall Bowie's work at the end of the 1960s; however, his lyrics include images of dead children, something quite a bit harsher than the kind of images he typically included in the work in his folk-rock period.

Bryan Ferry's "If There Is Something" is a far more musically edgy piece than either of the previous two tracks on the album, especially because of Gabrels's atonal leanings in his solos. Although some reviewers seem to have been somewhat taken aback by Gabrels's experimental playing,[2] his work on this song really is no more untraditional than some of the work of Robert Fripp and Carlos Alomar on earlier David Bowie solo albums. Gabrels does, however, exhibit more sheer technique, so his solos tend to stand out more than those of Fripp and Alomar. The album's next track, "Betty Wrong," is not among Bowie's most distinctive pieces. It is a fairly conventional new wave rock-style song, but lacks the melodic interest of Bowie's best.

The song "You Can't Talk," with lyrics by Bowie and music by all four Tin Machine members, perhaps is the song that most closely resembles the style of the band's first album. It is not as memorable as most of the songs on the first album, but it is a significant piece here in that it is very much a band presentation.

Hunt Sales and Bowie collaborated on the writing of "Stateside." The song is a vehicle for Sales, who provides lead vocals. The bluesy musical style and the overly obvious references to well-known American songs (the folk song "Home on the Range" along with the song "Horse with No Name," by the 1970s folkish pop band America) are decidedly outside of Bowie's standard points of musical and lyrical reference. For his part, Bowie contributes a baritone saxophone solo.

Bowie and Gabrels's "Shopping for Girls" contains urban imagery that resembles the work of Paul Simon. The character Bowie describes in the lyrics has his sights set on girls, whose lures seem to render him oblivious to the blight around him. It is not a pretty picture. The musical setting contains elements both of this urban bleakness (a melody that stays pretty much in a very narrow pitch range and contains little contrast) and a sunnier hope that the character will score (a tuneful pop, new-wavish keyboard figure that follows the line "he's shopping for girls").

"A Big Hurt" is the only song on *Tin Machine II* with words and music solely by Bowie. This piece would sound as though it came straight from the realm of 1977 British punk rock were it not for some harmonic changes that represent a beyond-punk sophistication. Bowie's lyrics concern a woman, his "roommate from hell," who leaves him with "a big hurt," apparently in spite of the fact that she is a "sex receiver." Bowie is fairly pointed in his disdain for the woman; however, as he usually does, he masks some of the sentiments by mixing clear, pointed lines with hazy, impressionistic lines. This might not be a song that is one of Bowie's best known, but it shows his mastery of the particular 1970s punk sound, á la Sex Pistols and the Damned. The problem with this is that Bowie made much of his musical reputation by either anticipating pop styles or at least being among the first artists to integrate new styles into his own. In his pre-Tin Machine solo career rarely did Bowie so obviously look to earlier parts of the rock era. "A Big Hurt" is a powerful rock song, but it finds David Bowie looking in the metaphorical rearview mirror. Additionally, his mix of pointed lines with somewhat more impressionistic lines means that his sod off (to use the British phrase that avoids the "f" word) statement to a former lover lacks the emotional intensity, not to mention the bitter irony, of a song such as Elvis Costello's 1986 composition "I Hope You're Happy Now."

With lyrics by Bowie, and music by Bowie and the Sales brothers, "Goodbye Mr. Ed" bids farewell to the innocence of the past by bidding farewell to "Mr. Ed," the talking horse of early television fame. Bowie's text highlights various symbols of the loss of innocence that occurred in the 1980s and 1990s, including corporate scandals, Andy Warhol's death, post-Sex Pistols punk and new wave rock, and racially motivated violence against blacks, and punctuates each one with the title's farewell to "Mr. Ed." The song's melody is built from short rhythmically related, but melodically contrasting phrases. It is, however, tuneful and easy to remember. The instrumental style and vocal harmony suggest the work of the Jam on some of their more pop-oriented material of the late 1970s, such as "Life from a Window." In fact, like the 1977 work of the Jam, "Goodbye Mr. Ed" includes instrumental signifiers that suggest the 1960s work of the Who, particularly in the suspended fourths in the guitar parts (a trademark of Pete Townshend's rhythm guitar playing with the Who). One of the striking features of the song is that it illustrates the extent to which Bowie had moved away from more than occasionally relying on titillation and the creation of vivid, but bizarre characters in order to make the strongest impact as a lyricist. Here, he deals with real issues poetically, and maturely. Still, it is not a flawless piece; the line "people are so dense" may be a near-perfect example of the vernacular of the era, but it is also such a cliché that it is also one of Bowie's most throwaway lines ever.

A brief (58 seconds) instrumental, "Hammerhead," concludes *Tin Machine II.* Despite its brevity, "Hammerhead" demonstrates Tin Machine's strength as a band. It is a tag that suggests that Tin Machine could have continued and perhaps charted new territory by increasing their work on instrumentals. *Tin Machine II,* however, was fated to be the band's last studio album. It was an album with some worthy songs, but an album that found the band largely abandoning its forward-looking alternative grunge style in order to return to clear hints of David Bowie's pre-Tin Machine solo career. The album was a compromise—something quite unusual for an artist who was not known for such obvious artistic compromises.

## OY VEY, BABY

*Tin Machine II*, however, was not quite the last gasp of Bowie's band project: the band released a live album, *Oy Vey, Baby,* in 1992. The live album consists primarily of songs taken from both of Tin Machine's studio albums. The unusual Yiddish title is a takeoff on U2's *Achtung, Baby. All Music Guide*'s Mark Allender gives *Oy Vey, Baby* two (out of a possible five) stars in his review. As Allender contends, "the polished songs of *Tin Machine II* do not translate well to a live recording."[3] Actually, the songs of *Tin Machine II* just did not work particularly well in a traditional rock concert venue, even with the presence of an additional rhythm guitarist. The arrangements are just too studio-conceived. The power of the band's first album is also only hinted at on this live package. What Tin Machine probably really needed in order to make their material work live was a so-called unplugged venue (such as that pioneered by MTV), which would have allowed them to adapt the arrangements more extensively, thereby avoiding the sound of a sonic compromise. One of the other problems with this recording is the way in which the harmony vocals recede into the background. *Oy Vey, Baby* is a difficult-to-find recording today: the David Bowie or Tin Machine fan will probably have to search online for a used copy. It is easily Tin Machine's least essential album, and among the least essential handful of albums associated with Bowie.

Bowie did not waste a great deal of time in resuming his solo career after the demise of Tin Machine. On April 20, 1992, he appeared at an AIDS benefit concert in London's Wembley Stadium. The concert saluted the late Freddie Mercury, lead singer of the band Queen, who had died of AIDS in November 1991. Bowie also quickly returned to the recording studio for his next solo album.

# New Sounds: 1992–1998

In the period spanning from 1992 to 1998, Bowie continued to record challenging music and lyrics, and explore such styles as metal and industrial. Throughout the period, he stepped away from the kind of pop accessibility that he fostered in the early 1980s; however, by doing so he returned to the kind of lyrical and musical relevance that he enjoyed in the 1970s. Bowie explored a variety of rock styles associated primarily with younger performers of the 1990s, and, to a large extent, his work was convincing. David Bowie continued to soak up cutting-edge styles and integrate them into his own compositional and performing vocabulary.

## BLACK TIE WHITE NOISE

Tin Machine fizzled out pretty much after its sophomore album. Conventional wisdom might have been for the band to put the *Tin Machine II* album behind them, and then move forward by attempting to perfect the alternative grunge style that had run throughout the band's first album; after all, that style was now starting to gain wider popularity with the emergence of the second wave of Seattle bands, such as Nirvana and Pearl Jam. Instead, Bowie made a bold about face. He did not return, however, to the easy accessibility of *Let's Dance* and the two lesser albums that followed Bowie's highly successful 1983 pop hit; instead he brought out *Black Tie White Noise*, an album that includes musical references to hip-hop rhythms, avant-garde jazz, Bowie's Plastic Soul work of the 1970s, and gospel. It seems almost like a continuation and refinement of Bowie's pre-Tin Machine, pre-dance club work. The album is not as challenging lyrically as much of Bowie's pre-*Let's*

*Dance* work, nor is it as unrelentingly gloomy as *Tin Machine*. This is an album of individual songs, situations, and instrumental pieces that loosely revolve around the theme of a wedding, and as such, represents a change from Bowie's character-oriented albums of the 1970s (Ziggy Stardust, the Thin White Duke). Bowie addressed this change in his *Rolling Stone* interview with David Wild. Wild asked Bowie if he ever thought about returning to his modus operandi of the 1970s—taking on a new character for each new album—to which Bowie replied "It has been gnawing at me, the idea of one more time developing a character. I do love the theatrical side of the thing—not only do I enjoy it, I also think I'm quite good at it. But for the time being, I'm quite happy being me."[1] In fact, unlike just about any previous David Bowie album, *Black Tie White Noise* is clearly autobiographical in spots. The album's twin themes of racial harmony and the events and emotions surrounding a wedding seem clearly to be related to Bowie's marriage to the black supermodel Iman.

Another major change that marks *Black Tie White Noise* is Bowie's return to saxophone playing, and with a vengeance. He took a huge chance by juxtaposing his sax playing with the trumpet playing of noted African-American jazz innovator Lester Bowie. David Bowie was never going to be confused with jazz greats Sonny Rollins on tenor sax or Gerry Mulligan on baritone sax; however, his playing of the larger members of the saxophone family on *Black Tie White Noise* is effective and credible. *Black Tie White Noise* received generally favorable critical reaction; however, that was not to a great deal of avail. Savage Records, which released the album, failed less than two months after the release of *Black Tie White Noise*.

That *Black Tie White Noise* represents something of a return to a mixture of aspects of David Bowie's pre-Tin Machine work is evident from the start of the first piece, "The Wedding." The piece focuses on Bowie's saxophone—it is *the* lead instrument throughout the five-minute piece. The sound of hip-hop also finds its way into the percussion tracks and the deep bass line. Given his expertise in the dance styles of the 1980s and 1990s, Bowie's co-producer Nile Rodgers (with whom Bowie had worked on *Let's Dance*) was probably largely responsible for these musical references, which run throughout *Black Tie White Noise*. Incidentally, although his presence is not felt on "The Wedding," Bowie's former Tin Machine bandmate Reeves Gabrels also plays guitar on the album.

"You've Been Around," a collaborative composition of Bowie and Gabrels, combines the percussion rhythms (acoustic and synthesized) of contemporary dance music, with elements of jazz, and Bowie's impressionistic lyrics. The song is a tale of someone who has "been around" and changed the singer's life. Set to a simple *ostinato*-like chord progression, the music gains a degree of sophistication with Lester Bowie's jazz trumpet solo. If one were forced to put a label on the combination of impressionistic lyrics, jazz-based instrumental work, and dance beat, it would have to be described as acid jazz, a popular style of the time.

*Black Tie White Noise* is notable for, among other things, Bowie's inter-pretation several cover songs. His take on Jack Bruce and Peter Brown's "I Feel Free" differs completely from the mid-1960s versions by Bruce's group Cream, the Amboy Dukes, and others. In fact, it is very different from solo versions by Eric Clapton (the most famous member of Cream) and others from later decades. The percussion rhythms all scream "1990s dance music," but the emotionless, otherworldly vocal style Bowie employs and the elec-tronic processing of his saxophone combine to give the track an eerie and ironic quality not found in a whole lot of dance music of the early 1990s.

The track "Black Tie White Noise" kicks off with a funky rhythm groove accompaniment made to sound old school by the superimposition of the sound of crackles, pops, and snaps from a record player. Bowie's piece deals with black-white race relations and incorporates quotes from the lyrics of earlier material, such as "We Shall Overcome" and Marvin Gaye's "What's Going On." He includes a dizzying number of disjointed lines, which are rendered even more dizzying by the fact that the album does not included printed lyrics. Al B. Sure!, a star of the then-prominent New Jack Swing subgenre of R&B, duets on lead vocals with Bowie. Both Bowies, Lester, on trumpet, and David, on tenor saxophone, provide occasional improvised jazzy filigree. What David Bowie really proves on this song is the fact that he can be more soulful as a singer than might commonly be believed. Musically, the slow groove, romantic string arrangement, and the tunefulness suggest the work of Marvin Gaye. While the we're-all-brothers theme might seem more like something from a Stevie Wonder album of the era than something that one would logically expect on a typical Bowie album, Bowie pulls it off, despite the fact that the theme is so foreign to his usual (or perhaps stereotypical) thematic material. This is due in part to the fact that he mixes cliché references to racial harmony with his patented impressionistic oblique lyrics.

The opening rhythmic groove of "Jump They Say" probably leaves fans of Bowie's mid-1970s albums expecting to hear him start singing about a "little girl with grey eyes," since the harmonic progression and rhythmic feel sounds so much like that of the song "What in the World," from Bowie's 1977 *Low* album. "Jump They Say," which was written entirely by Bowie, is somewhat oblique lyrically, but deals with observations and the resulting generaliza-tions that people can make about somewhat unconventional characters. The theme of mental illness (and perceptions of it) permeates the song, and the conventional wisdom is that the song was inspired in part by David Bowie's brother, who committed suicide.

"Jump They Say" was the feature release on the interactive Ion CD-ROM *Jump* in 1994. While the twenty-first century user of this interactive piece cannot be blamed for finding it somewhat quaint, the product was considered more cutting-edge when it was released. Among other things, the user can remix Bowie's music for "Black Tie White Noise," view a video of "Jump

They Say," and explore Bowie's thoughts about writing and performing by visiting a number of virtual rooms.

Scott Walker (real name, Scott Engel) was a member of the band the Walker Brothers, three Americans (none actually named Walker) transplanted to the United Kingdom who became part of the British Invasion in 1965. By the late 1970s, Walker became influenced by David Bowie's Berlin-period work. Walker's "Nite Flights," which originally appeared on a 1978 Walker Brothers album, includes the melodic, harmonic, and lyrical feel of Bowie's Berlin work, especially with its oblique lyrical references and obligato-style chord progression. Bowie's cover of the piece on *Black Tie White Noise* works well as an out-of-context isolated performance. It is difficult to ascertain, however, what role the song plays on the album.

Perhaps the most cutting-edge track on the album, Bowie's "Pallas Athena" is largely an instrumental piece that is clearly descended from his Berlin work. In contrast to the experimental pieces of *Low* and *Heroes,* however, "Pallas Athena" also finds Bowie referencing contemporary hip-hop dance rhythms. The minor key helps to establish the dark feel that runs throughout the piece. Bowie uses his tenor saxophone effectively, although the electronic processing of the saxophone seems unnecessary; Lester Bowie's trumpet presents the listener with a much more human effect since it is the one instrumental and vocal part that is not subjected to electronic manipulation.

Bowie's "Miracle Goodnight" resembles conventional 1980s pop, to its detriment. In fact, the piece recalls Paul McCartney's "Goodnight Tonight," and not just because of the similarity of the titles. Perhaps the song fits the wedding subtheme of the album, but sonically and texturally it stands so far apart from most of the songs that the listener can be left with the sense that it just does not quite belong on *Black Tie White Noise.* "Don't Let Me Down" is another popish track that supports the wedding theme, but is not a particularly strong piece; at least Bowie did not write this one.

Bowie's composition "Looking for Lester" is clearly a vehicle for trumpeter Lester Bowie, an artist perhaps best known for his work with the Afrocentric avant-garde jazz group the Art Ensemble of Chicago. David Bowie provides a tenor sax solo on the track. Unfortunately, the sound of his instrument is heavily processed electronically. This causes it to stand in too sharp a contrast to Lester Bowie's trumpet work. The effect to the listener is the feeling that somehow David Bowie's saxophone had to be processed in order to sound credible. However, there is nothing about the timbre (tone color) of Bowie's tenor playing on other recordings from throughout his career that suggests that his tone is anything less than acceptable in the jazz or rock genres.[2] The electronic treatment almost seems to suggest a feeling of insecurity. David Bowie need not have felt insecure about his tone, nor about his saxophone playing on this album. The composition is credible mid-1990s jazz. Listeners who are familiar with the sometimes-unexpected straight-ahead jazz knowledge and jazz appreciation of some rock, pop, and R&B musicians, such as Prince, Frank Zappa, and Stevie Wonder, might be surprised to find David

Bowie placed in that same category. However, Bowie's writing on this album, but especially on this track, reveals a side of him not often even hinted at in his previous recordings.

Bowie provides Morrissey's "I Know It's Gonna Happen" with a full-fledged gospel treatment. As is the case throughout *Black Tie White Noise*, Bowie proves that he has an affinity for African-American musical style to a far greater extent than his Plastic Soul of the mid-1970s suggested. The echo oft Bowie's lead vocal, as well as the sparse chords of the piano part in the accompaniment, also suggest the influence of John Lennon, particularly on Lennon's song "God," from the 1970 album *Plastic Ono Band*.

*Black Tie White Noise* basically ends with "The Wedding Song." This is Bowie's vocal version of the album's opener, "The Wedding." Despite the conventional pop musical setting and impressionistic love-related poetry, the song works. Bowie's blatantly romantic side as a songwriter had never really been exposed to the extent that it was on this album, which leads to the inescapable conclusion that his marriage to Iman, the supermodel, affected him quite deeply. The remaining two tracks on the Virgin and BMG reissues of the album (somewhat silly sounding, overly techno-oriented versions of "Jump They Say" and "Lucy Can't Dance") do not add much to *Black Tie White Noise*.

After the experience of the band Tin Machine, *Black Tie White Noise* represents a return to eclecticism (as opposed to a focus on hard rock) for Bowie. Although the album represents a return to styles that Bowie had integrated into his vocabulary before Tin Machine, the album tends to come off more as a transitional piece: the astute listener can hear everything from jazz to gospel to light hip-hop to twinges of alternative and grunge. One of the more problematic features of the album is that it is not the coherent whole that it could be. The overarching dual themes of a wedding (the Black Tie part) and the instrumentally focused, slightly experimental jazz pieces (the White Noise part) seem too much to be at odds with one another in order to work as an integrated whole. While the counterpoint between the two is interesting, the listener might be left with the sneaking suspicion that Bowie just didn't have quite enough wedding-related song material for an entire album, nor did he have quite enough instrumental material for an album. Should the listener be inclined to hear the album that way, some support could be found in the fact that *Black Tie White Noise* contains the largest number of covers of any David Bowie album before or since. The possible appearance, then, is that he combined two small sets of material into one to come up with an entire album's worth. Not all listeners will hear the album this way. It can also be heard as a sort of soundtrack for a movie or stage work that contains incidental music (the instrumentals) in between the songs that are part of the storyline, but that's a bit of a stretch.

Not only did Bowie's courtship of and marriage to Iman inspire his *Black Tie White Noise* album, it also gave *Rolling Stone*'s David Sinclair plenty to discuss with Bowie for his feature-length interview, "Station to Station."[3]

Although the interview contains a wealth of information about Bowie's reaction to fame and his recollections of recording his Ziggy Stardust-era albums, perhaps the most intriguing thoughts are on the subjects of love and sex. Bowie discusses courting Iman, bringing her flowers and chocolate, and sharing discreet kisses with her in doorways; in short, the kind of romantic expressions of affection that are almost completely absent from the lives of the characters of Bowie's songs. The other intriguing point of discussion revolves around Bowie's alleged bisexuality in the 1970s. He claims that, although he explored sexual experimentation during his glam period, it was largely heterosexual; he describes himself as a "closet heterosexual." The motivation for Bowie's claims of bisexuality have been the subject of much speculation over the years. Bowie's conversation with Sinclair suggests that it was largely inspired by a fascination with gay culture. At least one former business associate of Bowie, George Tremlett, suggests in his biography of Bowie[4] that it was as much a business ploy as anything else. Regardless of the motivation, however, David Bowie's frank discussion of sexual orientation and his own emotional attachment to Iman provides for a rare glimpse into his psyche completely devoid of the kind of character creation of Bowie's work as a songwriter and performer.

## THE BUDDHA OF SUBURBIA

In 1993 Bowie composed an album's worth of songs for the BBC2 series *The Buddha of Suburbia*. While a CD of the songs was released in the United Kingdom, it remained unheard in the United States until 1995. By the time *The Buddha of Suburbia* hit the United States Bowie had a new record company—Virgin—and a new official release: *Outside*. Musically and thematically, *The Buddha of Suburbia* and *Outside* are worlds apart. Unfortunately, *The Buddha of Suburbia* came out the loser in this somewhat confusing situation: it remains one of David Bowie's least-known works. It is, however, a thoroughly listenable album, and one that makes for interesting study, especially because it is so different in character from the new styles that Bowie turned to in 1995. The other particularly interesting feature of *The Buddha of Suburbia* is the fact that the project found Bowie returning to the fore as a songwriter: his previous album—*Black Tie White Noise*—contained more cover songs than any Bowie album before or since.

The album's opener, "Buddha of Suburbia" is mainstream British pop, at least musically. Bowie's lyrics are somewhat obscure, but it is clear is that his character feels himself to be an outsider in the south London suburbs. The melody of the verses is easy to remember—just the sort of thing that would work effectively as a television theme song. Unfortunately, the opening melodic motive, the thing that is the listener's first melodic impression of the piece, resembles the opening phrase of the theme song of the American television program *WKRP in Cincinnati*. To the extent that the listener recognizes the melodic descent from scale-step five as one of the signatures of the *WKRP in Cincinnati* theme, the opening of "Buddha of Suburbia" can be heard as one of the great groaners of David Bowie's songwriting career. The listener who does not make the connection will hear the song as a mood piece that sets up the premise of the story wrapped in a musical setting designed to appeal to the greatest possible number of viewers. The album closes with an alternate version of "Buddha of Suburbia," one that features Lenny Kravitz on electric guitar. Kravitz's solo work on the track adds just enough edge to make the reprise the more interesting version of the song.

"Sex and the Church" reprises the somewhat dark feel of *Black Tie White Noise*'s "Pallas Athena." Both tracks use spoken phrases to create a hook. Because of this, the two songs follow at least in part in the tradition of Yello's 1985 hit "Oh Yeah," perhaps best known for its appearance in the movie *Ferris Bueller's Day Off*, and R*S*F's 1992 hit "I'm Too Sexy." Unlike those two earlier, basically frivolous dance tracks, both "Pallas Athena" and "Sex and the Church" create a darker, more dramatic mood.

"South Horizon" extends Bowie's foray into jazz that he recently had undertaken on *Black Tie White Noise*. Structurally, however, the piece is more advanced than the jazz settings on *Black Tie White Noise*. The composition times out at 5 minutes, 24 seconds. The first 2 minutes, 26 seconds feature a fast-paced, straight-ahead jazz rhythm, over which Mike Garson (who had performed with Bowie in the early 1970s on *Aladdin Sane*) plays an atonal piano solo. Composer Bowie has Erdal Kizilcay add a short languid phrase on trumpet. This trumpet phrase is deliberately out of rhythm with respect to the rest of the soundscape, and it reappears unpredictably. Unlike small group jazz styles such as bebop, or hard bop, there is not a clear sense of progression and structure to the first section of "South Horizon"; instead, there is simply a sense of being—of timelessness. Although the percussion and bass change abruptly to a mix of jungle and hip-hop feel for the second section of the piece, the trumpet phrase recurs from time to time and Garson's avant-garde solo continues. In this section, too, Bowie creates a feeling of stasis through his non-traditional approach to harmonic progression. Whereas Bowie's state-of-being approach to jazz might be unfamiliar to some listeners who are more familiar with section-defining harmonic patterns of bop and bop-influenced jazz, there is a precedent for it in Ornette Coleman's free jazz of the 1960s. Even more to the point—at least in reference to the concept of the an eastern holy man as an outsider in south London—the sense of musical stasis is quite common in Asian music, in a variety of cultures. What Bowie does, then, is to merge Western culture (straight-ahead, and jungle- and hip-hop-based jazz) with the sense of stasis of eastern culture.

Clocking in at nearly seven and a quarter minutes, "The Mysteries" is the longest piece on *The Buddha of Suburbia*. A peaceful ambient texture features wave-like electronic sounds, synthesizer chords, and a synthesized piano-like melody. Unlike the other clearly ambient background piece on the album, "Ian Fish, U.K. Heir," this composition uses a longer-range harmonic progression in order to maintain its feel of needing to continue endlessly. Bowie establishes a tonality and then ends phrase after phrase on the dominant (V) chord. In conventional tonal writing, the dominant chord requires a resolution to the tonic (I) chord for the listener to feel a sense of completion. Bowie studiously avoids clear dominant-tonic resolutions in "The Mysteries." The listener, then, is left with a feeling of puzzles (or mysteries) that are never solved.

To the extent that the lyrics of "Bleed Like a Craze, Dad" are difficult to make out because of the way co-producers Bowie and Erdal Kizilcay treat Bowie's voice, the piece essentially functions best when considered as a manic, hard-driving, passionate rock track. It establishes a mood, which may be important in the context of the television miniseries, but it is not an essential David Bowie track. The song "Untitled No. 1" is another piece that—at least for this writer—fails to make a strong impression or a strong connection.

While I would not go as far as the *All Music Guide* critic William Ruhlmann, who writes "in another context songs like 'Strangers When We Meet' easily could become Bowie favorites,"[5] this particular song is one of the most memorable tracks on *The Buddha of Suburbia*. Bowie's poetry conjures up a wide variety of seemingly disconnected images of potential personality clashes that would tend to divide two individuals upon first meeting. And, it is important to note that the lyrics of the verse really are more like a poem than they are like conventional song lyrics. Of course, this had long been David Bowie's modus operandi, and one of the things that sets him aside from most pop and rock singer-songwriters: because of their unconventional themes, unconventional rhyme schemes, and disconnected imagery, many of Bowie's lyrics take on the character of impressionistic poetry set to vernacular music. The melody of the chorus is memorable, with its descending line, but is not as distinctive as Bowie's most memorable tunes.

"Dead Against It" is a highly effective rock piece. Musically, it calls to mind the best features of Bowie's work on *Station to Station, Low,* and *"Heroes."* There is an energy and new wave feel, instant accessibility, and enough interesting instrumental lines that the repetitive setting still holds the listener's interest. In fact, the music also recalls some of the similarly danceable, energetic, harmonically repetitive songs of Orchestral Manoeuvres in the Dark (OMD; Andy McCluskey's 1980 song "Enola Gay," in particular, comes to mind). Although Bowie doesn't use the old "Heart and Soul" chord progression (I-vi-IV-V) verbatim like McCluskey, the effect is the same. Bowie's singing, too, has some of the pretty character of OMD's McCluskey. The lyrics are typically Bowie-impressionistic, although some of the short, clipped phrases suggest a stream-of-consciousness progression of images that might result from a psychoanalysis session.

Bowie's "Ian Fish, U.K. Heir" is an eerie ambient mood piece that recaps some of the electronica of *"Heroes."* By 1993, however, Bowie had broadened his sense of time and overall progression: this piece maintains stasis effectively for a longer time than any of his previous minimalistic, static instrumental compositions. It remains quiet throughout, but builds just ever so slightly and slowly over six-and-a-half minutes. The sounds of static (pops and crackles) that introduce the piece are reminiscent of the sounds of a well-used vinyl; the static continues throughout the song, and lingers even after all other sounds have ceased, contributing to the overall ambient Zen feel of the piece.

Bowie's music for the series *The Buddha of Suburbia* might not have been his most cutting-edge work, but his measured and mature approach to ambient music is laudable, and his pop sensibilities are intact on the song "Dead Against It." He also demonstrations that his flirtation with jazz on *Black Tie White Noise* was not just a fluke. A copy of *The Buddha of Suburbia* remains difficult to obtain, but it is worth the hunt.

## OUTSIDE

Bowie decided in the mid-1990s that he wanted to tap into the end-of-the-millennium angst that pervaded western culture as the year 2000 approached. According to Bowie, he planned for *Outside* to be the first in a series of albums that would essentially "capture the atmosphere of the last five years of the millennium using the device of a storyline and characters."[6] *Outside* revolves around a story of intrigue and murder that Bowie penned for *Q Magazine,* entitled "The Diary of Nathan Adler or the Art-Ritual Murder of Baby Grace Blue." The story unfolds over the course of 23 years: 1977–1999. The album itself presents challenges to the listener, partly because Bowie portrays all of the story's seven characters, but mostly because the deliberately non-linear nature of the piece forces the listener to take a bunch of disconnected impressions (unsupported, by the way, by printed lyrics in the CD booklet) and then put the whole thing together. This requires considerably more thought, focus, and attentiveness than conventional concept albums and rock operas, because those sorts of pieces generally revolve around a more linear progression through time. In this respect, *Outside* ventures closer to the world of art music: it is more like a experimental song cycle or even John Cage-inspired cantata than a work such as, say, the Who's *Tommy.* The non-linear, cut-up nature of Bowie's presentation of what already seems like a difficult-to-follow storyline also suggests the non-linear writing technique of William S. Burroughs, a writer Bowie had earlier emulated. Even in Burroughs's cut-up works such as *Junky, Naked Lunch,* and *The Soft Machine,* however, the disjointed chunks of material are long enough that a greater degree of linearity is felt than in Bowie's narrative technique on *Outside.*

Bowie presents challenges in *Outside,* however, that go beyond a disturbing story of ritual murder and non-linear narrative technique. Another challenge that Bowie presents the listener is a dizzying variety of musical styles, from jazz to rock, from the electronica of industrial and its antithesis, ambient. Of course, in portraying seven characters and various relationships and scenarios in close to 20 pieces/songs/movements, there is bound to be quite a high level of variety. The final challenge that *Outside* presents is its length; the album is nearly an hour and a quarter of material that really begs to be listened to at the same sitting. Most of the individual songs stray from conventional pop style and are so tied to the album's theme, that listening to them piece-meal proves less effectual.

Sometimes it is tempting to pull a CD out of its box, pop it into the player, and simply listen. Since the development of such personal listening devices as the Walkman, Discman, mp3 players, and the iPod, it is easy to imagine that consumers of music have relied less and less on the conventional physical packaging of albums, such as liner sleeves and CD booklets. In the case of David Bowie's *Outside,* however, it would be a shame to ignore the CD booklet. The booklet contains the diary entries of Bowie's fictional character Detective Nathan Alder as he attempts to solve the ritual murders. Although these jump around chronologically, they are much easier to follow than the song cycle itself. In part, this is due to the fact that the booklet contains only a few snippets of the actual song lyrics. With these snippets, the fragmented diary of Detective Alder, the distorted and electronically manipulated photographs, and the music, one can experience *Outside* as a multi-media piece.

The entire cycle begins with the impressionistic musical and fragmented lyrical images of "Leon Takes Us Outside." The "Leon" of the title is Leon Blank, a 22-year-old, mixed-race male with a short string of previous convictions for petty crimes—none of which would be possible to ascertain were it not for the Alder diary entries of the CD booklet. The piece establishes a dark, mysterious mood, as well as the idea that what follows will not likely be presented in a nice, neat linear narrative form.

"Outside," with music by Bowie and Kevin Armstrong and lyrics by Bowie, is one of the few songs on the album that does not seem to support the Nathan Alder diaries in any substantial way. However, it is a strong song and deserving of being better known by Bowie's fans. The piece begins as a direct segue from the album's opener. A chord progression with slow harmonic rhythm (one chord per each two measures) gives way to an ominous minor-key bass line. Each of the bass notes lasts for a half-measure. Even though the beat speed remains constant, the quadrupling of the speed of the harmonic rhythm approximately 57 seconds into "Outside" represents a significant point in the piece's structure: the listener can perceive this as the start of the song proper, with the first section perceived as an extended transition from "Leon Takes Us Outside." Incidentally, Bowie includes several other transitions from song to song at other points on the album, all of which contribute to the listener's perception of the entire thing as a unified (although decidedly non-linear) whole.

Bowie's lyrics for "Outside" are decidedly minimal and "poem-like," in the sense that they read on paper more like a poem than conventionally structured song lyrics. Bowie and Brian Eno's musical setting counterpoints a generally descending, rhythmically syncopated melody against the steady half-note, rising bass line. Both the nature of the poem and the counterpoint of the music suggest a sophistication not all that common in the popular music of the mid-1990s.

"The Heart's Filthy Lesson" brings together elements of jungle and acid jazz together. A musical collaboration of Bowie, Eno, Reeves Gabrels, Mike Garson, Erdal Kizilcay, and Sterling Campbell—the album's core band—the track features lyrics by Bowie. When taken as a groove piece, it is successful; however, the full extent of Bowie's lyrics are difficult to grasp because of the recording's texture. Even as printed on a page—and, remember, the liner notes do not include a transcript of the lyrics—Bowie's poetry for this song, as well as most of the songs on *Outside,* are disjointed and impressionistic. The listener comes away with feelings, rather than a story, or even a narrative piece of the story. The problem with this is that, even within the Nathan Alder diaries printed in the album's booklet, the role of the songs, beyond establishing somewhat vague moods, remains unclear.

Because so many of the individual songs of *Outside* are mood pieces that work best within the context of the album, and because so few of them are known outside the context of the album, I will not dwell on each of the 19 pieces. I would point out that the pieces cover a wide musical scope. In "A Small Plot of Land," for example, Bowie sings a slow, chant-like melody over fast-paced jazz. In contrast, Bowie and Eno's "I Have Not Been to Oxford Town" features a forceful rhythm track that is reminiscent of Queen's "We Will Rock You," whereas Bowie and Eno's "Wishful Beginnings" features a mysterious, abstract melody over slowly building, layered, synthesized electronic sounds.

The final track on *Outside,* a new version of Bowie's 1993 song "Strangers When We Meet," sounds as though it was influenced by the songs on the first half of U2's 1987 classic album, *The Joshua Tree.* Bowie's vocal approach, the instrumental timbres, and the use of space all suggest the songs "With or Without You" and "I Still Haven't Found What I'm Looking For." This makes the track less distinctive than in its earlier form on the soundtrack for *The Buddha of Suburbia.*

Bowie's *Outside* is a formidable piece, showing wide musical range. It challenges listeners with an avant-garde, multi-media, performance art-like approach to a detective story that seems not too far removed from those of Raymond Chandler and his fictional detective, Philip Marlowe. Generally, music critics took issue with the difficult-to-follow storyline; for example, *People*'s Jeremy Helligar described the storyline as "a bit precious and pretentious,"[7] and *Rolling Stone*'s David Fricke panned the "tangled narrative conceit."[8] Both cited critics, however, gave better marks to Bowie's music.

Although Bowie had been involved in the film medium as an actor several times throughout his career, during the late eighties and early nineties he was largely absent from film. He reemerged as an actor in 1996 in Julian Schnabel's film *Basquiat.* In this biography of the famed graffiti artist Jean-Michel Basquiat, Bowie portrays Andy Warhol. In order to play the part as authentically as possible, Bowie donned one of Warhol's wigs. Critics and fans and associates of the late American pop artist were divided in their assessment of Bowie's portrayal. In his review of the film, *People*'s Tom Gliatto wrote, "Droll, thin and twittish, Bowie comes across more like Miss Hathaway from *The Beverly Hillbillies*."[9] On the other hand, film director Paul Morrissey, who worked at one time with Warhol, characterized Bowie's portrayal as "the best by far" of three different actors who had portrayed the artist in three different films. In particular, Morrissey noted that Bowie's portrayal was more three-dimensional and truer to Warhol's character than the others.[10] Bowie, who has had an interest in visual arts and has been active as a painter, wrote an op-ed piece for *Modern Painters* magazine on the importance of Jean-Michel Basquiat at the time of the film's release.[11] Bowie continued to contribute articles, op-ed pieces, and interviews with artists for the magazine through the end of the twentieth century. During this time, he also expanded his own work as a painter.

## EARTHLING

While Bowie's 1995 album *Outside* contains no fewer than 19 pieces, his 1997 offering, *Earthling,* contains nine songs. Freed of the constraints of a trying to create a series of mood pieces to fit a non-linear storyline, Bowie was able to use a more general concept to link the pieces together, which had long been his usual modus operandi. The CD features a cover photo of Bowie with his back to the camera wearing a geometric, space alien-like outfit. He looks out over what could be the British countryside. The only thing that is missing to complete the alien-comes-to-Britain visual premise is a crop circle. Once the listener opens up the CD package, however, one sees that the track listing and songwriting credits are presented in a circle. All of these things—the photograph, the circle of credits, and the album's title, combined with the techno music, the electronically manipulated photo collage that constitutes the colorful CD booklet, and the lyrics, which deal with various attributes and trappings of modern British and American society—establish Bowie as an outside, or in other words, alien, observer of the state of end-of-the-millennium western world. Compared with *Outside,* the music is more unified, too, with an emphasis on techno and jungle styles. Despite the intensity of these styles, the album is somehow more musically accessible than *Outside.* In large part, this is due to the stylistic consistency of the musical settings, but the album's accessibility is also helped by the presence of some strong melodic hooks. Critics have been somewhat divided over the merits of Bowie's use of the techno style on *Earthling.* On one hand, Carol Clerk and Andre Paine of *Melody Maker* include *Earthling* among the David Bowie albums best to avoid,[12] and Stephen Thomas Erlewine of *All Music Guide* writes that it sounds as if the jungle-style "beats were simply grafted on top of pre-existing songs."[13] On the other hand, Peter Castro of *People* credited Bowie with striking an "accessible" balance between "jungle" and rock styles that hearkens back to the balanced approach of *Lodger* and *Scary Monsters (And Super Creeps)*.[14]

*Earthling* begins with one of Bowie's strongest songs of the 1990s, "Little Wonder." Bowie's lyrics are highly impressionistic and contain disjointed references to everything from the trivial ("stinky weather") to pop culture (several of the Seven Dwarfs) to areas of fascination for males ("tits"). The "little wonder" of the song's title is not clearly identified, but is "so far away." It is easy to hear the lyrics referring to a person; however, given the space alien theme suggested by the whole gestalt of the album packaging, the distant "little wonder" could just as easily be Bowie's character's home star. In other words, "Little Wonder" can be heard as a modern, more adult version of "Twinkle, Twinkle Little Star." [It is not a huge leap from "Twinkle, twinkle little star, how I wonder what you are, Up above the world so high" to "You little wonder, little wonder you ... So far away."] As for the other lyrical references, they could be observations that the alien makes about Earth: lousy weather, males' obsession with female anatomy, pop culture.

The music, arrangement, and production are all catchy and hook-laden. All of these musical aspects of the piece set off the phrases "You little wonder you" and "So far away" so as to make them seem more significant than they are as pure text. It is, in short, a classic case of the whole being greater than the sum of its parts. Although the techno and jungle aspects of the arrangement and production are not necessary for the success of the piece—other interesting timbres and contrasts could have been used, perhaps to equally good effect—producer Bowie thoroughly integrates the electronic sounds and the rhythms of the contemporary popular music of the time, mixing them and contrasting them with more conventional rock sounds. In particular, the song finds Bowie grounding the double-time rhythms of jungle (in drum machines and acoustic drums) and the electronic effects of techno with an inspired chord progression. The chord progression and bass line of each of the lines of verses ends with an open feeling, which co-composers Bowie, Reeves Gabrels, and Mark Plati achieve by beginning each phrase on the tonic, but ending each on the dominant. In contrast, the music that accompanies the oft-repeated phrase "So far away" moves harmonically up by whole steps (G major, A major, B major) toward an ending on the B major tonic. The upward whole-step chord root movement comes right out of the harmonic vocabulary of some of the more adventurous nineteenth-century Romantic-era European composers, such as Franz Liszt. The contrast of a succession of open phrases in the verses and repeated closed-sounding phrases in the chorus gives the whole piece a nice, almost classical, long-range antecedent-consequent effect. The track is as good an illustration as any song on the album, then, of the sense of balance mentioned in the previously quoted *People* review of *Earthling*.[15]

In terms of the balance of the overt use of sound technology, dance beats, and musical references to more conventional pop, "Little Wonder" is strangely suggestive of Paul McCartney's "Goodnight Tonight," a non-album song from 1979. Even lyrically, the two songs are not all that far removed: both feature what on the surface seem like simple, almost inane lyrics that in reality are more complicated, as they manage to mask more sophisticated background meanings.

In case the lyrics of "Little Wonder" were not obscure enough, Bowie outdoes himself on the next track, "Looking for Satellites." The basic premise of looking for satellites, when none can be seen, is integrated with one- and two-word references to various parts of everyday life (e.g., "TV," "shampoo," and "slim tie"). There is a clear lyrical connection with "Little Wonder," though, in Bowie's reference to the a moon that is "far away." Despite the minimal nature of the lyrics and the fragmented (at least at first glance) images, one can actually read the lyrics in multiple ways. On one level, the listener can hear the piece as a continuation of the Bowie-as-alien theme: he misses his home, which is off somewhere far away in the heavens. On another level, this could be a song about a couple that has just about reached the end of their relationship. The moon, the satellites they are trying desperately to see perhaps represent their last hope to make the relationship work. This is one of Bowie's strengths as a lyricist: his poems may be intended (mostly) to mean one thing, but he often leaves just enough intentional ambiguity that multiple understandings are not only possible, but seem to be encouraged.

Even more so than "Little Wonder," this song relies on the musical setting to work. And, again, it is a piece that is much more than a musical setting of a poem. The challenge for a songwriter with this kind of mood piece with such minimal and disjointed lyrics is that the music carries a significant amount of weight in determining the overall success of the piece. Contrast this with, say, the work of a more folk-oriented singer-songwriter such as Leonard Cohen, in which the music may be fairly minimal and basically a medium for presentation of a poem. In the techno style that Bowie uses in this piece—indeed, throughout *Earthling*—the arrangement and the recording mix play a significant role in the overall effect of the piece. Increasingly, scholars acknowledge the importance of arrangement and mix in the role that they play in the overall meaning of the piece. Writing in the scholarly journal *American Music*, Albin Zak III quotes composer, singer, guitarist Frank Zappa on the subject of the role of arrangement and record production in defining a composition:

> On a record, the overall timbre of the piece (determined by equalization of individual parts and their proportions in the mix) tells you, in a subtle way, *WHAT* the song is about. The orchestration provides *important information* about what the composition *IS* and, in some instances, assumes a greater importance than *the composition itself*.[16]

Such is the case especially with Bowie's "Looking for Satellites." This is because the piece is based on an *ostinato* chant: there is not a great deal of melodic material, and the harmony remains static for significant periods of time. The piece is so thoroughly *ostinato* based that when there are harmonic changes underneath the *ostinato* vocal lines, they seem quite significant. Not so significant, however, that the harmonic changes take structural precedence over the arrangement and recording mix in defining the piece.

"Battle for Britain (The Letter)" combines the deep bass and drum sequences of techno music with the alternative hard rock guitar of Tin Machine and vocal melody and harmony that could easily have come out of a 1966 or 1967 British rock band. Aside from some of techno noises in the arrangement, the song does not overtly fit the space visitor theme of the previous songs on *Earthling*. The lyrics, in fact find Bowie in a rare optimistic mood. The real interest in the song, however, is the strong alternative rock setting. The brief backwards portion and some of the techno-related sounds are a bit of an annoyance, as they are not necessary, and can make for some confusion of genre among listeners.

"Seven Years in Tibet" also finds Bowie mixing genres. In this case a John Lennon-esque melody is set with a mix of early 1960s, late-1970s new wave Farfisa organ, the dynamic extremes of grunge, heavily distorted guitar, surf guitar, and an R&B-style horn line. Unlike the previous song, however, "Seven Years in Tibet" actually benefits from the stark sonic contrasts. Bowie's lyrics evoke vague impressions of a spiritual journey to Tibet; however, mostly because of the context in which they are placed by the title of the song. It betrays some of the spirituality that was starting to emerge in Bowie's work as the end of the millennium approached, a spirituality that would be more overt on the 1999 album *hours...*and the 2002 album *Heathen*. The song's most obvious tie to earlier David Bowie compositions was in his reference to the number seven. The storyline of *Outside*, for example, includes seven characters; "Little Wonder" refers to several of the Seven Dwarfs. It is one 1990s Bowie track that deserves a wider audience because of it richness musically and lyrically.

"Dead Man Walking" includes images of gay men embracing and dancing under a lamp post and a man repulsed by watching television because the program he is viewing reminds him of the tragedies of his past. Bowie uses these to compare with his own character's alienation from conventional society; he is "like a dead man walking." The music is largely conventional dance fare; however, at times there are hints of atonality in the piano, sequenced electronic keyboards, and electric guitar parts. There are also hints of Latin dance music and jazz. The disjointed nature of these unusual musical juxtapositions mirrors the lack of connectedness felt by Bowie's character and the other characters he describes. "Dead Man Walking" is not, however, a particularly distinctive song—Bowie has written and recorded more intriguing songs of alienation. Incidentally, this song was used in the soundtrack of the Paramount motion picture, *The Saint*. "Dead Man Walking" was joined by music from newer acts such as Sneaker Pimps, Fluke, and the Chemical Brothers.

"Telling Lies" comes from a different lyrical world than many of the other songs on *Earthling*. Here, Bowie includes more obvious rhymes than in most of the songs; however, the rhyme scheme of each verse is unique. This gives the poem a contradictory feeling of unity and unpredictability. Whereas the text is somewhat minimalistic, Bowie paints a picture of a world of gossip, exaggerations, and lies. The music is a mix of dance and alternative rock that does not blend as well as some of the other songs on *Earthling*.

"The Last Thing You Should Do" features even more minimal lyrics than "Telling Lies." In just a relatively few lines Bowie describes the lack of humor and the lack of self-love in late twentieth-century. Ultimately, he concludes that expressions of affection (a kiss, sharing a bus ride) are necessary because they bring safety. It is a pretty grim world that he paints, but in keeping with the spirit of millennial uncertainty of the time. The meaning of this song is also defined by the high-energy techno jungle musical setting. It is noisy, atonal in places, filled with a mixture of high-pitched noises, drum machine beats, and long synthesized string notes. "The Last Thing You Should Do" is dark and difficult to listen to: it is not a David Bowie track that the casual listener would be likely to seek out. The song really is most effective in the context of the overall *Earthling* gestalt of alienation and end-of-the-millennium uncertainty.

As the reader might suspect from the descriptions of the songs of *Earthling*, this album did not spawn much in the way of top-40 popular singles. One of the few tracks that found life outside the context of the album was "I'm Afraid of Americans." While critical reaction to the song was not unanimous, the single release of the song did receive favorable comment in *Billboard*.[17] Here, Bowie is joined by the industrial, techno musician Trent Reznor, of Nine Inch Nails fame. The musical setting is richer than some of the others on *Earthling*. In particular, there are sonic references not only to 1990s alternative rock, industrial, and techno, there are also discernable spiritual ties to 1980s techno á la the American band Devo. Bowie's lyrics pick up where his mid-1970s song "Young Americans" left off. He tells in a very matter-of-fact manner about Johnny, an American who is obsessed with sex and with his looks and self-importance. Bowie also touches on the sense of manifest destiny that has driven America's westward expansion, inventiveness, and slaughter of indigenous peoples. Although Bowie does not deal specifically with all these issues, the spirit of manifest destiny is definitely here and the problems it can bring are at the heart of Bowie's thoroughly ironic phrase, "God is an American."

The album's last track, "Law (Earthlings on Fire)," calls to mind Paul Hardcastle's 1985 British hit "19." It is a dance track that features the ominous spoken refrain, "I don't want knowledge; I want certainty." The image of a man falling to the floor dead is juxtaposed with the hackneyed expression "What a morning." It is the stark contrast that adds to the ominous nature of the piece. As an individual David Bowie composition, it does not rank among the most memorable. However, as an expression of the end-of-the-millennium sense of malaise that Bowie would explore on *Outside, Earthling,* and *hours...,* it captures a mood that many in the Western world felt in the late 1990s. One of the dangers of setting powerful images to dance music is that the listener can miss the meaning of the text for the beat. "Law (Earthlings on Fire)" ventures close to tipping the balance; however, it is so dark that it succeeds in the context of an alien's observation of humankind at what some people believed was a critical junction in history.

*Rolling Stone*'s Matt Diehl described recording sessions for *Earthling* in his article, "In the Studio: David Bowie Rumbles in the Jungle on *Earthling*." Among the more interesting observations were the images of Bowie instructing pianist Mike Garson. As Diehl writes, "'Lay off the chromatic things,' Bowie advises...'[The song] is more Kurt Weill than Hollywood strip. Keep it expressionistic, and float between the chords...Think Gil Evans—think of the long, plaintive notes in the *Taxi Driver* score!'"[18] In this brief explanation of his ideas for Garson's solo, Bowie demonstrates knowledge and appreciation of the German expressionist musical theater of Weill and the cool jazz of Evans. The passage also illustrates the way in which Bowie guides musicians toward his conceptual framework of a piece, while still allowing them creative elbow room for their improvisation.

By the time the listener finishes *Earthling*, it has become clear that the programmatic nature of the album that seemed to be very much in evidence on the first several tracks—that of the space alien visiting and observing Earth and earthlings—is really only one narrow aspect of the theme. The real overarching theme is alienation, which ends up taking a variety of forms. The challenge for the listener is that the album's artwork and the specifics of the opening songs focus so thoroughly on the alien from outer space that once this theme starts to disappear from the foreground of the songs, it causes confusion. The other major challenge of the album, and the one that caused the most consternation among critics, is the combination of musical styles. Sometimes it works and sometimes it is decidedly less than seamless.

David Bowie's exploration of new musical technology on *Earthling* expanded beyond the recording studio itself in the 1996–1999 period. In July 1996, Bowie's single "Telling Lies" was released through the Internet. And in September 1998, his Web site davidbowie.com went far beyond what the artists' Web sites of the day ordinarily did: it established itself as an Internet Service Provider, providing access to the Internet for $19.95 per month.

Bowie also created a huge stir in the financial world in 1998 and 1999 when it was announced that he would issue corporate bonds that would pay interest based on future income from Bowie's recordings and other entertainment projects. The so-called Bowie Bonds received extensive coverage from the popular financial press. Bowie proved to be a pioneer in this arena: other artists have followed his lead.

# The New Traditionalist: 1999–2007

David Bowie delved into jazz and then into several electronic styles in the early- and mid-1990s. Bowie's most recent three albums to date, however, have found him integrating the various styles with which he has been associated in the past. He has achieved a mature musical balance and has dealt increasingly with issues associated with spirituality, aging, and mortality.

## HOURS...

David Bowie had taken steps into the electronica worlds of industrial, jungle, and techno on the albums *Outside* and *Earthling*. *Outside* had been a relative commercial failure because the record company that originally released it went out of business. *Outside* also received less-than-stellar reviews because of its complex, non-linear storyline. *Earthling* was fairly well received; however, younger listeners did not seem to accept Bowie's incorporation into his overall style of what they perceived to be their exclusively their own, and some reviewers suggested that the techno and jungle style seemed to be somewhat artificially imposed on some of the songs. So, what was David Bowie to do? As he had done on more than one occasion in his long career, Bowie made an abrupt and dramatic stylistic change. His 1999 album *hours...* evokes 1960s soul and rock more than anything Bowie had recorded in years. Critics in major publications, such as *Rolling Stone* and *People,* praised the package as one of Bowie's best albums in years.[1] Despite this critical praise, the 1999 album *hours...* received perhaps even more press coverage for the album's marketing strategy than for the music itself. Bowie's record company, ISO, took the unusual step of releasing the album on the Internet two weeks before the CD itself was released to the public. So, although *hours...* may have found David Bowie eschewing the latest musical trends, it found him on the cutting edge of the recording industry in the distribution of his product.

One especially notable feature of *hours...* is that it represents the most completely conceived output of Bowie's and Reeves Gabrels's songwriting collaboration. This is especially interesting considering how different the arrangements on *hours...* are from the alternative grunge songs of Bowie and Gabrels's first work together a decade earlier on *Tin Machine*. In particular, the two songwriters weave memorable, singable melodies throughout the album, and Bowie's lyrics, though just as impressionistic as ever, focus on more easily accessible subjects than anything he had written for years. There are a couple of overarching themes: the ups and downs of relationships and the role of angels—the second of these being quite an unusual topic on a David Bowie album, given the subjects with which he had dealt in the past. Even the album's cover art suggests the dichotomy between heavenly intervention and the evils of earth that necessitate that intervention: the front of the CD shows Bowie resting his head in the lap of an angel (also portrayed by Bowie), while the back shows images of three less-than-at-ease Bowies seated in front of a black snake. Bowie and his angelic companion on the front cover are dressed in white, whereas the tense, wasted, and depressed-looking Bowies on the back cover are dressed in black. Despite the fact that the subject of angels might at first glance seem to be strange for Bowie, it is curiously in keeping with the end-of-the-millennium theme that had driven all of Bowie's work of the second half of the 1990s. The angst that had permeated Bowie's previous two albums was replaced on *hours...* by an eerie sense that, one way or another, angels would carry people through the change of the millennium. Tied into the theme of deliverance are references to numerology that run throughout the album. In particular, the number seven plays a significant role. Bowie had already made a few references to seven in just a few of his earlier songs. Here, the number that governs the passing of days into weeks appears in several guises. The listener is left with the feeling that not only is the passage of time controlled by some indefinable supreme power, but possibly so are the events of one's life.

Anyone who expected *hours...* to sound even remotely like the *Tin Machine* albums, or *Outside* and *Earthling,* for that matter, would have been in shock after the first few measures of "Thursday's Child," the album's opening track. Although synthesizers are very much in evidence, the song owes absolutely nothing to techno; from a musical standpoint this song is Quiet Storm R&B all the way. Bowie portrays a character who was "born out of [his] time," but who now sees hope for a brighter future. This hope for the formerly unlucky Thursday's Child comes from a new love relationship. Although Bowie, consistent with his poetic style from virtually his entire career, studiously avoids the word *love*, it is clear that the smile that warms his future is born of love. Because this character is so dramatically different than any of Bowie's previous characters, it seems almost as though all of the alienation his earlier characters have felt and have expressed has suddenly been lifted, literally after decades. In the context of Bowie's decades-long collection of social misfits, this is nothing short of dramatic and miraculous. This miraculous feeling does not end with "Thursday's Child": it pervades this, Bowie's angels album.

The reference to "Thursday's Child" of the song comes from the old Mother Goose poem that has been used for generations to teach children the days of the week:

> Monday's child is fair of face,
> Tuesday's child is full of grace;
> Wednesday's child is full of woe,
> Thursday's child has far to go;
> Friday's child is loving and giving,
> Saturday's child works hard for its living;
> But the child that is born on the Sabbath day
> Is bonny and blithe, and good and gay.

While Bowie had pursued his own brand of so-called Plastic Soul back in the mid-1970s and a couple of times subsequently, here he sounds less detached; therefore, he sounds more like a so-called real soul singer. Musically, it is as though the years of folk-rock, glam, punk, grunge, dance, techno, industrial, and jungle have been washed away. The listener is left with Bowie writing and singing in the manner of Al Green. Again, it is a miraculous stylistic change, and one that is intimately tied to the over-all theme of the album. Still, the melody of "Thursday's Child" is a little quirky: some difficult-to-sing intervals and some notes that are not necessarily intuitively harmonized tell the listener that the song is not the product of a conventional soul songwriter. The quirkiness of the melody helps to make the tune all the more memorable, and it is in keeping with Bowie's compositional style throughout his career. Many of his songs include melodies that, while suited for Bowie's voice, contain passages that would challenge singers who tend to excel at conventional melodic material. In the chorus and the song's run-out, however, there is a melody in the background vocals that is catchy and singable: the kind of hook that can be found in commercially successful Motown-style ballads. The balance between this hummable tune and the somewhat quirky tune of the verses supports the lyrical balance between the character's predestination ("Thursday's child has far to go," as the old poem goes), and the fact that he now seems to see that he finally is about to reach that brighter future.

"Something in the Air," not to be confused with the famous early-1970s song by the British band Thunderclap Newman, shares a stylistic feel with some of Bowie's Tin Machine-era songs, as well as with "Sunday" and "Slip Away," both from the 2002 album, *Heathen*. This song is the flip-side of "Thursday's Child"; not literally, in the sense of a two-sided vinyl record, but figuratively. Bowie's character is bemoaning the breakup of a relationship. Despite the fact that he knows that the relationship is over there is still "something in the air" that does not allow his character to feel a sense of closure. Apparently, he regrets his own decision, because he intimates that he was the one who asked the other character "to go."

It is important to note that both of these relationship songs are crafted in such a way as to make them applicable to a wide variety of poetic voices—they are pretty much gender neutral. In other words, "Something in the Air" (or "Thursday's Child," for that matter) could be about a male-female, female-male, male-male, or female-female relationship. Writing in the *Advocate*, Larry Flick referred to Bowie's writing on his next album, *Heathen*, as "gay friendly."[2] Flick's assessment could just as easily apply to *hours...* ; not because Bowie includes any gay-specific lyrical references, but because the characters and situations he creates are so frequently gender-neutral and sexual orientation–neutral.

Musically, "Something in the Air" sounds more conventional than "Thursday's Child," in large part because the minor-key chord progression is so timeless sounding. This harmonic pattern would not be out of place in Baroque-era art music, nor in the European Romantic period, nor in an alternative rock song of the end of the twentieth century. The arrangement hearkens back to some of the more gentle work of Tin Machine a decade earlier.

"Survive" is a broken relationship song from a similar perspective. Like "Something in the Air," in which it sounds as though Bowie's character initiated the breakup, here he also is the one who ended the relationship either actively ("I should have kept you") or passively ("I should have tried"). Despite the fact that he concludes, "I'll survive," he clearly harbors both a love for his former partner, a sense of loss, and some regret for his initiation of the breakup. Since Bowie had declared back in the mid-1990s that he planned to record a series of albums that would deal with the end of the millennium, the listener who was familiar with the pronouncement might hear the lyrics of this song (as well as the others on *hours...*) as metaphorical as well as literal. In the metaphorical sense, Bowie seems not to be singing about a relationship, but instead about his belief that something or someone will help him (and the rest of humankind) survive January 1, 2000. Admittedly, this is a bit of a stretch, but since Bowie set up this 1999 album as part of his commentary on the end of the millennium, it is an intriguing and entirely possible interpretation.

Musically, "Survive" recalls Bowie's pre-fame folk-rock music of the late 1960s. The melody is full of the kind of catchy hooks that defined Bowie's work in the 1960s and 1970s. Unlike some of his folk-rock songs of his early career, however, "Survive" does not meander musically or lyrically. It is the product of a master songwriter who knows what connects with an audience and what can lose an audience. With its strong melodic content, guitar and synthesizer-based arrangement, sustained lead guitar lines, and simple emotions expressed through poetic metaphor, it resembles the songs of Justin Hayward, the guitarist, lead singer, and principal songwriter of the Moody Blues. While the Moody Blues brand of progressive rock generally is fairly far removed from a lot of what Bowie wrote and recorded over the years, the song is effective.

The fourth track on *hours...*, "If I'm Dreaming My Life," makes musical references to the slow, heavy rock of Crosby, Stills, Nash, and Young's *Déja Vu*; early-1980s new wave; 1966- and 1967-period Brian Wilson; and the late 1960s psychedelic blues of Jimi Hendrix, mixed with some of the surf guitar tone color that pervades *hours...* . The lyrics of this over-seven-minute-long song speak of the alienation that Bowie's character feels not knowing if he is experiencing reality or "dreaming [his] life away." The range of musical styles Bowie references in this piece fit beautifully with the concept of his character reviewing his life.

The musical references to Bowie's late-1960s highly personal-sounding folk-rock style and to the music of his peers of the past three decades continue in the song "Seven." In fact, the multiple acoustic guitar and string synthesizer accompaniment, with a mellow-toned lead guitar line and easy melodic and harmonic accessibility all combine to suggest a combination of the styles of the Beatles's George Harrison and the Moody Blues's Justin Hayward. Perhaps more than any other song on *hours...*, "Seven" encapsulates the thematic dichotomy of the album. Bowie sings that he has "seven days to live [his] life, or seven ways to die." This, after disclosing that he has entered a new (gender neutral) love relationship. His references to forgetting what he was told by his mother and father suggest that this relationship represents a first sexual encounter. This relationship becomes a transcendent experience. It offers Bowie's character two paths: either this experience will lead to a lifetime of fulfillment, or a lifetime of pain. There is a feeling of sadness in the song that is expressed by the mournful lead guitar line, the small melodic range, and the even level of expression in Bowie's voice. This suggests that his character really is not sure which of the two possibilities he will experience. "Seven," then, rhetorically works as a predecessor of "Thursday's Child," a song in which Bowie's character has experienced his share of loss and struggle, but now is certain that he is poised on the cusp of a bright future.

This brings up one of the few minor problems with *hours...*: Although all the songs address a common theme and exhibit a unified musical vision, the order of the songs is non-linear. Certainly, it is not necessary that the album be a logical, ordered, linear, timeline of the trials and transcendent experiences of one character. The emotional ups and downs and apparent temporal jumping around of the album allows Bowie to explore the black-white, trial-transcendence themes perhaps more fully than would be possible with a timeline approach. The thing is, Bowie could have arranged the songs of *hours...* in a more linear sequence and provided the listener with a richer sense of one man's progression through life. Of course, those listeners who prefer the linear-progression approach can take advantage of the technology available today and resequence the album. Although this would cause the album to loose some of its structural integrity (by the end of *hours...* it becomes clear just why Bowie did not take a more linear approach), the individual songs are strong enough that a reordered version of the album can work.

"What's Really Happening," a collaboration of Bowie, Gabrels, and Alex Grant, maintains the 1960s feel of "Seven." In fact, the short descending melodic motive of the verses resembles the Motown song "You Keep Me Hangin' On," a hit for both the Supremes and Vanilla Fudge. Incidentally, Bowie would also include a melodic figure from this song as part of the lead guitar line in his song "Reality," the title track from his 2003 album. The lyrics of "What's Really Happening," which find Bowie's character contemplating just what led to the breakup of a relationship, feature a curious rhyme scheme. The first verse uses an A-A-A-B rhyme scheme, while all four of the lines in verse two include a final rhyme (A-A-A-A). The third verse, in contrast, has an A-B-A-A structure. Although the lyrics maintain a feel of speculation about what led to the couple's breakup, the unearthly vocal mix and lead guitar solo lines suggest that something sinister tore the couple apart. With its especially close (and a little too-obvious) ties to the music of the 1960s, "What's Really Happening" is not the most impressive, nor innovative, song on *hours*...; however, it works beautifully as a mood piece.

Bowie, Gabrels, and the other accompanying musicians step firmly into the late-1970s and early-1980s post-punk new wave with "The Pretty Things Are Going to Hell." Interestingly, this is the one song on *hours*... that received a review from *All Music Guide* separate from the album itself. *All Music*'s Dave Thompson, also a Bowie biographer, described the song as one of Bowie's "guitar-scything glam anthems," which reflects back to work of the Spiders from Mars era.[3] Actually, musically it is a little too reliant on new wave instrumental touches to really recall Bowie's work of the early 1970s. The theme of disillusionment and the decay of beauty, relationships, and meaning, however, do carry on the dark feel of 1972 and 1973. "The Pretty Things Are Going to Hell" is a strong counterbalance to the positivism of the album's opener, "Thursday's Child."

"Brilliant Adventures" is a brief Japanese-influenced, minimalistic composition of Bowie and Gabrels that hearkens back to some of Bowie's instrumental compositions of *Station to Station* and *"Heroes."* In the overall context of *hours*... it is difficult to understand the need for or the role of this particular piece. More substantial, but also somewhat disconnected from the overall theme of the album, is the final track before several alternative mixes: "The Dreamers." The dreamers in this song are social misfits who "eat in doorways" and "incline" their heads to the heavens, apparently awaiting some sort of heavenly answer to their problems. The song's melody resembles an ancient incantation to the gods. The characters Bowie describes seem to have escaped the touch of the angels that populated the earlier part of *hours*... This can almost leave the listener with the sense that this song might have made an ideal structural beginning to the album. Had it led off the collection, *hours*... would have started with a portrait of the desperate souls who need heavenly intervention. The album could then have moved into the more positive songs about finding meaning in life through love relationships, and so on. By placing "The Dreamers" at the end of the album proper, Bowie effectively inverts the narrative. Curiously, though this might not be the most conventional approach, it forces the listener to recall and mentally re-sequence the entire album, or at least to contemplate the meaning of the album's sequencing.

In terms of sheer accessibility, *hours...* found David Bowie exploring the mainstream more thoroughly than he had on any previous album, with the possible exception of *Let's Dance* and its immediate successors. Unlike his post-*Let's Dance* dance-focused albums of the 1980s, however, this one works. There is a lyrical richness of emotion that is closer to mainstream pop than the songs of desperate alienation of some of Bowie's best-known work. In particular, while *hours...* expresses a profound sadness that recurs throughout the album, there are hints of real hope—something previously rare in Bowie's output. Musically, Bowie references folk-rock, Quiet Storm soul, and top-40-style rock. He studiously avoids techno, dance, industrial, punk, grunge, jungle; in short, he avoids anything that might sound trendy, or specially aimed at an audience far younger than listeners of his own generation. One of the strengths of connectedness of *hours...*, and *Heathen*, its 2002 successor, is that the listener is left with the sense that the former punk, glam, bad boy has now grown up, and in the process has put aside characters that exhibit smugness, occasional insensitivity, self-importance, and a general alienation from society, in favor of developing characters who experience sadness, hope, and a more complex set of relationships. In Bowie's glam period songs—indeed in many songs throughout the 1970s—his characters were strangely almost completely alienated from mainstream society, while finding meaning for their lives through the strength of a counterculture clique. Here, the characters are part of mainstream society but are alienated from certain individuals. His characters are more mature. The album allows Bowie to show the audience more of his spiritual side—he had spent some time in a Buddhist monastery in his younger days—a side which he had allowed only glimpses of in his earlier work. *Hours...* picks up the sense of the spiritual and transcendent of some of his mid-1970s songs, such as "Word on a Wing" *(Station to Station)* and "Heroes" *("Heroes")*, except that now Bowie provides the listener with most of an entire album's worth of such material, rather than a few scattered overtly spiritual songs.

The end of the millennium was an especially busy time for Bowie, on several fronts. In 1999 he appeared in the film *Mr. Rice's Secret*. He and Gabrels also composed original music for the video game *Omikron: The Nomad Soul*. Bowie and members of his band appeared as a virtual band in the game. In doing so, Bowie managed to stay in touch with cutting-edge entertainment technology, just as he had done for so many years in the music world.

In 1999, David Bowie also was presented with an honorary doctorate in music by the Berklee College of Music in Boston. Bowie delivered the commencement address at the famed jazz and commercial music-focused institution. He discussed the music that he enjoys and that has influenced him throughout his career, including the jazz of Eric Dolphy, Sonny Stitt, and John Coltrane, the avant-garde compositions of John Cage, and the theatrical stylings of singers such as Anthony Newley, Edith Piaf, and Shirley Bassey. He also highlighted the importance of John Lennon, both as a friend and as a musical influence.

The start of the new millennium, too, found Bowie's work in the public eye. The 2000 film *Almost Famous* included Bowie's performance of the Lou Reed classic "I'm Waiting for the Man," and the 2001 film *Moulin Rouge!* included Bowie's song "Nature Boy," both in a solo Bowie version and in an alternate version by Bowie and British hip-hop giants Massive Attack. The iconic status of David Bowie's glam-era album covers was confirmed by the Absolut vodka company, which used the cover art from *Aladdin Sane* on its vodka bottles.

## HEATHEN

Given that an enormous amount of David Bowie's work exhibits such a strong fascination with the seediness of society—sometimes as a near voyeur and sometimes as a social commentator—he would seem to be logical choice for *the* artist of the past forty years to chronicle an apocalyptic event. *Heathen* chronicles New York City at the time of the September 11, 2001 terrorist attacks, but with a catch. The eerie catch is that Bowie had written the songs before the attacks.[4] *Heathen* also contains three notable covers: the Pixies's "Cactus", Neil Young's "I've Been Waiting for You," and the Legendary Stardust Cowboy's "I Took a Trip on a Gemini Spaceship." Critical reaction to this 2002 album generally was favorable, but there were a few complaints. In particular, Benjamin Nugent of *Time* suggested that the album's "only two really good songs... are the covers."[5] Kyle Smith of *People* complained about a general lack of melodicism on *Heathen*.[6] True, the two covers are quite effective and different enough from the originals that they stand out as notable achievements, and true, compared with *Let's Dance,* or some of Bowie's earlier hook-laden songs, his compositions on *Heathen* are not as melodically centered as his best-selling pop material. However, especially in the context of New York City in 2001 and 2002, songs such as "Sunday," "Slip Away," and "Heathen (The Rays)" are highly effective, and in response to Smith's observation about the melodic writing: Bowie's melodic material in many of the songs is based on short motives (small, easily identifiable fragments) and not the more expansive overarching phrase-oriented writing of songs such as "Changes." This is not the first album, however, on which Bowie has written songs based on short motives. Bowie's songs are tuneful enough; they are just a bit on the stark side. Considering the apocalyptic themes, though, there is nothing wrong with a slight lean in the direction of starkness.

*Heathen* begins with "Sunday," a solo Bowie composition. The controversial American electronic music composer, producer, and keyboardist Moby assisted Bowie in the electronic setting of the song (more on the arrangement later). The piece begins in a dark, somewhat ominous-sounding minor key. Curiously, Bowie's vocal melody almost studiously avoids the tonic pitch. In fact, it includes a fair number (for a pop song) of dissonant appoggiaturas (non-chord tones that are placed metrically on strong beats). Bowie's eerie lyrics about an apparently dead city in which "everything has changed" are made even more haunting by this searching-sounding melody. One of the more glorious moments in the entire Bowie compositional canon occurs at the end of the text when the repeated pitch of the melody suddenly is harmonized unexpectedly with a bright-sounding major chord. The song, then, becomes a play between dark and light, and the lyrical concepts that "nothing has changed" (life continues to go on) and "everything has changed" (life will never be the same again). On this song, as well as on "Slip Away" to a slightly lesser extent, Bowie and co-producer Tony Visconti incorporate electronic effects into the texture. Electronic artist Moby assisted with the creation of the effects on "Sunday." These effects are so thoroughly integrated that they seem far less "experimental" than the electronic effects of Bowie's Berlin era albums or his Moby-influenced work of the 1990s. Even more than as a result of its textures, however, "Sunday" works so beautifully because of its form. Bowie avoids conventional pop song form, with its verses, chorus, and middle eight. Instead, "Sunday" is more closely structured like nineteenth-century art songs by composers such as Franz Schubert and Robert Schumann, both of whom combined elements of strophic (repeated music with different words for each verse) and through-composed (freely flowing composition in which the music follows the text, rather than the text following a pre-set, repetitious musical structure) forms. The piece has an overarching shape that is not restrained by conventional form.

The Pixies's "Cactus" follows "Sunday." This composition by Black Francis contains lyrical references that fit the Bowie aesthetic. In particular, the image of proving one's love by bloodying one's hands "on the cactus tree" and then putting the blood on a dress and sending it to the singing character is just as vivid as Bowie's better images. It might not fit specifically into the 9/11 theme, but Black Francis's tale of obsession works well in Bowie's hands.

The album's third song, "Slip Away," returns to the New York City-centric focus of *Heathen*. In its intended pre-9/11 context, Bowie's tale of elderly New Yorkers dragging their bones "to see the Yankees play," with images of floating above Coney Island present the impression of old souls leaving their mortal bodies only to sail above the city in which they have lived for years. If the listener completely divorces the song from 9/11, it is easily understood as a song about the inevitable aging process. It is truly eerie, however, in a post-9/11 context. The song becomes a farewell to more than 2,000 people who died in the terrorists' attack on the World Trade Center. With references to the souls sailing over Coney Island seeing the "world in war torn," it is difficult to believe that "Slip Away" really is a pre-9/11 product, so closely does it reflect the state of the world after that fateful date. The electronic effects (which combine space-age synthesizer sounds and a reproduction of the crackles one would hear in the old days listening to a vinyl record) and the use of a deliberately out-of-tune piano give the song a curious mix of the ultra-modern with the nostalgic.

The next song, "Slow Burn," caused some critics to lament Bowie's underutilization of the talents of guest lead guitarist Pete Townshend. For example, Stephen Thomas Erlewine described Townshend's work as becoming too much part of the overall texture of the piece.[7] The apparent implication is that virtually any lead guitarist could fill that role. Compared with Bowie's almost anonymous use of the famed guitarist on "Because You're Young" on the 1980 album *Scary Monsters (And Super Creeps)*, however, "Slow Burn" seems like a feature concerto. Well, maybe not quite, but because Townshend's distinctive tone color and improvisational style can be hear throughout this track, there is no question that a different lead guitarist is playing on this track than plays on any other song on *Heathen*.

Bowie's lyrics on "Slow Burn" speak of a "terrible town" that is completely gripped with fear for the future. Like so many of the songs on *Heathen*, then, this song is even more applicable in the post-9/11 context in which the album saw release than it was at the time Bowie composed it. In the canon of David Bowie's work since the 1960s, this is not by any stretch of the imagination a hard rock song. However, Bowie sings the narrow-ranged melody of the verses with a sense of urgency that he more often than not keeps under wraps in his more recent recordings. Without the events of September 11, 2001 in New York City, Bowie's performance teeters on the edge of trying too hard to sell the meaning of the lyrics. In the context of 9/11, however, this sense of urgency matches the lyrics and the tenor of the times perfectly.

Melodically, "Slow Burn" features a low tessitura and narrow range in the verses, balanced by dramatic upper-range falsetto singing on the title words in the chorus. It is this contrast, as well as the chorus hook, that makes the song musically memorable. The arrangement, too, is strong, and reminiscent of Bowie's popular work on songs such as "Changes." The arrangement includes what can only be termed as a Bowian saxophone section (heavy on the lower-pitched tenor and baritone saxes); figures that recall his saxophone arrangement from throughout the 1970s. The steady eighth-note chords in the piano also suggest the pop-rock style of the David Bowie of about thirty years before. It is almost as though Bowie turned his back on trying to be au courant and trying to reach new audiences, and was now reaching out to the audience that had brought him to prominence three decades before. This, however, is not unique to "Slow Burn," or the whole of *Heathen*, for that matter: it was very much evident throughout the 1999 album *hours...* and would form the entire rhetorical basis for the 2003 album *Reality*. By coming full circle musically—while retaining the most effective of the various styles with which he had experimented over the decades—Bowie seems to have reached a new, higher level of maturity as a songwriter, arranger, and performer. It is as if he had achieved a sense of balance, which seemed to put to rest the image of Bowie as a musical chameleon once and for all.

"Afraid" shares melodic and harmonic patterns with both "Sunday" and "Slip Away," despite the fact that the tempo, as well as the guitar, bass, drums, and keyboard playing, suggest late-1970s new wave. By tying together the first, third, and fifth songs of the album, as well as some of the later ones, Bowie makes *Heathen* sound more like a unified song cycle than just about any of his previous albums. There is almost a sense of a loose theme and variations structure that runs through the album. The main difference between *Heathen* and Bowie's earlier albums is that in the past he included lyrical themes and lyrical structures that linked songs, whereas here he took the extra step of linking songs by means of obvious melodic, harmonic, and arrangement cues.

The lyrics of "Afraid" find Bowie's character coming to grips with his fears. Despite his faith in "the Beatles," in the growth of his "little soul," and in the belief that "we're not alone," he still fears for his own future, and presumably the future of humankind. It is an expression of searching and vulnerability and the complex interplay between faith and doubt. The urgency in the lyrics is well supported by the fast-paced musical setting.

At least one reviewer of *Heathen* stated that the main problem with the album was that the best songs were the covers.[8] Though I do not necessarily agree, it seems that one of the reasons for the previously mentioned reviewer's assessment may be the sheer strength of the covers Bowie performed on *Heathen*. Part of the reason for this assessment, I believe, also stems from an underappreciation for Bowie's compositions. Be that as it may, Bowie's performance of "Cactus" certainly holds up better than some of his more bizarre interpretations of others' songs on earlier albums: the overacted, Anthony Newley inspired version of the Beatles's "Across the Universe" on *Young Americans*, for example. Bowie's performance of Neil Young's "I've Been Waiting for You" should also be counted among his better cover performances. His vocal take on the Young song is matter-of-fact and straightforward. There is just a hint of an appropriate Young-inspired edge in Bowie's tone. Some of the credit for the success of the track goes to Bowie for his record production work. For one thing, he allows guest guitarist Dave Grohl (of the Foo Fighters) to evoke the essence of Neil Young's late-1960s soloing style and tone color; Grohl's performance manages to avoid coming off as a musical photocopy or caricature of Young.

In "I Would Be Your Slave" Bowie evokes images from the song "Slip Away," especially in his use of descending melodic motives and in the harmonic progression that marks the introduction and the verses. This continues the pattern of linkages between the odd-numbered tracks on *Heathen*. The gentle, almost melancholy nature of the vocal line, which is supported in mood by the sustained string lines, is eerie. Bowie's text of the verses suggests various scenarios in which the person to whom he is singing might present him with explicit or implicit rejection; however, the chorus finds him telling the other person that if they "open up their heart" to him, he "would be [their] slave." It is a song of undying devotion. Mostly because of some of Bowie's specific references in the verses and the middle eight of the song—"no footprints in the sand" stands out—the song can be read with religious connotations, provided that the listener is familiar with the famous, inspirational, Mary Stevenson-penned "Footprints in the Sand" poem.[9] In this reading, Bowie's character is in essence saying that he will make an unqualified declaration of faith ("I will be your slave") provided that the one in whom he believes "opens up [their] heart to [him]." Bowie is deliberately ambiguous enough that he could be addressing a deity or a lover. In either case, his character is a man who has never had a break and who needs to see evidence of love in order to live out the devotion he wants to, but is as of yet unable to express.

It is the vagueness of exactly who Bowie's character is addressing in "I Would Be Your Slave" that brings up another interesting feature of *Heathen*. As mentioned earlier in this chapter, at least one critic has referred to Bowie's lyrics on this album as "gay friendly."[10] This is not because of any specific gay references in Bowie's poetry, but rather because of the fact that he studiously avoids identifying a lover using any gender-specific references. But, this is not unique to *Heathen*: certainly, Bowie's lyrics on *hours...* are just as gender-neutral. What really makes his work on *Heathen* stand out in this regard is the stark contrast between the Bowie-penned songs and the Neil Young cover, "I've Been Waiting for You," a song in which the male-female relationship is absolutely clear.

The Legendary Space Cowboy's "I Took a Ride on a Gemini Spacecraft" is a rhythmically interesting workout for Bowie and his accompanying musicians; however, it really doesn't fit the nature of the rest of the album. The next song, "5:15 The Angels Have Gone," could have fit on *hours...*, because of the reference to angels; however, the sense of sadness Bowie's character expresses about the course his life has taken in a "new town" has New York City and *Heathen* written all over it. Bowie reprises the use of the metaphor of changing trains to represent a change of lifestyle that he had used back on the song "Station to Station" in the mid-1970s. Although the music does not stand out as one of Bowie's most memorable compositional efforts, the song succeeds in presenting the disillusionment one character feels when he becomes an anonymous face in unfamiliar surroundings.

Like "5:15 The Angels Have Gone," "Everyone Says 'Hi'" deals with a character leaving home for better and bigger opportunities. Here, however, Bowie's character remains home and addresses a character who has moved on. In a sense, then, it represents the flip side of "5:15 The Angels Have Gone." It is interesting that Bowie's characters in both songs express a sense of melancholy. Listening to the two songs in succession—the way they are ordered on *Heathen*—gives the impression that both people suffer from what is often termed buyer's remorse. One character is depressed because the new town did not meet his expectations, and the other character seems to be somewhat down about the fact that one of his group left town without a proper "good-bye." While "Everyone Says 'Hi'" supports the general sense of disillusion-ment and disconnection that runs throughout *Heathen,* it is not the most essential song on the album.

The song "A Better Future" is one that rings true both in the context of the sense of malaise that befell not only New York City, but the entire United States, in the wake of the September 11, 2001 attacks, as well as in the context of a person-to-person relationship. Bowie offers enough clues about the nature of the relationship and the attributes of the other party ("cloudless skies," for example) that make it most likely that he is addressing a location, in particular, a city. The most interesting thing about his ultima-tum, "I demand a better future," is what follows it: a declaration of love for the person or city to which he makes the demand. Bowie's melody, harmony, and arrangement for the song are simple, and reflect more than anything else early 1980s pop. The chorus hook may be simple, but it is catchy and com-mercial. To the extent that the listener hears the song as a set of demands that Bowie places on New York City to insure that he continues to love and live in the city, it is another of those *Heathen* tracks that takes on added significance in the context of 9/11. The simplicity of the music adds to its poignancy. Musically, its style foreshadows the songs of *Reality,* Bowie's last studio release to date.

The album *Heathen* concludes with the song "Heathen (The Rays)." Musi-cally, this piece recalls "Sunday" and "Sail Away," thereby tying the entire album together. It is not as interesting as most of Bowie's other *Heathen* compositions, mostly because it is a challenge for the listener to make a strong connection with the meandering melody. There is, however, reason behind the driftless melodic treatment. And, this hearkens back to the fact that it is very easy for the listener to interpret *Heathen* as a portrait of post-9/11 New York City. In the first verse of the song Bowie mentions a city made of steel and glass, and then concludes (as George Harrison had done back in 1971), "all things must pass." The second verse finds Bowie's character staring at his surroundings as if stunned by some sort of traumatic event; he is lost, per-haps both physically and emotionally. The meandering melody and sudden changes of musical texture suggest his character's lack of centeredness and lack of direction. Although this emotional state does not require the events of 9/11 as a context in order to make sense, it certainly fits in with the television images that were broadcast around the world of hordes of people wandering aimlessly after the destruction of the World Trade Center.

*Heathen* is unique in the David Bowie canon as a piece that captured the spirit of an epic tragedy, even though the songs were written before that tragedy. To the extent that there was any sense of foreboding in the air, Bowie captures it. The fact that the piece works so well in the context of its time, however, is at once a strength and a weakness. Unfortunately for the album, it seems like the kind of piece that future listeners may associate too closely with New York City on September 11, 2001 and the days immediately following and not give the album the attention it deserves because of a desire to not relive a great tragedy. That would be such a listener's loss; *Heathen* is one of the strongest late-Bowie albums.

## REALITY

Throughout his career, David Bowie has made more than his share of abrupt stylistic changes. However, such was not the case between the 2002 album *Heathen* and the 2003 album *Reality*. In fact, *Reality* also shares a great deal in common in approach and arrangement with Bowie's 1999 album *hours...* The lyrics on *Reality*, like those of *hours...* and *Heathen*, are more obviously autobiographical than anything Bowie recorded before. Even the cover material on *Reality* seems more autobiographical than the kinds of songs that Bowie had covered earlier in his career, most of which seemed to have been chosen for musical reasons or for their overall effect, rather than for specific references to Bowie's life. In particular, the last three songs on *Reality* find Bowie coming to grips with his past, and in some perhaps surprising ways. One of the more interesting musical features of Bowie's compositions and Bowie and co-producer Tony Visconti's arrangements is the way in which they reference music of the 1960s and 1970s.

*Reality* begins with Bowie's composition "New Killer Star." Bowie's impressionistic images include references to "the great white scar" near New York's Battery Park; Jesus of Nazareth appearing on the television news program *Dateline;* killer stars; and stars in a lover's eyes. It is a mix of images that call to mind the terror attacks of September 11, 2001 (the "great scar" in lower Manhattan, and killer stars), as well as the innocence of a love relationship. Musically, there are clear ties to the pop of the early 1960s. In particular, Bowie references the backing vocal chorus of the 1963 Little Peggy March hit "I Will Follow Him" for the backing vocal chorus of "New Killer Star." The electric guitar backing figures that accompany Bowie's lead vocal in the verses also uses the familiar "I Will Follow Him" rhythm.[11] Bowie's vocal melody, however, moves along in somewhat clipped phrases with a narrow pitch range, which are more characteristic of late-1970s songs written by David Byrne of Talking Heads than anything else. The mix of apocalyptic imagery with imagery of simple innocent beauty, and the mix of musical styles suggests the complexity of coping in a post-9/11 world. As the title of the album suggests, Bowie is trying to get at the complexity of the reality of the early twenty-first century.

Bowie next turns to Jonathan Richman's early-1970s composition "Pablo Picasso." As one first considers this choice as a representation of the "Reality" of the year 2003, it can seem to be quite a stretch. However, Richman's tale of Pablo Picasso's ability to "pick up girls" and otherwise succeed where the ordinary man fails is (in a way) a sort of universal tale of the guy who just doesn't understand why he is called "an asshole," to quote Richman, when he uses the same sort of pickup lines that another man uses without success. It is not, however, the most inspired Bowie cover, particularly within the context of the album; it's a tad too flippant.

The principle subtheme of *Reality* is that of how one grapples with the aging process. In several songs Bowie expresses his reflections on his youth and on the prospects for the future. "Never Grow Old" is a funky track in which Bowie declares in no uncertain terms that he will "never grow old." He rails against the inevitability of aging, while expressing anger that there will never "be enough money" and that he will "never get love." It is an expression both of desperation and denial. The strange thing about Bowie's denial is that it brings to mind Dr. Elisabeth Kübler-Ross's five stages of death from her well-known book *On Death and Dying*.[12] According to Kübler-Ross, the first reaction of those who are told that they are suffering from a terminal illness is denial. Throughout the rest of *Reality*, Bowie turns from denial of the aging process to the acknowledgement that he cannot escape it. Eventually, he deals with the realities of his present in the context of his past.

In "The Loneliest Guy," a slow-tempo minimalistic piece, Bowie's character also lives in denial: in spite of the chards of glass that he finds near his window, the solitary life he lives, and "all the pages that have turned," he expresses the belief that he is not "the loneliest guy" in the world, but, rather, "the luckiest guy." The slow, solemn pace of the piece, the long phrases sung with a slowly pulsing vibrato suggest a profound sadness. So, clearly, he is not the luckiest guy in the world, but in denial of the condition of his life. Bowie is effective in his portrayal of a lonely senior citizen ("all the pages that have turned"). The next song, "Looking for Water," brings to mind the minor-key, harmonically minimal songs of *Heathen*. Here, however, a rock beat predominates. Bowie's lyrics are more impressionistic than on some of the more direct tracks of *Reality*. His character is "looking for water," symbolic of the basic necessities of life, while he is surrounded by the unnecessary, but prevalent trappings of modern technological life. Despite their relevance to *Reality*'s overarching theme of dealing with the sometimes-contradictory realities of modern life, neither of these songs stand out within the David Bowie canon of works.

"She'll Drive the Big Car" is Bowie's story of a woman who dreams of glamour and wealth ("She'll drive the big car"), but is stuck in a mundane life of being "a husband's devoted wife." None of the things her husband promised have come to fruition. Bowie's music is even keeled and features a dissonant marimba line that appears at the end of some of the sections. Nothing about the melody, harmony, or arrangement (except for the curious marimba figure) draws a whole lot of attention; however, in the context of this song that is not a bad thing. The rather mundane, gently rocking music mimics the nothing-ever-changes nature of the character's life, and the marimba figure suggests the sense of bitterness she has developed over the years.

The next song, "Days," finds Bowie's character finally acknowledging a long-standing self-centeredness and a debt of gratitude to someone to whom he owes "all the days of [his] life." The gentle, mostly acoustic nature of the musical setting and the confessional style of the lyrics call to mind music of the early 1970s introspective singer-songwriter movement. Bowie includes a hint of ska and a just the tiniest of hints of American country music in the accompanying rhythms and arrangement, which makes for an intriguing and pleasant combination. The music makes heavy use of an oscillation between a root position G minor chord and a second-inversion B-flat major chord.[13] The constancy of this harmonic pivoting, the narrow melodic range, and the resigned quality with which Bowie sings all combine to make his character sound truly repentant.

"Fall Dog Bombs the Moon" is based on short melodic motives, the kind that seemed to permeate *Heathen*. The lyrics find Bowie's character describing himself as someone who is self-centered, "God damn rich," and basically, "just a dog." He has no respect for himself, for the girl who he asks to "blow [him] away," nor for the "morons" or "corporate ties" he sees around him. Musically, the song is not as interesting as the best songs on *Reality*. Because it finds Bowie's character dwelling on life in the present, it is not as rich as some of the songs on *Reality* that compare Bowie's characters' past and present.

George Harrison's "Try Some, Buy Some" seems to be especially appropriate for inclusion on an aging rock star's album about the realities of aging. The Harrison song concerns the recognition of the dangers of youthful overindulgence in sex, drugs, and rock and roll. Certainly, the debauchery associated with glam-rock in the pre-AIDS 1970s, the time period in which Bowie came to worldwide attention, fits the bill for the kind of lifestyle about which Harrison wrote. Bowie sings with a quality befitting a repentant former sinner. Despite the fact that this is one of Harrison's more challenging compositions harmonically—the chromatic shifts do not flow as intuitively as in some of his most successful songs—this is an effective cover. It fits *Reality* perfectly.

Bowie turns to hard rock for the title track, his own composition "Reality." While this song title might not be instantly recognizable to the casual fan of David Bowie's music, it is one of his better songs of recent years. It is not Bowie's most original musical piece, drawing on chord progressions that recall some of the songs of *Heathen* and a lead guitar lick in the chorus that closely resembles a melodic motive from the old Motown song "You Keep Me Hangin' On." The combination of the hard rock style; an easy-to-remember, catchy melody; and lyrics that detail the sexual escapades of a young male rock star and his female groupie companion, work beautifully together. It is as though Bowie tells his listeners with more specificity and in more graphic terms about the kinds of things at which he mostly only hinted at on the album *The Rise and Fall of Ziggy Stardust & the Spiders from Mars*. Perhaps even more interesting than the obvious ties to the characters of the *Ziggy Stardust* album, however, is the double meaning inherent in Bowie's lyrics about "tragic youth going down" on him. There is the obvious slang meaning of oral sex. Beyond that, though, the phrase can also be understood as Bowie's acknowledge that *his own* youth is now slipping away. This second meaning would be quite a stretch, though, were it not for the fact that so much of his material on *Reality* deals with the aging process as a whole, and his own in particular. "Reality" also finds Bowie acknowledging the fact that he hid behind the façade of aliens in his earlier songs and stage persona (Ziggy Stardust and the Spiders from Mars), and behind a wall of drugs that separated him from his audience (his pre-Berlin cocaine addiction). Ultimately, however, Bowie acknowledges that he is now staring into the face of reality. It is song with lyrical substance based on autobiographical-sounding situations from the life of an aging rock star; it is also a song with memorable vocal and instrumental hooks. It belongs on the Bowie canon's "A-list."

The final song on the album proper (the CD contains a bonus track, Bowie's cover of Ray Davies's "Waterloo Sunset") is the nearly-eight-minute-long composition "Bring Me the Disco King." The long-time Bowie sideman, pianist Mike Garson, and the relative newcomer, drummer Sterling Campbell, establish the jazzy underpinnings of the song right at the offset. Bowie's jazz singing style of the verses suggests a musical version of the improvisation of a 1990s poetry slam. The vague references suggest a look back at a lifetime of wasted moments. And, who is to blame for these wasted moments? Bowie's refrain, "Bring me the Disco King, dead or alive" tells the listener exactly whom he blames for all the wasted time "in the '70s." This moderately slow-paced jazz style is unusual for Bowie, which might explain the fact that critics did not universally warm to it.[14] The somewhat tired-sounding approach Bowie takes on the song works perfectly within the context of the album's focus on aging.

*Reality*'s bonus track, a cover of Ray Davies's "Waterloo Sunset," recalls Bowie's covers on *hours...* in that it is faithful to the spirit of its author, but takes on enough of a Bowie-esque style that he sounds as convincing singing the song as if he had written it. That Bowie covered a rather bright classic Kinks track from the critically acclaimed 1967 album *Something Else By the Kinks* provides a touch of balance to some of the gloomier recollections of the 1960s and 1970s that Bowie's lyrics provide on most of the album's other songs.

Bowie's record company, ISO, issued a DVD of his performance at the Hammersmith Riverside Studios, September 8, 2003, in the "Tour Edition" of *Reality*. The technology of 2003 is very much in evidence, from the dual earpieces Bowie and the members of his band wear, to the electronic sheet music system that some of the instrumentalists use in order to avoid difficult page turns. Twenty-first-century technology is also very much in evidence in the technical quality of this production, especially when it is compared with Bowie's earlier live audio and filmed recordings.

All in all, *Reality* is a strong album. Bowie establishes a theme and then—with the possible exception of "Fall Dog Bombs the Moon"—sticks with it and develops it to an extent he rarely has accomplished on his earlier concept albums. The cover songs are especially well chosen and fit in with Bowie's own compositions seamlessly. The fact that the theme Bowie uses, aging and reviewing one's present in the context of one's past, to shape the album is a universal theme only serves to strengthen the album more. And, throughout the album Bowie creates characters that, although they seem to be more or less autobiographical, are much easier to identify with than the characters that populated his albums in the 1970s and 1990s.

As is customary in the world of pop music, Bowie undertook a concert tour in support of *Reality*. Since *Reality* (and to some extent its immediate predecessors, *hours...* and *Heathen*) dealt with the issues of mortality and aging, it was eerily ironic that Bowie had to cancel a concert date in early July 2004 due to what he thought was severe shoulder pain from a pinched nerve. When Bowie sought medical help, it was found that the real source of the pain was a blocked artery in his heart. He underwent an emergency angioplasty to correct the situation.[15]

Although *Reality* is Bowie's last studio album to date, his music has continued to appear in various entertainment venues and forms. For example, the 2004 film *The Life Aquatic* included Bowie's recordings of "Queen Bitch" and "Life on Mars?," as well as Brazilian singer Seu Jorge's recording of "Rebel Rebel." The 2005 film *Stealth* included the song "(She Can) Do That," a collaboration of Bowie and B. T. (Brian Transeau). David Bowie's most recent project to date is his supporting role in the 2006 Christopher Nolan film *The Prestige*.

# Conclusions: Assessing Bowie's Significance

In the case of some singer-songwriters, one can gauge their significance at least in part from the number of cover recordings of their songs by other artists. For example, the importance of some of Stevie Wonder's more pop-oriented compositions, such as "You Are the Sunshine of My Life," can be seen through the fact that so many major artists in several genres recorded them. Carole King and Paul Simon wrote a number of songs that were so universal in their appeal that an incredible range of musicians recorded competent covers of their songs. Since so many of David Bowie's songs rely on such unconventional characters or musical and lyrical structures, there have been relatively few covers of his songs. Many of them rely on Bowie's theatricality as a performer to succeed. Bowie's significance as an artist needs to be established strictly on his own recordings. I believe that the only way to truly assess David Bowie as an artist of major importance over the past nearly four decades is to take a look at the musical styles he has incorporated, the lyrical styles he has used, and the challenging subjects that he has brought into the realm of pop music. Although not purely musical in nature, Bowie's significance also stems from his use of cutting edge technology on several fronts.

## BOWIE AND MUSICAL STYLES OF THE 1960s–2007

From the mid-1960s into the early twenty-first century, David Bowie has been associated with several distinctive styles within the world of popular music. He began his career with several compositions and commercially unsuccessful recordings that were squarely in the mid-1960s mod style. At the same time, he wrote and recorded songs that were more highly influenced by the British music hall, and more mainstream pop material that was typical of the Swinging London of the 1965–1967 period. While none of Bowie's recordings of this period resulted in stardom, at least one, "I Dig Everything," simultaneously established Bowie as a songwriter who excelled at portraying social outcasts—or those who at least on the fringes of society—and also as a near-prototypical representative of the Swinging London sound of the mid-1960s.

The close of the 1960s found Bowie recording his album *Man of Words, Man of Music* (later reissued as *Space Oddity*). Here, he adopted the psychedelic folk style of the Scottish singer-songwriter Donovan. Whereas the bulk of the album features meandering music and lengthy, impressionistic poetry, the album's first track, "Space Oddity," is more to the point. It is the song that eventually established Bowie as a star in the United States. Bowie's next album, *The Man Who Sold the World*, found him exploring heavy metal music. Although neither *Man of Worlds, Man of Music*, nor *The Man Who Sold the World* were smashes at the time of their initial release, they found Bowie producing credible music in two styles that would seem to be (at least from the standpoint of performance style and arrangement) mutually exclusive.

Bowie's next phrase found him on the forefront of the glam rock movement. With glam rock's lyrical focus on the sometimes sleazy side of sex, a fascination with androgyny, cross dressing, bisexuality, and hard rock music, the style ideally suited Bowie's *The Rise and Fall of Ziggy Stardust and the Spiders from Mars*. Glam rock might have had its strongest U.K. proponent in Marc Bolan, but David Bowie brought the style to a far wider audience. It was Bowie and not Bolan who came to be seen as the leader of the style among American audiences. Little by little, Bowie dropped the trappings of glam rock; however, he continued to develop some of the lyrical themes associated with the style. Some of his work with his so-called Spiders from Mars band, notably the song "Hang on to Yourself" anticipated the rhythms, timbres, and production style of British-style punk rock by a few years.

One of the more interesting aspects of the Ziggy Stardust-era David Bowie was the extent to which he (and, to be fair, other glam artists) blurred the lines between fiction and non-fiction. The fact that he played a theatrical role, confirmed by his costumes and makeup, that was at home on stage, in the recording studio, and (as far as the public could tell) in his private life, allowed his work to cross over into the realm of performance art. In fact, to the extent that David Bowie became a music industry insider in the early 1970s, yet continued almost exclusively to portray social outsiders until the end of the twentieth century, the bulk of his output could be seen as fitting into a decades-long performance art piece.

Although the pop music world of the 1970s is often defined by the introspective singer-songwriter movement (James Taylor, Carole King, Joni Mitchell, Carly Simon, and Paul Simon, for example), disco, and punk rock, there really was much more happening throughout the decade. One of the lesser-heralded styles that developed during the decade was ambient electronic music. The composer, keyboardist, and record producer Brian Eno was the leader of this style. Eno collaborated with Bowie in composing, arranging, and producing several pieces in this style on Bowie's mid- to late-1970s Berlin-period albums *Low* and *"Heroes."* While Bowie clearly did not invent this style, his iconic status helped ambient electronic experimental music reach a wider audience than it did through the recordings of musicians such as Brian Eno. Incidentally, Bowie reached an even higher level of quality and balance in this style in his early 1990s soundtrack for the British television program *The Buddha of Suburbia.*

Some of Bowie's Berlin-period music, the song "Be My Wife," for example, represented the new post-punk British new wave style. Again, while Bowie may not have invented the style, he was working along the same lines as such contemporary bands as the Stranglers. He has continued to use this late-1970s/early-1980s style from time to time into the twenty-first century.

Bowie reached the zenith of pure pop commercial success in the early 1980s. In particular, his album *Let's Dance* featured dance rhythms and styles that were better received by the public at large than anything Bowie had previously written and recorded. For a brief period in 1982 and 1983, Bowie captured the dance club spirit of the day better than perhaps any other artist. While his move to the mainstream would quickly cause Bowie to become almost an anonymous dance musician, his success in 1982–1983 is notable. For one thing, Bowie previously had not been associated with musical styles that were particularly dance-oriented. On the contrary: ambient, psychedelic-folk, heavy metal, and glam were more aimed at the listener than at the dancer. Bowie's success on the tracks of *Let's Dance* proved that he could reach the mainstream and the dance club underground in a way at which none of his previous music had even hinted.

When Bowie reemerged at the end of 1980s with his new band, Tin Machine, he was again anticipating musical trends. This time, though, the alternative/grunge style that could be heard in some of the songs of the album *Tin Machine* was just far enough away from gaining widespread popularity (the international success of the famed Seattle grunge bands was a couple of years in the future) that the album, potentially groundbreaking as it was, turned out to be a sort of musical dead end for Bowie.

Bowie would then turn to a mix of jazz and R&B for his *Black Tie White Noise* album. Some of the so-called acid jazz of the mid-1990s can be heard in this album. So, once again, David Bowie was very much part of a contemporary musical trend. By the end of the 1990s he would also explore the kinds of industrial and electronica associated with Nine Inch Nails, Moby, and others. His work with drum machines and synthesizers, and the beats of his late-1990s contemporaries would cause some consternation among young people who were fans of the styles. They saw Bowie as an older figure who was trying to cash in on a popular style in order to sound contemporary.

Between the 1999 album *hours...* and the present, Bowie has perhaps more than at any time in his career integrated all of these diverse styles. His work on *hours...*, *Heathen*, and *Reality* might not be musically groundbreaking, but it is among the most solid work he has done as a singer-songwriter. In fact, in some respects, Bowie's most recent three albums represent a sort of musical compendium of not only his work of the past four decades, but of some of the most significant styles of that entire era. Perhaps even more notable is the fact that these three albums seem to be more obviously autobiographical than anything he recorded earlier in his career. It is as though they represent his long-range coming of age and expression of self-understanding.

## BOWIE AND SONG AND LYRICAL STRUCTURE

Another area in which David Bowie has stood out among vernacular musicians of the past forty years is in his approach to musical and lyrical structure. His music, while exemplifying a number of styles, generally has fit easily within the established norms for those styles. From time to time, his songs exhibit attributes of both strophic and through-composed form,[1] but the structures of his vocal compositions has never been truly radical. Bowie's work as a composer of experimental instrumental pieces steps beyond that which most pop musicians were doing in the late 1970s. It would be, for example, a couple of years after Bowie's Berlin period that Stevie Wonder would compose and record his similar ambient experimental pieces for *Journey Through the Secret Life of Plants*. It should be noted, however, that Bowie's work in ambient and minimalist music, while considered experimental in the context of pop music, is more closely tied to traditional pop song structures than the work of leading ambient composers of the time, such as Brian Eno, or leading experimental minimalists, such as Terry Riley, Philip Glass, and Steve Reich.

Bowie was more of a consistent innovator as a lyricist and as an assembler (for want of a better term) of thematic albums. He consistently proved himself to be free of the customary constraints of pop song lyrical structures, conventional pop song subject matter, and customary narrative schemes.

Bowie's early pre-fame songs featured conventional pop song rhyme schemes. While Bowie tended to avoid this type of poetry in his wordier, meandering psychedelic-folk songs on *Man of Words, Man of Music,* the poetic structure of his Ziggy Stardust-era songs was not at all far removed from that of conventional rock songs of the time. As the 1970s progressed, however, Bowie turned to free verse writing, often pairing a free treatment of lyrical structure with music in conventional four- and eight-measure phrases. Throughout the 1980s and into the present, Bowie has written in such free structures that when he does juxtapose conventionally rhyming couplets, what for most pop song writers is standard procedure, the couplets stand out as noticeably unusual and unexpected.

Even when he was struggling to establish a career on his early Pye and Deram recordings Bowie created characters that were on the fringes of society, or even were out-and-out social outcasts. While sometimes he plays the role of observer of these characters in his songs, more often than not he writes in a first-person form, actually portraying these members of society's fringe. He has dealt with a wide range of challenging subjects, including homelessness, mental illness, homosexuality, bisexuality, suicide, drug abuse, among others. And, he has done so not just in a few, select songs. Bowie has made his career as a writer in dealing with subject matter that other pop songwriters only dabble in from time to time. This has been an important contribution because it has exposed many things that are everyday occurrences in society, but that have largely been swept under the rug in pop music. When Bowie does deal with conventional pop song material, such as one-on-one relationships, he does so in highly unconventional ways. For example, one can listen to song after song from the late 1970s through the present and never hear the word *love* once. "Be My Wife," for example, is a proposal of marriage in which the word does not occur even once.

Bowie is also unusual in his approach to narrative structure, both on a microlevel (song) and on a macrolevel (album). The early Pye and Deram singles, and even the impressionistic songs of *Man of Words, Man of Music,* generally followed a linear timeline. Beginning with the concept album *The Rise and Fall of Ziggy Stardust and the Spiders from Mars,* Bowie has avoided linear narrative structure on the macro level. On the *Ziggy Stardust* album, for example, the logical progression of events encapsulated in the song "Ziggy Stardust" can be found on the album, but only when the listener experiences the entire package and then mentally resequences the songs. *Diamond Dogs,* too, is a concept album that avoids a timeline-like structure. Despite its focus on a wedding, *Black Tie White Noise* similarly avoids linear structure. Perhaps the ultimate example of the challenges posed by Bowie's avoidance of a linear narrative, however, is his detective fantasy *Outside,* an album that demands repeated listenings in order to sort out the sequence of events.

On the microlevel, too, Bowie often avoids the traditional linear narrative. In his songs, incongruous images and events are often juxtaposed. By writing in this way on various levels of structure, Bowie forces the listener to react, to analyze, to reshuffle; in short, Bowie demands the one thing that perhaps is most difficult in listening to pop songs: active listening.

The cut-up techniques Bowie employed on various levels of lyrical structure were not his invention. Although there are precedents in the Dada movement of the early twentieth century, the most immediate influences on Bowie are the American experimental artists of the 1940s and 1950s. In particular, the composer and philosopher John Cage, who actively encouraged chance to play a role in the compositional process; the painter Jackson Pollack, who pioneered action painting; and the Beat writer William S. Burroughs can all be seen as influences on Bowie's technique. When he delivered his commencement address to graduates of Boston's Berklee College of Music in 1999, Bowie himself acknowledged the influence of

Cage.[2] The cut-up technique of Burroughs, found in such books as *Junky, Queer, The Soft Machine*, and *Naked Lunch*, however, also clearly influenced Bowie. In addition to Burroughs's non-linear narrative technique, Bowie also seems to have been influenced by the Beat author's fascination with psychology and with the seamy side of urban life. While the use of non-linear, impressionistic lyrics in pop songs of the past forty years is not unique to David Bowie, he stands alone among his peers in terms of the extent to which he carried forth the aesthetics of experimenters such as Burroughs and Cage into pop music of the second half of the period—Bowie alone has stood committed to forcing active listening through the use of these structures.

## BOWIE AND GENDER

As far back as his pre-fame singles of 1966 and 1967 (notably "The London Boys"), David Bowie dealt with questions of masculinity, femininity, and gender roles. During the glam period of the early 1970s Bowie brought sexual orientation into the mix, first by cross-dressing on the cover of *The Man Who Sold the World*, then by claiming that he was bisexual, and then by creating characters in his songs who were bisexual or homosexual.

In hindsight, Bowie's iconic Ziggy Stardust character, however, does not wear particularly well. What may have been intriguing, shocking, and titillating in the early 1970s, now can tend to come off as a near self-parody. Bowie's costumes and posing in the concert video *Ziggy Stardust and the Spiders from Mars: The Motion Picture* (30th anniversary DVD release, Virgin 72434–90388–9–9, 2003) just seems hopelessly dated today. Some of Bowie's songs of 1972–1973—notably "Queen Bitch"—in hindsight rely too much on stereotypes to be considered serious songs about sexual orientation.

Bowie's main lyrical contribution to the questions of gender and sexuality really come from his work in more recent years. With rare exceptions, Bowie's more recent songs about one-on-one relationships have been remarkably gender neutral. This feature of Bowie's approach to lyrics especially is noticeable on his most recent three albums to date: *hours...*, *Heathen*, and *Reality*, mostly because the cover songs on those albums are by contrast so explicit in painting the relationships as male-female. Bowie's lyrics, though, are so nonspecific that they by and large could apply to male-male, female-female, or male-female relationships. He does this by avoiding gender role stereotypes and by almost studiously avoiding references of any kind to gender. In short, he allows for all sexual orientations, thereby allowing the listener to project himself or herself (regardless of their own gender *or* orientation) into Bowie's music. Another result of this approach is that it places female and male characters on equal footing, something that is rare among male pop musicians of Bowie's generation.

## BOWIE AND TECHNOLOGY

David Bowie's role as a cutting-edge pop musician who either anticipated or was on the ground floor of such genres as heavy metal, punk, new wave, glam, grunge, and industrial is well established. Various critics and other writers have commented on Bowie's use of non-traditional lyrical structures and his unusual use of gender-neutral language in relationship songs. What perhaps is not so obvious is the extent to which he has embraced emerging technologies in the distribution and marketing of his music.

The end of the 1990s, in particular, saw Bowie embrace technologies to an extent that was rare among musicians of his generation. In July 1996, he released his single "Telling Lies" exclusively through the Internet. In the late 1990s, record companies and artists (especially well-established acts) generally viewed the Internet as more of a threat than a usable technology. Not Bowie; in September 1998 his davidbowie.com Web site ventured beyond what many artists' Web sites of the day did. Davidbowie.com went into business as an Internet Service Provider, delivering access to the Internet for $19.95 per month. The site also provided Bowie fans with other Internet-only releases. By 2004, Bowie actively encouraged fans' rearrangements ("mashes") of his songs, going so far as to sponsor a contest to find the best fan mashes of his music.

Bowie created a stir in the financial community in late 1990s when it was announced that he would issue corporate bonds that would pay interest based on future income from Bowie's recordings and other entertainment projects. Although the practice is not necessarily widespread today, Bowie proved to be a pioneer in this arena: other artists and entertainment figures have followed his lead.

## THE *LOW* AND "*HEROES*" SYMPHONIES

The significance of some singer-songwriters can in part be assessed by looking at how many times their songs have been covered and how those covers fared critically and commercially. Generally, David Bowie's compositions have just been too idiosyncratic to have been covered very often by other pop artists. Perhaps the best-known covers of Bowie's songs actually come from a very unusual source relative to pop music of the late twentieth century: from the world of concert/classical music. In 1992, the American minimalist Philip Glass wrote his *Low Symphony,* an orchestral work based on songs and instrumental pieces composed by Bowie and Brian Eno for the album *Low.* According to Glass's program notes for the piece, Bowie's *Low* "was widely appreciated by musicians working both in the field of 'pop' music and in experimental music and was a landmark work of that period."[3] In 1996, Glass turned to Bowie and Eno's compositions on Bowie's 1977 album "*Heroes*" for the *Heroes Symphony,* a six-movement work composed for famed choreographer Twyla Tharp's dance company. In describing his attraction to the music of "*Heroes,*" Glass said, "In a series of innovative recordings made in the late 70s, David and Brian combined influences from world music, experimental avant-garde and rock & roll and thereby redefined the future of popular music. The continuing influence of these works has secured their stature as part of the new 'classics' of our time."[4]

The rock music journal *Rolling Stone,* and the Academy of Recording Arts and Sciences, however, get the final word in assessing David Bowie's importance in the pop music of the 1970s into the present time. In a special article listing that commemorated the fiftieth anniversary of rock, *Rolling Stone* named Bowie the 39th most important person in the history of rock music.[5] This 2004 article quotes singer-songwriter Lou Reed as saying that Bowie's primary contribution to music was the richness of his voice and the level of sophistication that Bowie brought to songwriting.[6] Also in 2004, *Rolling Stone* listed four Bowie songs among the 500 greatest songs of all time: "Heroes" (No. 46), "Changes" (No. 127), "Ziggy Stardust" (No. 277), and "Young Americans" (No. 481).[7] More recently, the Academy of Recording Arts and Sciences presented David Bowie with its 2006 Lifetime Achievement Award.

# Selected Discography

## THE ALBUMS OF DAVID BOWIE

*David Bowie*. David Bowie, vocals; assisting instrumental trio. "Uncle Arthur" (Bowie), "Sell Me a Coat" (Bowie), "Rubber Band" (Bowie), "Love You Till Tuesday" (Bowie), "There Is a Happy Land" (Bowie), "When I Live My Dream" (Bowie), "Little Bombadier" (Bowie), "Silly Boy Blues" (Bowie), "Come and Buy My Toys" (Bowie), "Join the Gang" (Bowie), "She's Got Medals" (Bowie), "Please Mr. Gravedigger" (Bowie). 33–1/3 rpm LP. Deram DE-16003, 1967.

*Man of Words, Man of Music*. David Bowie, vocals, guitar, organ, stylophone, kalimba; various assisting musicians. "Space Oddity" (Bowie), "Unwashed and Somewhat Slightly Dazed" (Bowie), "Letter to Hermione" (Bowie), "Cygnet Committee" (Bowie), "Janine" (Bowie), "An Occasional Dream" (Bowie), "The Wild-Eyed Boy from Freecloud" (Bowie), "God Knows I'm Good" (Bowie), "Memory of a Free Festival" (Bowie). Produced by Tony Visconti. 33–1/3 rpm LP. Mercury SR 61246, 1969. Reissued as RCA Victor LSP-4813, 1972 under the title *Space Oddity*. Reissued on compact disc with additional material as *Space Oddity*, Rykodisc RCD 10131, 1990. Reissued on enhanced compact disc as *Space Oddity*, Virgin 7243 521898 0 9, 1999.

*The Man Who Sold the World*. David Bowie, vocals and guitar; various assisting musicians. "The Width of a Circle" (Bowie), "All the Madmen" (Bowie), "Black Country Rock" (Bowie), "After All" (Bowie), "Running Gun Blues" (Bowie), "Saviour Machine" (Bowie), "She Shook Me Cold" (Bowie), "The Man Who Sold the World" (Bowie), "The Supermen" (Bowie). Produced by Tony Visconti. 33–1/3 rpm LP. Mercury SR-61325, 1971. Reissued as RCA Victor AFL1–4816, 1972. Reissued as RCA Victor 003540, 1972. Reissued on compact disc with additional material, Rykodisc RCD 10132, 1990. Reissued on enhanced compact disc, Virgin 7243 521901 0 2, 1999.

*Hunky Dory.* David Bowie, vocals, guitar, alto and tenor saxophone, piano; various assisting musicians. "Changes" (Bowie), "Oh! You Pretty Things" (Bowie), "Eight Line Poem" (Bowie), "Life on Mars?" (Bowie), "Kooks" (Bowie), "Quicksand" (Bowie), "Fill Your Heart" (Biff Rose, Paul Williams), "Andy Warhol" (Bowie), "Song for Bob Dylan" (Bowie), "Queen Bitch" (Bowie), "The Bewlay Brothers" (Bowie). Produced by Ken Scott (assisted by the actor). 33–1/3 rpm LP. RCA LSP-4623, 1971. Reissued with additional material on two 33–1/3 LPs as Ryko RALP 0133–2, 1990. Reissued with additional material on compact disc, Ryko-disc RCD 10133, 1990. Reissued on enhanced compact disc, Virgin 7243 521899 0 8, 1999.

*The Rise and Fall of Ziggy Stardust and the Spiders from Mars.* David Bowie, vocals, guitar, saxophone; various assisting musicians. "Five Years" (Bowie), "Soul Love" (Bowie), "Moonage Daydream" (Bowie), "Starman" (Bowie), "It Ain't Easy" (Ron Davies), "Lady Stardust" (Bowie), "Star" (Bowie), "Hang on to Yourself" (Bowie), "Ziggy Stardust" (Bowie), "Suffragette City" (Bowie), "Rock 'n' Roll Suicide" (Bowie). Produced by David Bowie and Ken Scott. 33–1/3 rpm LP. RCA Victor LSP-4702, 1972. Reissued on two 33–1/3 rpm LPs with additional material, Ryko RALP 0134–2, 1990. Reissued with additional material on compact disc, Rykodisc RCD 10134, 1990. Reissued on enhanced compact disc, Virgin 7243 521900 0 3, 1999.

*Aladdin Sane.* David Bowie, vocals, guitar, harmonica, saxophone; various assisting musicians. "Watch that Man" (Bowie), "Aladdin Sane (1913–1938–197_)" (Bowie), "Drive in Saturday" (Bowie), "Panic in Detroit" (Bowie), "Cracked Actor" (Bowie), "Time" (Bowie), "The Prettiest Star" (Bowie), "Let's Spend the Night Together" (Mick Jagger, Keith Richards), "The Jean Genie" (Bowie), "Lady Grinning Soul" (Bowie). Produced by David Bowie and Ken Scott. 33–1/3 rpm LP. RCA Victor LSP-4852, 1973. Reissued on 33–1/3 rpm LP, Ryko RALP 0135–2, and compact disc, Rykodisc RCD 10135, 1990. Reissued on enhanced compact disc, Virgin 7243 521902 0 1, 1999.

*Pin Ups.* David Bowie, vocals, saxophone, harmonica, synthesizer; various assisting musicians. "Rosalyn" (Duncan, Farley), "Here Comes the Night" (Berns), "I Wish You Would" (Arnold), "See Emily Play" (Syd Barrett), "Everything's All Right" (Stavely, James, Karlson, Crouch, Konrad), "I Can't Explain" (Pete Townshend), "Friday on My Mind" (Vanda, Young), "Sorrow" (Bob Feldman, Jerry Goldstein, Richard Bottehrer), "Don't Bring Me Down" (Dee), "Shapes of Things" (Paul Samwell-Smith, Jim McCarty, Keith Relf), "Anyway, Anyhow, Anywhere" (Pete Townshend, Roger Daltrey), "Where Have All the Good Times Gone" (Ray Davies). 33–1/3 rpm LP. RCA Records AQL-0291, 1973. Also issued as RCA AYL1–4653, 1973. Reissued with additional material as Ryko RALP 0136–2, 1990. Reissued with additional material on compact disc, Rykodisc RCD 10136, 1990. Reissued on enhanced compact disc, Virgin 7243 52190 30 0, 1999.

*Diamond Dogs.* David Bowie, vocals, guitars, saxophones, synthesizer, mellotron; various assisting musicians. "Future Legend" (Bowie), "Diamond Dogs" (Bowie), "Sweet Thing" (Bowie), "Candidate" (Bowie), "Sweet Things" [reprise] (Bowie), "Rebel Rebel" (Bowie), "Rock 'n' Roll with Me" (Bowie, Warren Peace), "We Are the Dead" (Bowie), "1984" (Bowie), "Big Brother" (Bowie), "Chant of the Ever-Circling Skeletal Family" (Bowie). Produced by David Bowie. 33–1/3 rpm LP. RCA CPL1–0576, 1974. Reissued with additional material on compact disc, Rykodisc RCD 10137, 1990. Reissued on enhanced compact disc with additional material, Virgin 7243 521904 0 9, 1999.

*David Live.* David Bowie, vocals, guitar; various assisting musicians. "1984" (Bowie), "Rebel Rebel" (Bowie), "Moonage Daydream" (Bowie), "Sweet Thing" (Bowie), "Changes" (Bowie), "Suffragette City" (Bowie), "Aladdin Sane" (Bowie), "All the Young Dudes" (Bowie), "Cracked Actor" (Bowie), "Rock 'n' Roll with Me" (Bowie, Warren Peace), "Watch that Man" (Bowie), "Knock on Wood" (Steve Cropper, Eddie Floyd), "Diamond Dogs" (Bowie), "Big Brother" (Bowie), "The Width of a Circle" (Bowie), "The Jean Genie" (Bowie), "Rock 'n' Roll Suicide" (Bowie). Produced by Tony Visconti. Two 33–1/3 rpm LPs. RCA CPL2–0771, 1974. Reissued with additional material on two compact discs, Rykodisc RCD 10138/39, 1990. Reissued on compact disc, EMI 795362, 1995.

*Young Americans.* David Bowie, vocals, guitar, keyboards; various assisting musicians.[1] "Young Americans" (Bowie), "Win" (Bowie), "Fascination" (Luther Vandross, Bowie), "Right" (Bowie), "Somebody Up There Likes Me" (Bowie), "Across the Universe" (John Lennon, Paul McCartney), "Can You Hear Me" (Bowie), "Fame" (Bowie, John Lennon, Carlos Alomar). Produced by Tony Visconti. 33–1/3 rpm LP. RCA Victor APL 1–0998, 1975. Reissued with additional material on compact disc, Rykodisc RCD 10140, 1991. Reissued on enhanced compact disc, Virgin 7243 521905 0 8, 1999.

*ChangesOneBowie.* David Bowie, vocals and various instruments; various assisting musicians. "Space Oddity" (Bowie), "John, I'm Only Dancing" (Bowie), "Changes" (Bowie), "Ziggy Stardust" (Bowie), "Suffragette City" (Bowie), "Jean Genie" (Bowie), "Diamond Dogs" (Bowie), "Rebel Rebel" (Bowie), "Young Americans" (Bowie), "Fame (Bowie, Carlos Alomar, John Lennon), "Golden Years" (Bowie). Various producers. 33–1/3 rpm LP. RCA Victor AFL1–1732, 1976. Contains previously released material.

*Station to Station.* David Bowie, vocals, guitars, saxophones, synthesizer, mellotron; various assisting musicians. "Station to Station" (Bowie), "Golden Years" (Bowie), "Word on a Wing" (Bowie), "TVC15" (Bowie), "Stay" (Bowie), "Wild Is the Wind" (Dmitri Tiomkin, Ned Washington). Produced by David Bowie and Harry Maslin. 33–1/3 rpm LP. RCA Victor APL 1–1327, 1976. Reissued with additional material on compact disc, Rykodisc RCD 10141, 1991. Reissued on enhanced compact disc, Virgin 7243 521906 0 7, 1999.

*Low.* David Bowie, vocals, guitar, pump bass, synthesizers, piano, taped stringed and wind instruments, saxophones, percussion; various assisting musicians. "Speed of Life" (Bowie), "Breaking Glass" (Bowie, Dennis Davis, George Murray), "What in the World" (Bowie), "Sound and Vision" (Bowie), "Always Crashing in the Same Car" (Bowie), "Be My Wife" (Bowie), "A New Career in a New Town" (Bowie), "Warszawa" (Bowie, Brian Eno), "Art Decade" (Bowie), "Weeping Wall" (Bowie), "Subterraneans" (Bowie). Produced by David Bowie and Tony Visconti. 33–1/3 rpm LP. RCA Victor CPL1–2030, 1977. Reissued with additional material on compact disc, Rykodisc RCD 10142, 1991. Reissued on enhanced compact disc, Virgin 7243 521907 0 6, 1999.

*"Heroes."* David Bowie, vocals, keyboards, guitar, saxophone, koto; various assisting musicians. "Beauty and the Beast" (Bowie), "Joe the Lion" (Bowie), "'Heroes'" (Bowie, Brian Eno), "Sons of the Silent Age" (Bowie), "Blackout" (Bowie), "V-2 Schneider" (Bowie), "Sense of Doubt" (Bowie), "Moss Garden" (Bowie,

Eno), "Neuköln" (Bowie, Eno), "The Secret Life of Arabia" (Bowie, Eno, Carlos Alomar). Produced by David Bowie and Tony Visconti. 33–1/3 rpm LP. RCA AFL1–2522, 1977. Reissued with additional material on compact disc, Rykodisc RCD 10143, 1991. Reissued on enhanced compact disc, Virgin 7243 521908–0, 1999.

*Stage.* David Bowie, vocals, guitar; various assisting musicians. "Hang on to Yourself" (Bowie), "Ziggy Stardust" (Bowie), "Five Years" (Bowie), "Soul Love" (Bowie), "Star" (Bowie), "Station to Station" (Bowie), "Fame" (Bowie, John Lennon, Carlos Alomar), "TVC15" (Bowie), "Warszawa" (Bowie, Eno), "Speed of Life" (Bowie), "Art Decade" (Bowie), "Sense of Doubt" (Bowie), "Breaking Glass" (Bowie, Dennis Davis, George Murray), "'Heroes'" (Bowie, Eno), "What in the World" (Bowie), "Blackout" (Bowie), "Beauty and the Beast" (Bowie). Produced by David Bowie and Tony Visconti. Two 33–1/3 rpm LPs. RCA Victor CPL-2–2913, 1978. Reissued on two compact discs, Rykodisc RCD-10144/45, 1992.

*Lodger.* David Bowie vocals, piano, synthesizer, chamberlain, guitar; various assisting musicians. "Fantastic Voyage" (Bowie, Brian Eno), "African Night Flight" (Bowie, Eno), "Move On" (Bowie), "Yassassin (Turkish for Long Live)" (Bowie), "Red Sails" (Bowie, Eno), "D.J." (Bowie, Eno, Carlos Alomar), "Look Back in Anger" (Bowie, Eno), "Boys Keep Swinging" (Bowie, Eno), "Repetition" (Bowie), "Red Money" (Bowie, Alomar). 33–1/3 rpm LP. RCA AQL 1–3254, 1979. Reissued on enhanced compact disc, Virgin 7243 521909 0 4, 1999.

*Scary Monsters (And Super Creeps).* David Bowie, vocals and keyboards; various assisting musicians. "It's No Game (Part 1)" (Bowie), "Up the Hill Backwards" (Bowie), "Scary Monsters (And Super Creeps)" (Bowie), "Ashes to Ashes" (Bowie), "Fashion" (Bowie), "Teenage Wildlife" (Bowie), "Scream Like a Baby" (Bowie), "Kingdom Come" (Tom Verlaine), "Because You're Young" (Bowie), "It's No Game (Part 2)" (Bowie). Produced by David Bowie and Tony Visconti 33–1/3 rpm LP. RCA Victor AQL 1–3647, 1980. Reissued on enhanced compact disc, Virgin 7243 521895 0 2, 1999.

*Another Face.* David Bowie, vocals; various assisting musicians. "Rubber Band" (Bowie), "The London Boys" (Bowie), "The Gospel According to Tony Day" (Bowie), "There Is a Happy Land" (Bowie), "Maid of Bond Street" (Bowie), "When I Live My Dream" (Bowie), "Liza Jane" (Bowie), "The Laughing Gnome" (Bowie), "In the Heart of the Morning" (Bowie), "Did You Ever Have a Dream" (Bowie), "Please Mr. Gravedigger" (Bowie), "Join the Gang" (Bowie), "Love You till Tuesday" (Bowie), "Louie, Louie Go Home" (Bowie). Various producers. 33–1/3 rpm LP. Decca TAB 17, 1981. Includes material previously issued in the 1960s on Deram. Reissued on compact disc with additional material as *The Deram Anthology 1966–1968* (see separate entry).

*Changestwobowie.* David Bowie, vocals and various instruments; various assisting musicians. "Aladdin Sane (1913–1938–197?)" (Bowie), "Oh! You Pretty Things" (Bowie), "Starman" (Bowie), "1984" (Bowie), "Ashes to Ashes" (Bowie), "Sound and Vision" (Bowie), "Fashion" (Bowie), "Wild Is the Wind" (Dmitri Tiomkin, Ned Washington), "John, I'm Only Dancing" (Bowie), "D.J." (Bowie, Brian Eno, Carlos Alomar). 33–1/3 rpm LP. RCA Victor AFL 1–4202, 1981. Contains previously released material.

*Christiane F.* David Bowie, vocals and various instruments; various assisting musicians. "V-2 Schneider" (Bowie), "TVC15" (Bowie), "Heroes/Helden" (Bowie,

Brian Eno), "Boys Keep Swinging" (Bowie, Eno), "Sense of Doubt" (Bowie), "Station to Station" (Bowie), "Look Back in Anger" (Bowie, Eno), "Stay" (Bowie), "Warszawa" (Bowie, Eno). Various producers. CBS Records ABL 1–4239, 1982. Note: This is the soundtrack from the motion picture *Christiane F.*

*Ziggy Stardust.* David Bowie, vocals and guitar; various assisting musicians. "Hang on to Yourself" (Bowie), "Watch that Man" (Bowie), Wild-Eyed Boy from Freecloud" (Bowie), "All the Young Dudes" (Bowie), "Oh! You Pretty Things" (Bowie), "Moonage Daydream" (Bowie), "Space Oddity" (Bowie), "My Death" (Eric Blau, Mort Shuman, Jacques Brel), "Cracked Actor" (Bowie), "Time" (Bowie), "Width of a Circle" (Bowie), "Changes" (Bowie), "Let's Spend the Night Together" (Mick Jagger, Keith Richards), "Suffragette City" (Bowie), "White Light/White Heat" (Lou Reed), "Rock 'n' Roll Suicide" (Bowie). Produced by Tony Visconti. Two 33–1/3 rpm LPs. RCA Victor CPL 2–4862, 1983. Note: This is the soundtrack from the motion picture *Ziggy Stardust and the Spiders from Mars.* Reissued on two compact discs, EMI 72435–82209–2-6, 2003.

*Let's Dance.* David Bowie, vocals; various assisting musicians. "Modern Love" (Bowie), "China Girl" (Bowie, Iggy Pop), "Let's Dance" (Bowie), "Without You" (Bowie), "Ricochet" (Bowie), "Criminal World" (Peter Godwin, Duncan Browne, Sean Lyons), "Cat People (Putting Out Fire)" (Bowie, Giorgio Moroder), "Shake It" (Bowie). Produced by David Bowie and Nile Rodgers. Simultaneously issued on 33–1/3 rpm LP, EMI-America SO-17093; and compact disc, EMI-America CDP7 46002 2, 1983. Reissued on enhanced compact disc, Virgin 521896–0, 1999.

*Fame and Fashion.* David Bowie, vocals and various instruments; various assisting musicians. "Space Oddity" (Bowie), "Changes" (Bowie), "Starman" (Bowie), "1984" (Bowie), "Young American" (Bowie), "Fame" (Bowie, Carlos Alomar, John Lennon), "Golden Years" (Bowie), "TVC15" (Bowie), "'Heroes'" (Bowie, Brian Eno), "D.J." (Bowie, Eno, Alomar), "Fashion" (Bowie), "Ashes to Ashes" (Bowie). Various producers. 33–1/3 rpm LP. RCA Victor AFL 1–4919, 1984. Contains previously released material.

*Tonight.* David Bowie, vocals; Iggy Pop, vocals; Tina Turner, vocals; various assisting musicians. "Loving the Alien" (Bowie), "Don't Look Down" (Iggy Pop, James Williamson), "God Only Knows" (Brian Wilson, Tony Asher), "Tonight" (Bowie, Pop), "Neighborhood Treat" (Bowie, Pop), "Blue Jean" (Bowie), "Tumble and Twirl" (Bowie, Pop), "I Keep Forgetting" (Jerry Leiber, Mike Stoller), "Dancing with the Big Boys" (Bowie, Pop, Carlos Alomar). Produced by David Bowie, Derek Bramble, and Hugh Padgham. 33–1/3 rpm LP. EMI America SJ-17138, 1984.

*Never Let Me Down.* David Bowie, vocals, guitar, keyboards, percussion, rap; various assisting musicians. "Day-In Day-Out" (Bowie), "Time Will Crawl" (Bowie), "Beat of Your Drum" (Bowie), "Never Let Me Down" (Bowie, Carlos Alomar), "Zeroes" (Bowie), "Glass Spider" (Bowie), "Shining Star (Makin' It My Love)" (Bowie), "New York's in Love" (Bowie), "'87 and Cry" (Bowie), "Bang Bang" (Pop Kraal). Produced by David Bowie and David Richards. 33–1/3 rpm LP. EMI America PJ-17267, 1987. Reissued on compact disc (with bonus tracks), Virgin 7243 8 40986 2 9, 1987.

*1966.* David Bowie, vocals; The Lower Third, various instruments and backing vocals. "I'm Not Losing Sleep" (Bowie), "I Dig Everything" (Bowie), "Can't Help Thinking About Me" (Bowie), "Do Anything You Say" (Bowie), "Good

Morning Girl" (Bowie), "And I Say to Myself" (Bowie). Compact disc. PRT
PYC 6001, 1987. Contains previously released material.

*Sound + Vision.* David Bowie, vocals and various instruments; various assisting musi-
cians. Volume One: "Space Oddity" (Bowie), "Wild-Eyed Boy from Freecloud"
(Bowie), "The Prettiest Star" (Bowie), "London Bye Ta-Ta" (Bowie), "Black
Country Rock" (Bowie), "The Man Who Sold the World" (Bowie), "The Bewlay
Brothers" (Bowie), "Changes" (Bowie), "Round and Round" (Chuck Berry),
"Moonage Daydream" (Bowie), "John, I'm Only Dancing" (Bowie), "Drive
in Saturday" (Bowie), "Panic in Detroit" (Bowie), "Ziggy Stardust" (Bowie),
"White Light/White Heat" (Lou Reed), "Rock 'n' Roll Suicide" (Bowie); Vol-
ume Two: "Anyway, Anyhow, Anywhere" (Roger Daltrey, Pete Townshend),
"Sorrow" (Bob Feldman, Jerry Goldstein, Richard Bottehrer), "Don't Bring
Me Down" (Dee), "1984" (Bowie), "Dodo" (Bowie), "Big Brother" (Bowie),
"Rebel Rebel" (Bowie), "Suffragette City" (Bowie), "Watch that Man"
(Bowie), "Cracked Actor" (Bowie), "Young Americans" (Bowie), "Fascination"
(Bowie, Luther Vandross), "After Today" (Bowie), "It's Hard to Be a Saint in
the City" (Bruce Springsteen), "TVC15" (Bowie), "Wild Is the Wind" (Dmitri
Tiomkin, Ned Washington); Volume Three: "Be My Wife" (Bowie), "Speed of
Life" (Bowie), "Helden" (Bowie, Brian Eno), "Joe the Lion" (Bowie), "Sons
of the Silent Age" (Bowie), "Station to Station" (Bowie), "Warszawa" (Bowie,
Eno), "Breaking Glass" (Bowie, Dennis Davis, George Murray), "Red Sails"
(Bowie, Eno), "Look Back in Anger" (Bowie, Eno), "Boys Keep Swinging"
(Bowie, Eno), "Up the Hill Backwards" (Bowie), "Kingdom Come" (Tom Ver-
laine), "Ashes to Ashes" (Bowie). Various producers. Reissued on three compact discs, Rykodisc RCD-0120/21/23-2, 1989. Contains previously released
material.

*Tin Machine.* Tin Machine (David Bowie, vocals and guitar; Reeves Gabrels, lead
guitar; Hunt Sales, drums and vocals; Tony Sales, bass and vocals); Kevin Arm-
strong, rhythm guitar and organ. "Heaven's in Here" (Bowie), "Tin Machine"
(Bowie, Hunt Sales, Tony Sales, Reeves Gabrels), "Prisoner of Love" (Bowie,
Sales, Sales, Gabrels), "Crack City" (Bowie), "I Can't Read" (Bowie, Gabrels),
"Under the God" (Bowie), "Amazing" (Bowie, Gabrels), "Working Class
Hero" (John Lennon), "Bus Stop" (Bowie, Gabrels), "Pretty Thing" (Bowie),
"Video Crime" (Bowie, Sales, Sales), "Run" (Bowie, Kevin Armstrong), "Sac-
rifice Yourself" (Bowie, Sales, Sales), "Baby Can Dance" (Bowie). Produced
by Tin Machine and Tim Palmer. 33-1/3 rpm LP. EMI 1004/EMI America
E1-91990, 1989. Reissued on compact disc, Capitol 91990, 1990. Reissued on
enhanced compact disc as Virgin 7243 521910 0 0, 1999.

*ChangesBowie.* David Bowie, vocals and various instruments; various assisting musi-
cians. "Space Oddity" (Bowie), "John, I'm Only Dancing" (Bowie), "Changes"
(Bowie), "Ziggy Stardust" (Bowie), "Suffragette City" (Bowie), "Jean Genie"
(Bowie), "Diamond Dogs" (Bowie), "Rebel Rebel" (Bowie), "Young Amer-
icans" (Bowie), "Fame '90" [remix] (Bowie, Carlos Alomar, John Lennon),
"Golden Years" (Bowie), "Heroes" (Bowie, Brian Eno), "Ashes to Ashes"
(Bowie), "Fashion" (Bowie), "Let's Dance" (Bowie), "China Girl" (Bowie, Iggy
Pop), "Modern Love" (Bowie), "Blue Jean" (Bowie). Compact disc. Rykodisc
RCD 20171, 1990. Contains previously released material.

*Tin Machine II.* Tin Machine (David Bowie, vocals, guitar, piano, saxophone; Reeves
Gabrels, guitar, vocals, vibrators, Drano, organ; Hunt Sales, drums, percussion,

vocals; Tony Sales, bass, vocals); other accompanying musicians. "Baby Universal" (Bowie, Reeves Gabrels), "One Shot" (Bowie, Gabrels, Hunt Sales, Tony Sales), "You Belong in Rock & Roll" (Bowie, Gabrels), "If There Is Something" (Bryan Ferry), "Amlapura" (Bowie, Gabrels), "Betty Wrong" (Bowie, Gabrels), "You Can't Talk" (Bowie, Gabrels, Sales, Sales), "Stateside" (Bowie, Hunt Sales), "Shopping for Girls" (Bowie, Gabrels), "A Big Hurt" (Bowie), "Sorry" (Hunt Sales), "Goodbye Mr. Ed" (Bowie, Sales, Sales). Produced by Tin Machine, Tim Palmer, and Hugh Padgham. Compact disc. Polygram 511216, 1991. Also issued as Polygram 511575 and Victory Music 314 511 216–2, 1991. Reissued as JVC Victor 5075, 1996 and JVC Japan 63333, 2006.

*Oy Vey, Baby.* Tin Machine (David Bowie, vocals, guitar; Reeves Gabrels, guitar, vocals; Hunt Sales, drums, vocals; Tony Sales, bass guitar, vocals); Eric Schermerhorn, guitar and backing vocals. "If There Is Something" (Bryan Ferry), "Amazing" (Bowie, Reeves Gabrels), "I Can't Read" (Bowie, Gabrels), "Stateside" (Bowie, Hunt Sales), "Under the God" (Bowie), "Goodbye, Mr. Ed" (Bowie, Hunt Sales, Tony Sales), "Heaven's in Here" (Bowie), "You Belong in Rock & Roll" (Bowie, Gabrels). Compact disc. Victory Music 383 480 004 2, 1992.

*Black Tie White Noise.* David Bowie, vocals, guitar, saxophone; various assisting musicians. "The Wedding" (Bowie), "You've Been Around" (Bowie, Reeves Gabrels), "I Feel Free" (Jack Bruce, Peter Brown), "Black Tie White Noise" (Bowie), "Jump They Say" (Bowie), "Nite Flights" (Scott Engels), "Pallas Athena" (Bowie), "Miracle Goodnight" (Bowie), "Don't Let Me Down & Down" (Tarha, Michel Valmont), "Looking for Lester" (Bowie), "I Know It's Gonna Happen Someday" (Morrissey), "The Wedding Song" (Bowie), "Jump They Say" [alternative mix] (Bowie), "Lucy Can't Dance" (Bowie). Produced by David Bowie and Nile Rodgers. Compact disc. Savage Records 74785–50212–2, 1993.

*The Buddha of Suburbia.* Performed by David Bowie and Erdal Kizilcay; various assisting musicians. "Buddha of Suburbia" (Bowie), "Sex and the Church" (Bowie), "South Horizon" (Bowie), "The Mysteries" (Bowie), "Bleed Like a Craze, Dad" (Bowie), "Strangers When We Meet" (Bowie), "Dead Against It" (Bowie), "Untitled No. 1" (Bowie), "Ian Fish, U.K. Heir" (Bowie), "Buddha of Suburbia" (Bowie). Produced by David Bowie and David Richards. Compact disc. BBC, 1993. Released in the United States as Virgin 40988, 1995.

*Bowie: The Singles 1969 to 1993.* David Bowie, vocals and various instruments; various assisting musicians. "Space Oddity" (Bowie), "Changes" (Bowie), "Oh! You Pretty Things" (Bowie), "Life on Mars?" (Bowie), "Ziggy Stardust" (Bowie), "Starman" (Bowie), "John, I'm Only Dancing" (Bowie), "Suffragette City" (Bowie), "Jean Genie" (Bowie), "Sorrow" (Bob Feldman, Jerry Goldstein, Richard Bottehrer), "Drive-in Saturday" (Bowie), "Diamond Dogs" (Bowie), "Rebel Rebel" (Bowie), "Young Americans" (Bowie), "Fame" (Bowie, Carlos Alomar, John Lennon), "Golden Years" (Bowie), "TVC15" (Bowie), "Be My Wife" (Bowie), "Sound and Vision" (Bowie), "Beauty and the Beast" (Bowie), "Heroes" (Bowie, Brian Eno), "Boys Keep Swinging" (Bowie, Eno), "D.J." (Bowie, Eno, Alomar), "Look Back in Anger" (Bowie, Eno), "Ashes to Ashes" (Bowie), "Fashion" (Bowie), "Scary Monsters (and Super Creeps)" (Bowie), "Under Pressure" (Bowie, John Deacon, Brian May, Freddie Mercury, Roger Taylor), "Cat People (Putting out the Fire)" (Bowie, Giorgio Moroder), "Let's Dance" (Bowie), "China Girl" (Bowie, Iggy Pop), "Modern Love" (Bowie),

"Blue Jean" (Bowie), "Loving the Alien" (Bowie), "Dancing in the Street" (Marvin Gaye, Ivy Hunter, William "Mickey" Stevenson), "Absolute Beginners" (Bowie), "Day-In Day-Out" (Bowie), "Never Let Me Down" (Bowie, Carlos Alomar), "Jump They Say" (Bowie), "Peace on Earth"/"Little Drummer Boy" (Dennis Davis, Ian Fraser, Larry Grossman, Kohan, Henry Onorati, Harry Simone). Compilation produced by Jeff Rougvie. Three compact discs. Rykodisc 10218/19, 1993. Contains previously released material.

*Outside: The Nathan Adler Diaries: A Hyper-Cycle.* David Bowie, vocals, saxophone, guitar, keyboards; Brian Eno, synthesizers, treatments & strategies; various assisting musicians. "Leon Takes Us Outside" (Bowie, Brian Eno, Reeves Gabrels, Mike Garson, Erdal Kizilcay, Sterling Campbell), "Outside" (Bowie, Kevin Armstrong), "The Heart's Filthy Lesson" (Bowie, Eno, Gabrels, Garson, Kizilcay, Campbell), "A Small Plot of Land" (Bowie, Eno, Gabrels, Garson, Kizilcay, Campbell), "Segue—Baby Grace (A Horrid Cassette)" (Bowie, Eno, Gabrels, Garson, Kizilcay, Campbell), "Hallo Spaceboy" (Bowie, Eno), "The Motel" (Bowie), "I Have Not Been to Oxford Town" (Bowie, Eno), "No Control" (Bowie, Eno), "Segue—Algeria Touchshriek" (Bowie, Eno, Gabrels, Garson, Kizilcay, Campbell), "The Voyeur of Utter Destruction (As Beauty)" (Bowie, Eno, Gabrels), "Segue—Romona A. Stone/I Am with Name" (Bowie, Eno, Gabrels, Garson, Kizilcay, Campbell), "Wishful Beginnings" (Bowie, Eno), "We Prick You" (Bowie, Eno), "Segue—Nathan Adler" (Bowie, Eno, Gabrels, Garson, Kizilcay, Campbell), "I'm Deranged" (Bowie, Eno), "Thru' These Architects Eyes" (Bowie, Gabrels), "Segue—Nathan Adler" (Bowie, Eno), "Strangers When We Meet" (Bowie). Produced by David Bowie and Brian Eno. Compact disc. BMG/Arista 74321369002, 1995.

*The Deram Anthology (1966–1968).* David Bowie, vocals and guitar; various assisting musicians. "Rubber Band" [single version] (Bowie), "The London Boys" (Bowie), "The Laughing Gnome" (Bowie), "The Gospel According to Tony Day" (Bowie), "Uncle Arthur" (Bowie), "Sell Me a Coat" (Bowie), "Rubber Band" (Bowie), "Love You 'till Tuesday" (Bowie), "There Is a Happy Land" (Bowie), "We Are Hungry Men" (Bowie), "When I Live My Dreams" (Bowie), "Little Bombardier" (Bowie), "Silly Boy Blue" (Bowie), "Come and Buy My Toys" (Bowie), "Join the Gang" (Bowie), "She's Got Medals" (Bowie), "Maid of Bond Street" (Bowie), "Please Mr. Gravedigger" (Bowie), "Love You 'till Tuesday" [single version] (Bowie), "Did You Ever Have a Dream" (Bowie), "Karma Man" (Bowie), "Let Me Sleep Beside You" (Bowie), "In the Heat of the Morning" (Bowie), "Ching-a-Ling" (Bowie), "Sell Me a Coat" [alternate version] (Bowie), "When I Live My Dream" [alternate version] (Bowie), "Space Oddity" (Bowie). Various producers. Compact disc. Deram 844 784–2, 1997. Contains previously released material recorded by Bowie in 1966–68.

*The Best of Bowie 1969–1974.* David Bowie, vocals, guitar, keyboards, and saxophone; various assisting musicians. "The Jean Genie" (Bowie), "Space Oddity" (Bowie), "Starman" (Bowie), "Ziggy Stardust" (Bowie), "John, I'm Only Dancing" (Bowie), "Rebel Rebel" (Bowie), "Let's Spend the Night Together" (Mick Jagger, Keith Richards), "Suffragette City" (Bowie), "Oh! You Pretty Things" (Bowie), "Velvet Goldmine" (Bowie), "Drive-In Saturday" (Bowie), "Diamond Dogs" (Bowie), "Changes" (Bowie), "Sorrow" (Bob Feldman, Jerry Goldstein, Richard Bottehrer), "The Prettiest Star" (Bowie), "Life on Mars" (Bowie), "Aladdin Sane" (Bowie), "The Man Who Sold the World" (Bowie), "Rock 'n'

Roll Suicide" (Bowie), "All the Young Dudes" (Bowie). Various producers. Compact disc. EMI 72438–21849-2-8, 1997.

*Earthling.* David Bowie, vocals, keyboards, guitars, alto saxophone, samples; various assisting musicians. "Little Wonder" (Bowie, Reeves Gabrels, Mark Plati), "Looking for Satellites" (Bowie, Gabrels, Plati), "Battle for Britain (The Letter)" (Bowie, Gabrels, Plati), "Seven Years in Tibet" (Bowie, Gabrels), "Dead Man Walking" (Bowie, Gabrels), "Telling Lies" (Bowie), "The Last Thing You Should Do" (Bowie, Gabrels, Plati), "I'm Afraid of Americans" (Bowie, Brian Eno), "Law (Earthlings on Fire)" (Bowie, Gabrels). Produced by David Bowie. Compact disc. ISO/BMG 7432144944 2, 1997.

*The Best of Bowie 1974–1979.* David Bowie, vocals, guitar, keyboards, and saxophone; various assisting musicians. "Sound and Vision" (Bowie), "Golden Years" (Bowie), "Fame" (Bowie, John Lennon, Carlos Alomar), "Young Americans" (Bowie), "John, I'm Only Dancing" (Bowie), "Can You Hear Me" (Bowie), "Wild Is the Wind" (Dmitri Tiomkin, Ned Washington), "Knock on Wood" (Steve Cropper, Eddie Floyd), "TVC15" (Bowie), "1984" (Bowie), "It's Hard to Be a Saint in the City" (Bruce Springsteen), "Look Back in Anger" (Bowie, Brian Eno), "The Secret Life of Arabia" (Bowie, Eno, Alomar), "D.J." (Bowie, Eno, Alomar), "Beauty and the Beast" (Bowie), "Breaking Glass" (Bowie, Dennis Davis, George Murray), "Boys Keep Swinging" (Bowie, Eno), "Heroes" (Bowie, Eno). Various producers. Compact disc. Virgin 7243 4 94300, 1998. Also issued as EMI 4943002, 2000.

*hours...* David Bowie, vocals, keyboards, guitar, drum programming; various assisting musicians. "Thursday's Child" (Bowie, Reeves Gabrels), "Something in the Air" (Bowie, Gabrels), "Survive" (Bowie, Gabrels), "If I'm Dreaming My Life" (Bowie, Gabrels), "Seven" (Bowie, Gabrels), "What's Really Happening?" (Bowie, Gabrels, Alex Grant), "The Pretty Things Are Going to Hell" (Bowie, Gabrels), "New Angels of Promise" (Bowie, Gabrels), "Brilliant Adventure" (Bowie, Gabrels), "The Dreamers" (Bowie, Gabrels). Produced by David Bowie and Reeves Gabrels. Compact disc. ISO 0152518, 1999. Also released as Virgin 48157, 1999.

*Bowie at the BEEB.* David Bowie, vocals and guitar; various assisting musicians. "In the Heat of the Morning" (Bowie), "London Bye Ta Ta" (Bowie), "Karma Man" (Bowie), "Silly Boy Blue" (Bowie), "Let Me Sleep Beside You" (Bowie), "Janine" (Bowie), "Amsterdam" (Jacques Brel, Mort Shuman), "God Knows I'm Good" (Bowie), "The Width of a Circle" (Bowie), "Unwashed and Somewhat Slightly Dazed" (Bowie), "Cygnet Committee" (Bowie), "Memory of a Free Festival" (Bowie), "Wild Eyed Boy from Freecloud" (Bowie), "Bombers" (Bowie), "Looking for a Friend" (Bowie), "Almost Grown" (Chuck Berry), "Kooks" (Bowie), "It Ain't Easy" (Ray Davies), "The Supermen" (Bowie), "Eight Line Poem" (Bowie), "Hang on to Yourself" [two versions] (Bowie), "Ziggy Stardust" [two versions] (Bowie), "Queen Bitch" (Bowie), "I'm Waiting for the Man" (Lou Reed), "Five Years" (Bowie), "White Light/White Heat" (Lou Reed), "Moonage Daydream" (Bowie), "Suffragette City" (Bowie), "Starman" (Bowie), "Space Oddity" (Bowie), "Changes" (Bowie), "Oh! You Pretty Things" (Bowie), "Andy Warhol" (Bowie), "Lady Stardust" (Bowie), "Rock 'n' Roll Suicide" (Bowie). Various producers. Two compact discs. EMI 7243 528629 2 4, 2000. Contains material originally recorded 1968–72 for broadcast on the BBC.

*Heathen.* David Bowie, vocals, keyboards, guitar, saxophone, stylophone, drums; various assisting musicians. "Sunday" (Bowie), "Cactus" (Black Francis), "Slip Away" (Bowie), "Slow Burn" (Bowie), "Afraid" (Bowie), "I've Been Waiting for You" (Neil Young), "I Would Be Your Slave" (Bowie), "I Took a Trip on a Gemini Spaceship" (Legendary Stardust Cowboy), "5:15 The Angels Have Gone" (Bowie), "Everyone Says 'Hi'" (Bowie), "A Better Future" (Bowie), "Heathen (The Rays)" (Bowie). Produced by Tony Visconti and David Bowie. Compact disc. ISO/Columbia CK 86630, 2002.

*The Best of Bowie.* David Bowie, vocals, guitar, keyboards, and saxophone; various assisting musicians. "Space Oddity" (Bowie), "The Man Who Sold the World" (Bowie), "Changes" (Bowie), "Life on Mars?" (Bowie), "Moonage Daydream" (Bowie), "Suffragette City" (Bowie), "Ziggy Stardust" (Bowie), "All the Young Dudes" (Bowie), "The Jean Genie" (Bowie), "Panic in Detroit" (Bowie), "Rebel Rebel" (Bowie), "Diamond Dogs" (Bowie), "Young Americans" (Bowie), "Fame" (Bowie, Carlos Alomar, John Lennon), "Golden Years" (Bowie), "TVC15" (Bowie), "Sound and Vision" (Bowie), "'Heroes'" (Bowie, Brian Eno), "D.J." (Bowie, Eno, Alomar), "Ashes to Ashes" (Bowie), "Fashion" (Bowie), "Scary Monsters (And Super Creeps)" (Bowie), "Under Pressure" (Bowie, John Deacon, Brian May, Freddie Mercury, Roger Taylor), "Cat People (Putting Out Fire)" (Bowie, Giorgio Moroder), "Let's Dance" (Bowie), "China Girl" (Bowie, Iggy Pop), "Modern Love" (Bowie), "Blue Jean" (Bowie), "This Is Not America" (Bowie), "Dancing in the Street" (Marvin Gaye, Ivy Hunter, William "Mickey" Stevenson), "Absolute Beginners" (Bowie), "Time Will Crawl" (Bowie), "Under the God" (Bowie), "Jump They Say" (Bowie), "The Heart's Filthy Lesson" (Bowie, Eno, Reeves Gabrels, Mike Garson, Erdal Kizilcay, Sterling Campbell), "I'm Afraid of Americans" (Bowie, Eno), "Thursday's Child" (Bowie, Gabrels), "Slow Burn" (Bowie). Various producers. Three compact discs. EMI 7243 5 4193026, 2002. Contains previously issued material.

*Reality.* David Bowie, vocals, guitar, keyboards, stylophone, baritone saxophone, percussion, synthesizers; various assisting musicians. "New Killer Star" (Bowie), "Pablo Picasso" (Jonathan Richman), "Never Get Old" (Bowie), "The Loneliest Guy" (Bowie), "Looking for Water" (Bowie), "She'll Drive the Big Car" (Bowie), "Days" (Bowie), "Fall Dog Bombs The Moon" (Bowie), "Try Some, Buy Some" (George Harrison), "Reality" (Bowie), "Bring Me the Disco King" (Bowie). Produced by David Bowie and Tony Visconti. Compact disc. ISO Columbia CK 90576, 2003. Also issued in a special tour edition as ISO Columbia COL 512555 3, 2003. Note: The tour edition also includes the track "Waterloo Sunset" (Ray Davies), as well as a DVD live performance of "Reality."

# Notes

## INTRODUCTION

1. "David Bowie," *Wikipedia*, http://en.wikipedia.org/wiki/David_bowie, Accessed May 17, 2006. Although as a college professor I discourage my students from citing any encyclopedia as a primary source, in the early twenty-first century *Wikipedia* stands as a pretty good gauge of popular perception.

2. Stephen Thomas Erlewine, "David Bowie: Biography," *All Music Guide,* http://www.allmusic.com, Accessed January 30, 2006.

3. Brock Helander, *Baker's Biographical Dictionary of Musicians, s.v.* "Bowie, David," (New York: Schirmer Books, 2001), vol. 1, p. 418.

4. Bowie would reveal in a 1993 interview that he considered himself to be a "closet heterosexual" and that bisexuality and homosexuality was not his true nature. David Sinclair, "Station to Station," *Rolling Stone* no. 658, June 10, 1993, pp. 56ff.

5. Readers looking for complete Bowie discographies are encouraged to consult the latest edition of Roy Carr and Charles Saar Murray's *David Bowie: An Illustrated Record.* Due to the extensive coverage of Bowie on the Internet, readers may also wish to consult fan sites with discographies. Perhaps the most authoritative Internet source, however, is *All Music Guide:* http://www.allmusic.com.

## CHAPTER 1

1. Reportedly, Bowie's early bands the King Bees and the Mannish Boys recorded singles. These, however, seem to be unavailable at the time of this writing.

2. The Roman numerals refer to the scale degrees on which each chord is built, with capital numerals representing major chords, and lowercase numerals representing minor chords.

3. Mark Adams, Liner notes to *The Deram Anthology 1966–1968,* Compact disc, Deram 844 784–2, 1997.

4. Hugh Mendl, Liner notes to *Days of Future Passed,* 33 1/3 rpm LP, Deram DES 18012, 1967.

5. Mark Adams, Liner notes to *The Deram Anthology 1966–1968.*

## CHAPTER 2

1. The original American release of *The Man Who Sold the World* featured a cartoon cover that resembled the style of 1967 summer of love drawings such as the album cover of Big Brother and the Holding Company's *Cheap Thrills.*

2. Victor Bockris, *The Life and Death of Andy Warhol* (New York: Bantam Books, 1989), p. 263; and Bob Colacello, *Holy Terror: Andy Warhol Close Up* (New York: HarperCollins, 1990), p. 68.

3. Ibid.

4. David Sinclair, "Station to Station," *Rolling Stone* no. 658, June 10, 1993, pp. 56ff.

5. Dave Thompson, Review of "The Bewlay Brothers," *All Music Guide,* http:// allmusic.com/cg/amg.dll?p=amg&token=&sql=33:hu67men39fco, Accessed June 21, 2006.

6. One of the few crystal clear autobiographical references is to schoolyard fights: it was one such fight that left Bowie with a permanently dilated left pupil.

7. The title is sometimes abbreviated as *Ziggy Stardust;* therefore the reader who looks for the album or information about it is advised to look under both *r* and *z.*

8. Critic Stephen Thomas Erlewine, for example, writes, "the story falls apart quickly." Erlewine, Review of *Ziggy Stardust, All Music Guide,* http://allmusic.com/ cg/amg.dll?p=amg&sql=10:38q8g4gttv2z, Accessed June 21, 2006.

9. Mick Woodmansey's stylistic resemblance to the early-1970s work of Palmer is also particularly noticeable on the song "Ziggy Stardust."

10. The roman numerals represent the scale degrees on which the chords are built; upper-case numerals represent major chords and lower-case numerals represent minor chords. In the key of C major, the I-vi-IV-V progression would consist of the following chords: C major, A minor, F major, and G major. Bowie's progression is a bit more complicated, because he uses a substitute for the IV chord, but it has the same sort of retro, 1950s effect as "Heart and Soul."

11. The notable exception is the *Diamond Dogs* album, on which Bowie handles nearly all of the guitar work.

12. Incidentally, this is an even bigger problem in the album's compact disc reissue on Virgin at the end of the twentieth century.

13. In typical Bowie fashion, however, the gender of the prostitute is open to speculation.

14. Stephen Thomas Erlewine, "Aladdin Sane," *All Music Guide,* http://allmusic. com/cg/amg.dll?p=amg&token=&sql=10:7s220roac48n, Accessed July 3, 2006.

15. Ibid.

16. The minimal liner notes of *Pin Ups* does not include performer credits. *All Music Guide,* however, includes full performer and production credits at their Web site, http://allmusic.com/cg/amg.dll?p=amg&sql=10:i2jp7i3jg77r~T2, Accessed June 20, 2006.

17. Bruce Eder, Review of *Pin Ups, All Music Guide,* http://allmusic.com/cg/amg.dll?p=amg&sql=10:rt7uak2k5m3m, Accessed June 20, 2006.

18. Liner notes to *Rock 'n' Roll* by John Lennon, 33–1/3 rpm LP, Apple SK-3419, 1975.

19. The listener should note, however, that Bowie's tenor saxophone work on the album is far superior to his alto work, particularly in the area of intonation.

## CHAPTER 3

1. He also, thankfully, never tackled country music.

2. I discuss this aspect of the 1966–1967 Stevie Wonder repertoire extensively in my book *The Sounds of Stevie Wonder: His Words and Music* (Westport, CT: Praeger, 2006).

3. A slightly different mix of the Beatles's recording of the song had been issued on a limited edition charity album a couple of years earlier.

4. It appears that Lennon wrote the song with little or no contribution from Paul McCartney.

5. An *ostinato* is a musical figure that is repeated over and over, sometimes throughout an entire composition.

## CHAPTER 4

1. Musical motives are short melodic fragments, the basic building blocks of a tune.

2. The printed lyrics in the liner notes of the compact disc reissue use the British spelling (grey) of gray. Liner notes to *Low,* enhanced compact disc, Virgin 7243 521907 0 6, 1999.

3. Jerry Stahl, "David Bowie," In Sean Manning, *The Show I'll Never Forget* (Cambridge, MA: Da Capo Press, 2007), pp. 258–262.

4. Glass's popularity would reach its zenith in 1982, when his album *Glassworks* dominated the *Billboard* Classical album charts and even appeared on the Pop charts.

5. An all-star rock orchestra McCartney assembled for several recordings and live benefit concerts in the late 1970s.

6. Bowie has been interviewed a number of times in the three decades since he began working in earnest in electronic music, and has shown a strong knowledge of what is current in music technology.

7. Incidentally, the Nick Lowe EP, as well as the album from which it was culled *(Pure Pop for Now People)*, is notable for the superb song "Marie Provost," a catchy mid-1960s-style pop-rock tune about the American silent film actress of the same name, who died in obscurity and was eaten by her pet dog. The sharp disconnection between musical style and text is as strange, thought provoking, and ironic as probably any recording of the 1970s, including those of David Bowie.

8. The album cover includes the quotation marks as part of the album's title.

9. The reader must keep in mind that although Bowie's instrumental pieces on *Low* and *"Heroes"* are experimental within the context of pop music, they are all clearly tonal and therefore not necessarily experimental in the context of twentieth-century classical compositions.

10. *Sprechstimme* (German for "speech-song") was a singing style associated with the early twentieth-century composers Arnold Schoenberg and Alban Berg, who were known for their expressionistic and twelve-tone work. In this style, the singer would consciously slide between pitches in what might be called a melodically heightened version of speech.

11. *Rolling Stone* 500 Greatest Songs of All Time: David Bowie—'Heroes,'" *Rolling Stone* no. 963, December 9, 2004, p. 102. Incidentally, three other Bowie songs made the list: "Changes" (No. 127), "Ziggy Stardust" (No. 277), and "Young Americans" (No. 481).

12. The liner booklet published with the Virgin CD reissue includes this intriguing range of visual images, as well as photographs of an entirely conventional-looking David Bowie. It is easily the widest and wildest range of collected images of any Bowie album.

13. Stephen Thomas Erlewine, Review of *Lodger* by David Bowie, *All Music Guide,* http://allmusic.com/cg/amg.dll?p=amg&token=&sql=10:am6zefbkhgfj, Accessed August 27, 2006.

14. "On Second Thought: David Bowie—*Lodger,*" *Stylus,* http://www.stylusmagazine.com/feature.php?ID=1120, Accessed August 27, 2006.

15. "On Second Thought: David Bowie—*Lodger,*" *Stylus,* http://www.stylusmagazine.com/feature.php?ID=1120, Accessed August 27, 2006.

16. The semi-autobiographical Burroughs novel *Junky* (also known as *Junkie*) belies an especially strong interest in psychology. William S. Burroughs, *Junky* (New York: Penguin Books, 1977); originally published: William Lee, *Junkie* (New York: Ace Books, 1953).

## CHAPTER 5

1. Bowie never did, thankfully, delve into country music.

2. Chic was best-known for their 1978 mega-hit "Le Freak," a dance single that spent over a month at No. 1 on the *Billboard* pop charts.

3. Boy George and Culture Club's best-known hit "Karma Chameleon" shares a basic production feel with Bowie's "Modern Love." Probably not coincidentally, Boy George adopted Bowie's use of eye makeup and androgynous dress of Bowie's glam period.

4. This reference provided the name for Bowie's concert tour of the era: the Serious Moonlight Tour.

5. Stephen Thomas Erlewine, Review of *Tonight, All Music Guide,* http://www.allmusic.com, Accessed September 20, 2006.

6. Ibid.

7. Ibid.

8. Stephen Thomas Erlewine, Review of *Never Let Me Down, All Music Guide,* http://www.allmusic.com, Accessed September 21, 2006.

9. Ibid.

10. Aside from his soundtrack work of the late 1980s, perhaps Bowie's main musical contribution between 1985 and 1989 was his writing, production, and performance work on Iggy Pop's 1986 album *Blah, Blah, Blah.*

## CHAPTER 6

1. Whereas bands such as the Melvins, Soundgarden, Mudhoney, and Green River were representative of the style for a few years in the late 1980s, before Nirvana

and Pearl Jam cultivated a national audience for grunge, it was largely a regional style of the American Pacific Northwest.

2. Mark W. B. Allender, Review of *Tin Machine II*, *All Music Guide*, http://allmusic.com/cg/amg.dll?p=amg&sql=10:8eanqjkbojja, Accessed October 12, 2006.

3. Mark W. B. Allender, Review of *Oy Vey, Baby*, *All Music Guide*, http://allmusic.com/cg/amg.dll?p=amg&sql=10:31juea104xs7, Accessed September 29, 2006.

## Chapter 7

1. David Wild, "David Bowie," *Rolling Stone* no. 648, January 21, 1993, p. 14.

2. Bowie's tone color on the saxophone fits within mainstream rock and jazz approaches to the tenor and baritone saxophone. His intonation in solos, particularly in extreme registers, does however, tend to wander somewhat.

3. David Sinclair, "Station to Station," *Rolling Stone* no. 658, June 10, 1993, pp. 56ff.

4. George Tremlett, *David Bowie: Living on the Brink* (New York: Carroll & Graf, 1997).

5. William Ruhlmann, "*The Buddha of Suburbia*," *All Music Guide*, http://allmusic.com/cg/amg.dll?p=amg&sql=10:cqn8b5b4nsqj, Accessed October 28, 2006.

6. Melinda Newman, "David Bowie Returns to Drama," *Billboard* 107, August 19, 1995, p. 8.

7. Jeremy Helligar, "*Outside*," *People* 44, October 16, 1995, p. 32.

8. David Fricke, "Recordings," *Rolling Stone* no. 724–725, December 28, 1995–January 11, 1996, p. 126.

9. Tom Gliatto, "*Basquiat*," *People* 46, August 19, 1996, p. 19.

10. Dan Jewel, "The Art of Being Andy," *People* 46, August 26, 1996, p. 18.

11. David Bowie, "Basquiat's Wave," *Modern Painters* 9, Spring 1996, pp. 46–47.

12. Carol Clerk and Andre Paine, "Headlines: David Bowie—So Which of His Albums Should You Buy?" *Melody Maker* 77, July 5, 2000–July 11, 2000, p. 12.

13. Stephen Thomas Erlewine, Review of *Earthling*, *All Music Guide*, http://allmusic.com/cg/amg.dll?p=amg&sql=10:9y3m963ofepc, Accessed November 6, 2006.

14. Peter Castro, "*Earthling*," *People* 47, February 17, 1997, p. 27.

15. Ibid.

16. Frank Zappa, with Peter Occhiogrosso, *The Real Frank Zappa Book* (New York: Poseidon Press, 1989), p. 188 (capitalizations and italics in the original). Quoted in Albin J. Zak III, "'Edition-ing' Rock," *American Music* 23, Spring 2005, p. 96.

17. Larry Flick and Shawnee Smith, "Singles: Rock Tracks," *Billboard* 109, October 18, 1997, p. 80.

18. Matt Diehl, "In the Studio: David Bowie Rumbles in the Jungle on *Earthling*," *Rolling Stone* no. 749, December 12, 1996, p. 25.

## Chapter 8

1. Matt Hendrickson, "Bowie's Golden *Hours*," *Rolling Stone* no. 822, September 30, 1999, p. 24; Steve Dougherty, Ralph Novak, and Alec Foege, "Picks & Pans: Song," *People* 52, October 11, 1999, pp. 43ff.

2. Larry Flick, "Zowie! Bowie!" *Advocate* no. 867, July 9, 2002, p. 67.

3. Dave Thompson, "'The Pretty Things Are Going to Hell,'" *All Music Guide,* http://allmusic.com/cg/amg.dll?p=amg&sql=33:wc6xlf3e5ccq, Accessed November 27, 2006.

4. Elysa Gardner, "Bowie Has Faith in the *Heathen,*" *USA Today,* June 11, 2002, Life, p. 10d. Bowie discusses the timing of the writing of the songs in this interview.

5. Benjamin Nugent, "Space Slacker," *Time* 159, June 17, 2002, p. 76.

6. Kyle Smith, "*Heathen,*" *People* 57, June 17, 2002, p. 41.

7. Stephen Thomas Erlewine, Review of *Heathen, All Music Guide,* http://allmusic.com/cg/amg.dll?p=amg&sql=10:g2k0iklabbf9, Accessed October 31, 2006.

8. Benjamin Nugent, "Space Slacker," *Time* 159, June 17, 2002, p. 76.

9. For more information on this poem and the intriguing story of the legal determination of its authorship, see *The Official Footprints in the Sand Page,* http://www.footprints-inthe-sand.com/.

10. Larry Flick, "Zowie! Bowie!" *Advocate* no. 867, July 9, 2002, p. 67.

11. Readers who are unfamiliar with "I Will Follow Him" may wish to look up the song at *Allmusic.com* (http://allmusic.com). This Web site provides a brief downloadable audio sample of the famous chorus figure.

12. Elisabeth Kübler-Ross, *On Death and Dying* (New York: Macmillan, 1969).

13. A chord in root position has its root—G in the case of a G minor chord—in the bass; a second inversion chord has its fifth—F in the case of a B-flat major chord—in the bass.

14. Kyle Smith of *People* singles out "Bring Me the Disco King" as the weakest song on the album. Kyle Smith, "*Reality,*" *People* 60, September 22, 2003, p. 47

15. Bowie's emergency surgery and subsequent recovery received extensive press coverage. See, for example, Mitch Schneider, "David Bowie Recovering," *New York Times,* July 10, 2004, p. B16.

## CONCLUSIONS

1. In strophic songs, each verse is set to the same music. In through-composed songs, the musical form is completely fluid. Despite the fact that the bulk of pop songs are in strophic form, Bowie sometimes incorporates elements of both strict repetition and fluid form.

2. David Bowie, "Changes: Memories from a Life in Music," *Billboard* 111, May 29, 1999, p. 4.

3. Philip Glass, Quoted in liner notes to *Bowie & Eno Meet Glass; Heroes, Low Symphonies,* Two compact discs, Philips B0000840–02, 2003.

4. Ibid.

5. "The 50th Anniversary of Rock: The Immortals—39: David Bowie," *Rolling Stone* no. 946, April 15, 2004, pp. 128–129.

6. Ibid.

7. "*Rolling Stone* 500 Greatest Songs of All Time," *Rolling Stone* no. 963, December 9, 2004, pp. 102, 120, 137, 162.

## SELECTED DISCOGRAPHY

1. Among the luminaries that appear on *Young Americans* are John Lennon, Luther Vandross, and David Sanborn.

# Bibliography

"Absence Makes the Heart Grow Fonder?" *Melody Maker* 54, May 26, 1979, pp. 9–10. This article concerns Bowie's work in Berlin in the late 1970s.

Adams, Mark. Liner notes to *The Deram Anthology 1966–1968*. Compact disc. Deram, 844 784-2, 1997. These liner notes contain information about Bowie's pre-fame recordings.

"Albums: *Aladdin Sane*." *Melody Maker* 56, January 31, 1981, p. 17. A review of the Bowie album.

"Albums: *Bowie Rare*." *Melody Maker* 58, January 29, 1983, p. 17. A review of the Bowie album.

"Albums: *The Buddha of Suburbia*." *Melody Maker* 70, November 27, 1993, p. 41. A review of the Bowie television soundtrack album.

"Albums: *Changesbowie*." *Melody Maker* 66, March 17, 1990, p. 37. A review of the reissue of the Bowie compilation.

"Albums: *Changestwobowie*." *Melody Maker* 56, November 21, 1981, p. 23. A review of the Bowie greatest hits album.

"Albums: *Diamond Dogs*." *Melody Maker* 56, January 31, 1981, p. 17. A review of the Bowie album.

"Albums: *Earthling*." *Melody Maker* 74, February 8, 1997, p. 51. A review of Bowie's techno album.

"Albums: *Fame and Fashion*." *Melody Maker* 59, May 19, 1984, p. 31. A review of the Bowie album.

"Albums: '*Heroes*.'" *Melody Maker* 52, October 1, 1977, p. 23. A review of the Bowie album.

"Albums: Funky Dory." *Melody Maker* 69, April 10, 1993, p. 29. A review of *Black Tie White Noise*.

"Albums: *Let's Dance*." *Melody Maker* 58, April 16, 1983, p. 25. A review of the Bowie album.

"Albums: *Lodger*." *Melody Maker* 54, May 26, 1979, p. 28. A review of the Bowie album.

"Albums: *Love You 'Til Tuesday*." *Melody Maker* 59, May 19, 1984, p. 31. A review of this reissue of pre-fame material recorded by Bowie in the 1960s.

"Albums: *Low*." *Melody Maker* 52, January 22, 1977, pp. 16ff. A review of Bowie's first Berlin album.

"Albums: *Never Let Me Down*." *Melody Maker* 62, April 18, 1987, p. 29. A review of the Bowie album.

"Albums: *Scary Monsters*." *Melody Maker* 55, September 20, 1980, p. 32. A review of the Bowie album.

"Albums: *Stage*." *Melody Maker* 53, September 30, 1978, p. 18. A review of the Bowie album.

"Albums: *Tonight*." *Melody Maker* 59, September 29, 1984, p. 28. A review of the Bowie album.

"Albums: *Ziggy Stardust*." *Melody Maker* 66, June 23, 1990, p. 44. A review of the reissue of the Bowie album.

"Albums: *Ziggy Stardust—The Motion Picture*." *Melody Maker* 58, November 5, 1983. A review of the Bowie album and concert video.

Allender, Mark W. B. Review of *Tin Machine II*. *All Music Guide*. http://allmusic. com/cg/amg.dll?p=amg&sql=10:8eanqjkbojja. Accessed October 12, 2006. A generally unfavorable review of the album.

Allender, Mark W. B. Review of *Oy Vey, Baby*. *All Music Guide*. http://allmusic.com/cg/amg.dll?p=amg&sql=10:31juea104xs7. Accessed September 29, 2006. A generally unfavorable review of the album.

"At the American Museum." *Natural History* 99, August 1990, pp. 70–71. Among the happenings at the American Museum of Natural History in New York City covered in this article was a laser light show at Hayden Planetarium set to the music of Bowie.

Atwood, Brett. "Bowie Gets Graphic; Garbage Clips 'Queer'." *Billboard* 107, September 16, 1995, p. 82. A report on the video for Bowie's "The Hearts Filthy Lesson," from the album *Outside*, and its depiction of ritualistic murder.

Atwood, Brett. "David Bowie Single Exclusive to Internet." *Billboard* 108, September 21, 1996, p. 58. A discussion of Bowie's "Telling Lies," which is being issued exclusively over the Internet.

Austin, April. "Oh, the Irony: Bowie Upstaged by an Angry Young Rebel." *Christian Science Monitor* 87, September 20, 1995, p. 13. A report on the contrasts between Bowie and Trent Reznor of Nine Inch Nails on their then-current concert tour.

Bambarger, Bradley. "*The Rise and Fall of Ziggy Stardust & the Spiders from Mars*." *Billboard* 114, July 20, 2002, p. 18. A favorable review of the 2002 compact disc reissue of Bowie's *Ziggy Stardust* album. According to the reviewer, the reissue "should help remind those at major companies how music that seems hopelessly idiosyncratic and excessively provocative at the time can eventually be celebrated as utterly timeless."

Berger, A. "Music: Funky Dory." *The Village Voice* 40, October 24, 1995, pp. 58ff.

Bockris, Victor. *The Life and Death of Andy Warhol*. New York: Bantam Books, 1989. This biography of Warhol includes several references to Bowie's meeting with the artist in the early 1970s.

Bowie, Angela, with Patrick Carr. *Backstage Passes: Life on the Wild Side with David Bowie*. New York: G. P. Putnam's Sons, 1993. New York: Cooper Square Press, 2000. A behind-the-scenes biography of Bowie by his former wife.

"Bowie, David." *Current Biography* 55, November 1994, pp.14–18. A detailed biography of Bowie.

Bowie, David. "Basquiat's Wave." *Modern Painters* 9, Spring 1996, pp. 46–47. An op-ed piece on the importance of artist Jean-Michel Basquiat.

Bowie, David. *Bowie in His Own Words*. London: Omnibus, 1980. Bowie's autobiography compiled by Barry Miles from various sources.

Bowie, David. "Changes: Memories from a Life in Music." *Billboard* 111, May 29, 1999, p. 4. An adaptation of Bowie's commencement address at the Berklee College of Music. Berklee presented Bowie with an honorary doctorate at the event. Bowie reveals his love of a wide range of music, from the jazz of Eric Dolphy, Sonny Stitt, and John Coltrane, to the avant-garde of John Cage, to Anthony Newley, Edith Piaf, and Shirley Bassey. He highlights the importance of John Lennon as a friend and as a musical influence.

Bowie, David. "It's Art, Jim, But As We Know It." *Modern Painters* 10, Autumn 1997, pp. 24ff. An interview with artist Tracey Emin.

Bowie, David. *Musical Storyland*. San Diego: Worlds in Ink, 2003. A children's book that is packaged with a sing-along compact disc.

Bowie, David. "(s)now." *Modern Painters* 9, Summer 1996, pp. 36ff. Bowie discusses meeting with artist Damien Hirst, and the importance of Hirst's work.

Bowie, David. "Stardust Memories." *New York Times Magazine* 149, March 19, 2000, pp. 38ff. A fictional interview between the Bowie of 2000 and his early 1970s persona on the subject of fashion.

Bowie, David and Mick Rock. *Moonage Daydream: The Life and Times of Ziggy Stardust*. Guildford, UK: Genesis Publications, 2002. Available in a limited edition of 2,500 copies signed by Bowie. Also published New York: Universe, 2005.

"Bowie Rules NYC." *New York* 36, September 29, 2003, pp. 30ff. This article deals with Bowie's move to and love of life in New York City.

"Bowie: Trees Rule." *Rolling Stone* no. 931, September 18, 2003, p. 36. A brief report on David Bowie's purchase of the 64-acre retreat outside Woodstock, New York.

"Bowie's *Lodger:* Where New Muzik Meets Errol Flynn." *Melody Maker* 54, May 19, 1979, p. 13. A report on Bowie's *Lodger*.

Brazier, C. "Seriously, It's Bowie." *Melody Maker* 53, June 24, 1978, p. 13.

Brown, Ethan. "Staged Oddity." *New York* 34, October 8, 2001, p. 104. A report on Kustard Kings performance of songs of David Bowie at their Westbeth Theatre Center concerts in New York City, October 4–6, 2001.

Brown, Liz, et al. "CD Reviews." *Christian Science Monitor* 89, February 25, 1997, p. 15. A brief favorable review of *Earthling*.

Buckley, Bill. "*B&S* Soul: Starters." *Blues & Soul* no. 949, July 19, 2005–August 1, 2005, pp. 48–49. Among the other items reported in the article is the fact that a recent article in the Sunday *London Times* named David Bowie the definitive blue-eyed soul singer.

Buckley, Christopher. "*Architectural Digest* Visits David Bowie." *Architectural Digest* 49, September 1992, 100. A profile of Bowie's refuge, a residence on the island of Mustique.

Buckley, David. *Strange Fascination: David Bowie, the Definitive Story*. London: Virgin, 2000. A major biography of Bowie.

Burpee, Geoff. "Bowie's No. 1 'Moment' Unusual in Hong Kong." *Billboard* 109, July 26, 1997, pp. 45ff. A report on Bowie's Mandarin-language recording of the song "A Fleeting Moment," which at the time of the report was at the No. 1 position on radio play lists in Hong Kong.

Burroughs, William S. *Junky*. New York: Penguin Books, 1977. Beat writer Burroughs' non-linear, semi-autobiographical novel about heroin addiction published by Ace Books in 1953, under his pen name William Lee, and under the title *Junkie*. The non-linear techniques that Burroughs applied in this and other books greatly influenced David Bowie.

Burroughs, William S. *The Soft Machine*. New York: Grove Press, 1961. Perhaps more obviously than his other influential books *Junky* and *Naked Lunch*, *The Soft Machine* incorporates non-linear techniques on a foreground level. David Bowie was greatly influenced by this cut-up technique on several structural levels, especially in his songs of the 1970s.

Cann, Kevin. *David Bowie: A Chronology*. New York: Simon & Schuster, 1984. A biography, discography, and filmography of Bowie.

Carr, Roy and Charles Saar Murray. *David Bowie: An Illustrated Record*. New York: Avon, 1981; London: Eel Pie Publishers, 1981. This reference work provides information on Bowie's recordings through the start of the 1980s.

Castro, Peter. "*Earthling*." *People* 47, February 17, 1997, p. 27. A favorable review of *Earthling*, which credits Bowie with striking an "accessible" balance between the "jungle" and rock style that hearkens back to *Lodger* and *Scary Monsters*.

Cave, Damien. "Ziggy Stardust Reaches Earth." *Rolling Stone* no. 951, June 24, 2004, p. 129. A report on Bowie's contributions to the popularization of the British glam style in 1972, and its impact on Lou Reed and Iggy Pop.

Charlesworth, Chris. *David Bowie, Profile*. New York: Proteus, 1981. A brief biography.

Chezzi, Derek. "Feel Free to Mix and Mash." *Maclean's* 117, September 20, 2004, p. 81. This article deals in part with Bowie's invitation to his fans to "mash" his songs (fuse different songs to create new songs). Bowie ran a contest on the Web site neverfollow.com devoted to this music mixing technique.

Christman, Ed. "Bowie Predicts End of Stores & Labels; Numbers Say Otherwise." *Billboard* 111, November 13, 1999, pp. 56ff. A report on Bowie's prediction that music stores and record labels will become obsolete in the United States in the not too distant future. The author contrasts Bowie's remarks with the relatively low Internet sales statistics for Bowie's *hours...* album.

Clark, Rick. "Recording Notes: Classic Tracks: David Bowie's 'Five Years'/'Soul Love'/'Moonage Daydream.'" *Mix* 28, March 2004, pp. 130–132. A detailed discussion of the impact of the opening three tracks of Bowie's *Ziggy Stardust* album on rock music. Clark also discusses the studio techniques used in the recordings.

Clerk, Carol and Andre Paine. "Headlines: David Bowie—So Which of His Albums Should You Buy?" *Melody Maker* 77, July 5, 2000–July 11, 2000, p. 12. According to the authors, Bowie's best albums are *The Rise and Fall of Ziggy Stardust & the Spiders from Mars, Heroes, Hunky Dory, Young Americans, Low, Scary Monsters (And Super Creeps), Aladdin Sane, Let's Dance, Station to Station, ChangesOneBowie*, and *ChangesTwoBowie*. They suggest avoiding *Tin Machine, Tin Machine II, Tonight, Never Let Me Down*, and *Earthling*.

Clover, J. "Fables of the Self-Construction: A User's Guide to Velvet Goldmine." *Spin* 14, November 1998, pp. 92–99.

Colacello, Bob. *Holy Terror: Andy Warhol Close Up.* New York: HarperCollins, 1990. This biography of Warhol includes several references to Bowie's meeting with the artist in the early 1970s.

Coleman, Mark. "New Rock Bios Dish the Dirt on Aerosmith, Van Halen and David Bowie." *Rolling Stone* no. 771, October 16, 1997, p. 31. A somewhat critical review of George Tremlett's biography *David Bowie: Living on the Brink.*

"The Column." *Audio* 62, May 1978, pp. 95–96. Includes a review of *Heroes.*

"Confessions of an Elitist." *Melody Maker* 53, February 16, 1978, pp. 36–40. An interview with Bowie.

Considine, J. D. "*Fi* Interview: David Bowie." *Fi: The Magazine of Music & Sound* 2, October 1997, pp. 36ff. An interview with Bowie on the subject of his use of techno music on the *Earthling* album.

Considine, J. D. "Out of the Box." *Rolling Stone* nos. 672–673, December 23, 1993–January 6, 1994, p. 148. Includes a brief favorable review of *Bowie: The Singles 1969 to 1993.* According to the review, "Bowie's best still manages to startle."

Crowe, C. "Space Face Changes the *Station;* David Bowie Pulls a Lazarus." *Creem* 7, May 1976, pp. 38ff. A feature report on *Station to Station.*

Cunningham, Thomas. "The Return of The Thin White Duke." *Daily News Record* 34, February 23, 2004, p. 14. A report on clothing designer Tommy Hilfiger's enlisting of Iman and David Bowie to support Federated Department Stores' launch of Hilfiger's new clothing line.

"David Bowie Bonds, Anyone?" *Business Week,* March 11, 2002, p. 58. A report on the performance of Bowie's bonds.

"David Bowie Is at His Best Doing Other People's Stuff." *Time,* June 17 2002, pp. 76–77. Echoing sentiments expressed by several reviewers, this article praises Bowie's cover recordings on the *Heathen* album.

"David Bowie Returns to Earth (Loudly)." *New York Times,* September 14, 2003, Section 2, p. 28. A review of Bowie's *Reality* album.

"David Bowie: *Scary Monster* on Broadway." *Rolling Stone* no. 330, November 13, 1980, pp. 8–11.

"David Bowie (What I've Learned)." *Esquire* 141, March 2004, pp. 128–129. Bowie discusses fashion, his relationship with his family, religion, and philosophy.

de Angelis, Davide. "Digital Frankenstein—Collaborations with David Bowie." *Art & Design* 12, no. 9–10, 1997, p. 79.

DeCurtis, Anthony. "Truth Hurts." *Rolling Stone* no. 932, October 2, 2003, p. 117. A generally favorable review of Bowie's *Reality* album. DeCurtis identifies the key tracks as "New Killer Star," "Reality," and George Harrison's "Try Some, Buy Some."

DeMain, Bill. "The Sound and Vision of David Bowie." *The Performing Songwriter* 11, September-October 2003, pp. 44–52. An interview with Bowie with a focus on the *Reality* album and his life with his wife, supermodel Iman.

Denisoff, R. Serge. "Music Videos: *Serious Moonlight.*" *Popular Music and Society* 10, no. 1, 1985, p. 74. Although I deliberately have included only a few citations to reviews of videos, this one is included to illustrate the extent to which Bowie has been given serious attention in scholarly journals.

"Der Abgang des 'Thin White Duke': Die Abschiedstournee von David Bowie." *Neue Musikzeitung* 39, June-July 1990, p. 15.

Diehl, Matt. "In the Studio: David Bowie Rumbles in the Jungle on *Earthling*." *Rolling Stone* no. 749, December 12, 1996, p. 25. A discussion of the electronic dance "jungle" style of Bowie's *Earthling* album.

Diliberto, John. "Rock-Pop Recordings." *Audio* 79, December 1995, p. 94. Includes information on Bowie's *Outside*.

Di Perna, Alan. "Bring up Bowie." *Pulse* no. 217, July 2002, p. 48. A description of *Heathen*, which is described as reminiscent of his dark late-1970s work from the Berlin period.

Doerschuk, Robert L. "Frontman: David Bowie." *Musician* no. 221, April 1997, p. 11. An interview with Bowie concerning his *Earthling* album and the influence of contemporary dance club rhythms on it.

Dougherty, Steve, Ralph Novak, and Alec Foege. "Picks & Pans: Song." *People* 52, October 11, 1999, pp. 43ff. Includes a favorable review of *hours...*, which was *People*'s Album of the Week.

Dunn, Jancee and Nilou Panahpour. "Hall of Fame '96." *Rolling Stone* no. 728, February 22, 1996, pp. 18–19. A report on the Rock and Roll Hall of Fame induction ceremony at which Bowie was inducted in absentia.

Durbin, Jonathan. "Nothing Says 'I Love You' Like a Box Set." *Maclean's* 116, December 15, 2003. A brief favorable review of the compact disc reissue of Bowie's *Sound Vision* compilation.

Eder, Bruce. Review of *Pin Ups*. All Music Guide. http://allmusic.com/cg/amg.dll?p=amg&sql=10:rt7uak2k5m3m. Accessed June 20, 2006.

Edwards, Henry and Tony Zanetta. *Stardust: The David Bowie Story*. New York: McGraw-Hill, 1986. A biography of Bowie.

"The Eighties—A Vinyl Documentary: *Scary Monsters*." *Melody Maker* 65, February 4, 1989, pp. 28–29.

Erickson, S. "Movies: Jon Bon Jovi, Renaissance Man; Or, Why Bad Musicians Make Good Movie Actors, and Vice Versa." *Spin* 14, February 1998, pp. 52ff. Includes discussion of Bowie's acting career.

Erlewine, Stephen Thomas. Biography of David Bowie. *All Music Guide*. http://www.allmusic.com. Accessed January 30, 2006. Due to the high quality and up-to-date nature of All Music Guide's biographies, this concise on-line biography is highly recommended.

Erlewine, Stephen Thomas. Review of *Earthling*. *All Music Guide*. http://allmusic.com/cg/amg.dll?p=amg&sql=10:9y3m963ofepc. Accessed November 6, 2006.

Erlewine, Stephen Thomas. Review of *Ziggy Stardust*. *All Music Guide*. http://allmusic.com/cg/amg.dll?p=amg&sql=10:38q8g4gttv2z. Accessed June 21, 2006.

Erlewine, Stephen Thomas. Review of *Heathen*. *All Music Guide*. http://allmusic.com/cg/amg.dll?p=amg&sql=10:g2k0iklabbf9. Accessed October 31, 2006.

Evans, Paul. "David Bowie. *Black Tie White Noise* Brings the Thin White Duke Back with One of the Smartest Records of a Very Smart Career." *Rolling Stone* no. 655, April 29, 1993, pp. 59–60. A favorable review of the Bowie album. The review describes New Jack Swing and house music as "congenial" forms for Bowie.

Falcon, Richard. "Features—Urban Legends: Berlin." *Sight and Sound* 11, no. 11, 2001, pp. 28ff. A feature report on West Berlin's "anti-glamour" reputation in the arts in the 1970s and the role that Bowie's Berlin recordings played in this reputation.

Farren, M. "Surface Noise: The Trouble with Bowie." *Trouser Press* 10, December 1983-January 1984, p. 55.

Flagg, Gordon. "Adult Books: Nonfiction." *Booklist* 94, June 1–June 15, 1998, p. 1703. Includes a review of Bowie's *The Rise and Fall of Ziggy Stardust and the Spiders from Mars.*

Flanagan, Bill. "Music." *GQ* 67, January 1, 1997, p. 46. A profile of Bowie's latest work and the fact that it goes into musical styles that are not necessarily favorites of his earlier audience.

Fletcher, David Jeffrey. *David Robert Jones Bowie: The Discography of a Generalist, 1962–1979.* Chicago: F. Fergeson Productions, 1979. A discography of Bowie's work through his Berlin period.

Flick, Larry. "Bowie Has Believers for *Heathen*." *Billboard* 114, June 1, 2002, p. 15. A report on Bowie's decision to turn to Columbia Records as the home for his new ISO label and Columbia's willingness to allow Bowie complete artistic freedom for his *Heathen* album.

Flick, Larry. "Dance Trax: Bowie Jumps into Action." *Billboard* 105, March 13, 1993, p. 42.

Flick, Larry. "Dance Trax: Bowie's Chameleon Act Can't Hide New Single." *Billboard* 105, February 6, 1993, p. 26.

Flick, Larry. "Rock Tracks." *Billboard* 107, December 2, 1995, p. 83. Includes a generally favorable review of the Bowie single "Strangers When We Meet." While the song may not have easy pop accessibility, "those who are willing to give this a few spins will uncover a pleasant but subtle pop track that is worth the wait."

Flick, Larry. "Virgin Pulls out all Stops for Bowie Set." *Billboard* 111, September 11, 1999, pp. 19ff. A report on the marketing of *hours...*, including the Internet download option that will be offered two weeks before the album's official release.

Flick, Larry. "Zowie! Bowie!" *Advocate* no. 867, July 9, 2002, p. 67. A favorable review of Bowie's *Heathen* album. The author focuses on the gay-friendliness of the album, as well as the high quality of the poetry, both of which mark a return to Bowie's great work of the 1970s.

Flick, Larry and Doug Reece. "Singles: Rock Tracks." *Billboard* 109, April 12, 1997, p. 66. Includes a highly favorable review of Bowie's "Dead Man Walking," from the *Earthling* album.

Flick, Larry and Shawnee Smith. "Singles: Rock Tracks." *Billboard* 109, October 18, 1997, p. 80. Includes a brief favorable review of Bowie's "I'm Afraid of Americans," a single take from the *Earthling* album.

Forget, Thomas. *David Bowie.* New York: Rosen Central, 2002. A biography of Bowie for juvenile readers.

Frere-Jones, Sasha. "When I'm Sixty-Four." *New Yorker* 80, January 17, 2005. Includes a favorable review of Bowie's 2004 Jones Beach, New York concert on his "Reality Tour."

Fricke, David. "Art Crime." *Rolling Stone* no. 719, October 19, 1995, p. 148. A lukewarm review of Bowie's *Outside,* which suffers under the weight of its "superfluous wordage."

Fricke, David. "Bowie Playing Bowie." *Rolling Stone* no. 898, June 20, 2002, p. 82. A review of Bowie's *Heathen* album. According to Fricke, the high point of the album is the fact that it resembles Bowie "essentially covering himself," since the best tracks sound like his best work on several disparate albums from 1970–1980.

Fricke, David. "The Dark Soul of a New Machine." *Rolling Stone* no. 554, June 15, 1989, pp. 137ff. A feature review of Bowie's *Tin Machine* album.

Fricke, David. "David Bowie." *Musician* no. 74, December 1984, pp. 46ff.

Fricke, David. "George Clinton." *Rolling Stone* no. 587, September 20, 1990, pp. 74ff. Funk superstar Clinton acknowledges the influence of Bowie on Parliament-Funkadelic's shows and costumes.

Fricke, David. "Recordings." *Rolling Stone* nos. 724–725, December 28, 1995–January 11, 1996, p. 126. A brief review of Bowie's *Outside* that pans the "tangled narrative conceit" but praises the music of "I Have Not Been to Oxford Town and "The Voyeur of Utter Destruction (As Beauty)." According to Fricke, "Next time, Bowie should retire the gumshoe—with extreme prejudice."

Fricke, David. "20 Concerts that Changed Rock and Roll." *Rolling Stone* no. 501, June 4, 1987, pp. 44ff.

Fricke, David. "The Year in Recordings." *Rolling Stone* no. 776–777, December 25, 1997–January 8, 1998, pp. 155ff. Includes a brief review of Bowie's *Earthling*. According to Fricke, Bowie tried to keep up with current trends (the "jungle," bass-and-drums style, in this case) too hard, to the detriment of his material.

Frith, S. "How Low Can You Get?" *Creem* 8, May 1977, pp. 56ff.

Gandee, Charles. "A Perfect Match." *Vogue* 184, June 1994, p. 194. A profile of Iman and David Bowie.

Gardner, Elysa. "Bowie Has Faith in the *Heathen*." *USA Today*, June 11, 2002, Life, p. 10d. According to this interview with Bowie, he had written the songs *Heathen* before the September 11, 2001 terrorist attacks on New York City, where Bowie lived at the time. Bowie discusses the religious references on the album.

Garrity, Brian. "New Music-Centric Games Coming from Sony, Eidos." *Billboard* 115, March 8, 2003, p. 49. A brief report on *Amplitude,* a music-mixing game for PlayStation 2; David Bowie is among the artists whose work is included in the game.

Gaughn, Michael. "David Bowie's Future." *Sound & Vision* 65, January 2000, pp. 113ff. An interview with Bowie in which he discusses his *hours...* album, as well as his belief in the power of the Internet as a resource for entertainment and information.

Gett, Steve. *David Bowie.* Port Chester, NY: Cherry Lane Books, 1985. A brief biography.

Giangrande, Mark. "Take David Bowie, for Instance." *Stereo Review* March 1976, p. 74.

Gill, Chris. "Rock-Pop Recordings." *Audio* 81, April 1997, pp. 84ff. Includes a review of Bowie's *Earthling*.

Gillen, Marilyn A. "Interactive David Bowie Bows on New CD-ROM." *Billboard* 106, March 26, 1994, p. 18. A report on *Jump: The David Bowie Interactive CD-ROM*. The product will allow users to construct a music video for the song "Jump, They Say" and to remix the song to their liking.

Gillen, Marilyn A. "Ion Does CD-ROMs with Eno, Residents." *Billboard* 106, August 20, 1994, p. 80. A report that includes discussion of Bowie's interactive CD-ROM *Jump*.

Gillman, Peter and Leni Gillman. *Alias David Bowie: A Biography.* New York: Henry Holt, 1987. A thorough biography of Bowie through the mid 1980s. The focus is on his life and career moves.

Glass, Philip. Liner notes to *Bowie & Eno Meet Glass; Heroes, Low Symphonies.* Two compact discs, Philips B0000840–02, 2003.

"Glass Revives Bowie's *Heroes*." *Classic CD* no. 84, April 1997, p. 37. A brief interview with Philip Glass concerning his *Heroes Symphony,* which incorporates themes from Bowie's "*Heroes*" album.

Gliatto, Tom. "*Basquiat*." *People* 46, August 19, 1996, p. 19. Bowie's portrayal of Andy Warhol is panned in this review of the film *Basquiat.* "Droll, thin and twittish, Bowie comes across more like Miss Hathaway from *The Beverly Hillbillies*."

Goddard, Peter and Philip Kamin. *David Bowie: Out of the Cool.* New York: Beaufort Books, 1983. A biography and photo essay.

Goins, Liesa. "Worth Your Time." *Men's Health,* November 18, 2003, p. 76. A brief favorable review of Bowie's *Reality* album.

Gordinier, Jeff. "Playlist." *Fortune* 142, October 30, 2000, p. 326. Includes a brief review of Bowie at the BEEB, on which "you hear Bowie learning how to rock."

"*GQ* Critiques: David Bowie Releases His Twenty-Third Album." *GQ* 69, November 1, 1999, p. 191. A review of Bowie's *hours...*

Gutterman, J. "The Wooing of David Bowie." *Rolling Stone* no. 552, May 18, 1989, p. 28. A report on Bowie's choice of Rykodisc to handle the compact disc reissue of his eighteen RCA albums.

Haddad, M. G. "Bowie: Just a Gigolo." *Creem* 10, September 1978, pp. 38ff. An extensive interview with Bowie.

Haley, Frank-John. "David Bowie: Rock's One-Man Cult of Personality." *Pulse* no. 217, July 2002, pp. 42–45. A profile of Bowie and his various personae.

Harris, Keith. "Reviews: Iggy Pop—*Skull Ring*; David Bowie—*Reality*." *Spin* 19, December 2003, pp. 123–124. A review of Bowie's *Reality* album.

Hatch, Robert. "Films." *The Nation* 222, June 19, 1976, pp. 765–766. Includes a review of the film *The Man Who Fell to Earth,* which starred Bowie.

Hay, Carla. "Gorillaz, Fatboy Slim Top Video Awards." *Billboard* 113, November 17, 2001, p. 10. Includes a report on Bowie being selected for a Hall of Fame award at the 2001 *Billboard* Music Video Awards.

Hay, Carla. "Music & Showbiz." *Billboard* 114, May 11, 2002, p. 55. Includes a brief report on the retrospective exhibit *David Bowie: Sound + Vision* at the Museum of Television and Radio in New York and Los Angeles.

Hay, Carla. "VH1 Polls Artists on Rock's Greats." *Billboard* 110, March 21, 1998, pp. 10ff. A report on the poll conducted by VH1 on the 100 Greatest Artists of Rock and Roll; Bowie is ranked higher than Elvis Presley.

"Head-Scratching Music Choices for Ad Campaigns." *Advertising Age* 76, December 19, 2005, p. 24. Included is the fact that Bowie and Queen's "Under Pressure" will be used in television advertisements for Zale Corporation.

Hedegaard, Erik. "Iggy Pop's Trail of Destruction." *Rolling Stone* no. 937, December 11, 2003, pp. 70–81. A feature-length profile of Iggy Pop (James Hewell Osterberg, Jr.), who worked with and influenced Bowie. In particular, Hedegaard attributes the roots of Bowie's Ziggy Stardust persona to Iggy Pop's act in the late 1960s and early 1970s.

Hein, Helmut. "Pop: Der Mann, der vom Himmel Fiel: Viel Zukunfts-Fantasie: David Bowie geht an die Börse." *Neue Musikzeitung* 49, March 2000, p. 39. A report on Bowie's *hours...* album, as well as a report on Bowie's desire always to be, above all else, modern.

Helander, Brock. *Baker's Biographical Dictionary of Musicians. s.v.* "Bowie, David." New York: Schirmer Books, 2001. A brief biographical sketch of Bowie and assessment of his career. Helander expresses the view that Bowie's career was based more on style than substance.

Helligar, Jeremy. "*Outside.*" *People* 44, October 16, 1995, p. 32. Although this review describes the storyline of *Outside* as "a bit precious and pretentious," Bowie's music for the album is praised.

Hendrickson, Matt. "Bowie's Golden *Hours.*" *Rolling Stone* no. 822, September 30, 1999, p. 24. Bowie's *hours...* is called "his strongest album in years," in this favorable review.

Hiatt, Brian. "Downloads." *Rolling Stone* no. 985, October 20, 2005, p. 83. Among other recordings that are reviewed is Bowie's collaboration with Arcade Fire's song "Wake Up." Hiatt praises Bowie's " 'Heroes'-style lead vocals."

Hisama, Ellie M. "Postcolonialism on the Make: The Music of John Mellencamp, David Bowie, and John Zorn." *Popular Music* 12, 1993, pp. 91–104. Reprinted in Middleton, Richard. *Reading Pop: Approaches to Textual Analysis in Popular Music.* New York: Oxford University Press, 2000.

Hodenfield, C. "Bad Boys in Berlin: David Bowie, Iggy Pop and the Terrible Things an Audience Can Make You Do." *Rolling Stone* no. 301, October 4, 1979, pp. 41–45.

Hoggard, Stuart. *David Bowie: An Illustrated Discography.* London: Omnibus Press, 1980. An indexed discography of Bowie's work through the end of his Berlin period.

Holden, Stephen. "Rock Kings, Drag Queens: A Common Strut." *New York Times,* June 14, 1998, Section 2, p. 1. This article deals in part with Bowie's self-proclaimed bisexuality during his glam period.

Hopkins, Jerry. *Bowie.* New York: Macmillan, 1985. A biography.

Hunter, James. "Book List." *Rolling Stone* no. 801, December 10, 1998, p. 38. Includes a favorable review of Christopher Sanford's book *Bowie: Loving the Alien.*

Huwig, Pam. "Reality." *Lesbian News,* November 29, 2003, p. 36. A generally favorable review of Bowie's *Reality* album.

"IMMedia Video: *Ricochet.*" *Melody Maker* 60, October 5, 1985, p. 42. A review of Bowie's "Serious Moonlight" tour video, *Ricochet.*

*Inside Bowie and the Spiders.* Sound recording. Compact disc. Classic Rock Productions CRL 1607, 2003. Contains interviews with Bowie's band members, other musicians, and various music critics, all related to Bowie's work in 1969–1972.

"Investing." *Money* April 1999, pp. 64–65. A report on David Pullman, the creator of the Bowie Bonds.

"Investing: Here Come the Celebrity Bonds." *Time,* August 17, 1998, p. 39. A report on the issuance of the Bowie Bonds.

Isler, S. "David Bowie Opens up a Little." *Musician,* August 1987, pp. 60ff. A profile of and interview with Bowie.

"It Was a Civil Ceremony, Yes. But Lovebirds David Bowie and Iman insist that the Real Wedding Is Still to Come." *People Weekly* 37, May 18, 1992. A report on Iman and David Bowie's wedding.

Itzkoff, Dave. "Bowie." *New Yorker* 81, September 26, 2005, pp. 16–18. A Q&A with Bowie on the subject of fashion. Bowie acknowledges the influence of

Stanley Kubrick's film *A Clockwork Orange* on his Ziggy Stardust costumes. He also discusses contemporary bands that he likes.

Jackson, Blair. "David Bowie's '*Heroes.*'" *Mix* 21, February 1997, pp. 162ff. An interview with Bowie's producer Tony Visconti on the writing and recording of the songs of *Low* and "*Heroes.*"

Jerome, Jim. "A Session with David Bowie." *Life* 15, December 1, 1992, p. 90. Bowie reminisces about his glam rock career in the 1970s.

Jewel, Dan. "The Art of Being Andy." *People* 46, August 26, 1996, p. 18. A discussion of three actors who portrayed artist Andy Warhol in three different films; Bowie's portrayal in *Basquiat* is characterized by director Paul Morrissey (who worked with Warhol) as "the best by far."

Johnson, Holly. "Real People in Cork Street." *Modern Painters* 8, Summer 1995, pp. 48ff. A report on Bowie's painting style and his exhibition at the Gallery on Cork Street in London.

Jones, A. "Goodbye to Ziggy and All That." *Melody Maker* 52, October 29, 1977, pp. 8–10. An interview with Bowie.

Jones, P. "BBC Bans Bowie Videoclip." *Billboard* 99, April 18, 1987, p. 84.

Jones, Sarah. "Tour Profile: David Bowie & Nine Inch Nails." *Mix* 20, January 1996, pp. 113ff. Presents technical details on the equipment used for Bowie's tour with the industrial band Nine Inch Nails.

Juby, Kerry, ed. *In Other Words—David Bowie.* London and New York: Omnibus Press, 1986. Contains Bowie's personal observations culled from various sources.

Kamp, Thomas. *David Bowie, the Wild-Eyed Boy, 1964–1984: A Comprehensive Reference and World-Wide Discography Guide.* Phoenix, AZ: O'Sullivan Woodside, 1985. A discography and guide to Bowie's recordings.

Kane, P. "Cash for Questions: David Bowie." *Q* no. 166, July 2000, pp. 8ff.

Kemp, Mark. "David Bowie: *Diamond Dogs:* 30th Anniversary Edition." *Rolling Stone* nos. 952–953, July 8, 2004. A generally unfavorable review of the compact disc reissue of Bowie's *Diamond Dogs* album.

Kemp, Mark. "Sound + Fission." *Rolling Stone* no. 754, February 20, 1997, pp. 65ff. A favorable review of *Earthling.* Kemp compares the "forced story line" and "spoken interludes and overblown avant-garde flourishes that marred *Outside,*" with the sonic power and conceptual clarity of *Earthling.* The last two songs on the album, "I'm Afraid of Americans" and "Law (Earthlings on Fire)," however, are described as not being up to the high standards of the rest of *Earthling.*

Kimmelman, Michael. "A Musician's Parallel Passion." *New York Time,* June 14, 1998, Section 2, p. 1. A report on Bowie's work as a painter and as an interviewer of artists for *Modern Painters* magazine.

King, Rachael. "Backstage Pass on the Net." *Inter@ctive Week* 5, December 7, 1998, pp. S8ff. A report on BowieNet and the songwriting contest Bowie is sponsoring on his Internet service provider.

Koranteng, Juliana. "Bowie Blends His Artistic Tastes for Meltdown 2002." *Billboard* 114, June 15, 2002, p. 20. A report on Bowie's work as artistic director for Meltdown 2002, the British music and creative arts festival.

Kübler-Ross, Elisabeth. *On Death and Dying.* New York: Macmillan, 1969.

Lake, S. "Bowie." *Melody Maker* 58, May 28, 1983, pp. 23–26.

Lanker, Brian. "A Session with David Bowie." *Life* 15, December 1, 1992. An interview with Bowie.

Larson, Mark and Barney Hoskyns. "The Hairstyle of the Gods." *GQ* 70, January 1, 2000, p. 112. Larson and Hoskyns chronicle the influence of David Bowie on male hairstyles. They find evidence of Bowie's Ziggy Stardust-era influence in late-twentieth century hard rock musicians, hockey stars, and televangelists.

Lenig, S. "The Theatre of Rock." *Popular Music and Society* 17, no. 1, 1993, pp. 1–21. This scholarly article deals in part with Bowie's cultivation of the Ziggy Stardust image and his use of androgyny in his early 1970s act.

Lipke, David. "Bowie to Star in H Hilfiger Ads." *Daily News Record* 33, October 27, 2003, p. 12. A report on David Bowie and his wife Iman starring in advertisements for Tommy Hilfiger's H Hilfiger line of fashions.

Loder, Kurt. "David Bowie." *Rolling Stone* no. 498, April 23, 1987. Reprinted in *Rolling Stone* no. 641, October 15, 1992, pp. 141ff. An extensive interview with Bowie in which he discusses early influences (such as Little Richard), the development of his Ziggy Stardust character, Prince's relationship to glam-rock, his favorite film appearances, among other things.

Loder, Kurt. "Straight Time." *Rolling Stone* no. 395, May 12, 1983, pp. 22ff.

Luscombe, Belinda. "Seen & Heard." *Time* 145, April 24, 1995, p. 78. Includes a brief report on Bowie's collaboration with designer Laura Ashley on two wallpaper designs based on his paintings.

Lynch, Kate. *David Bowie: A Rock 'n' Roll Odyssey.* London and New York: Proteus Books, 1984. A biography and discography.

Mallon, Tom. "Wishful Beginnings: David Bowie Liked His Music so Much, He Bought the Company." *CMJ New Music Monthly* 103, July 2002, pp. 28–31. A report on Bowie's new independent record label, ISO.

"*The Man Who Fell to Earth.*" *New Yorker* 62, August 11, 1986, p. 16. A review of the video release of the film *The Man Who Fell to Earth,* which starred Bowie.

"*The Man Who Fell to Earth.*" *Rolling Stone* no. 983, September 22, 2005, p. 118. A review of the DVD release of the Nicolas Roeg film *The Man Who Fell to Earth.* The reviewer calls the casting of Bowie to star in the 1976 film as "inspired."

Martin, Rick. "Radar: Seeking out the Best New Music—Star-Gazing Glam-Pop Brilliance!" *New Musical Express,* September 17, 2005, p. 25. A profile of the rock band Duels; David Bowie was one of the band's inspirations.

Matthew-Walker, Robert. *David Bowie: Theater of Music.* Bourne End, Buckinghamshire: Kensal Press, 1985. This study of Bowie focuses on the use of the techniques of theater in his poetry, music, and stage persona.

Matthews, Jay. "Securities Oddity: The Bowie Bond." *The Washington Post,* February 6, 1997, P. C1. A report on Bowie issuing ten-year bonds that will pay 7.9 percent per year.

McCormick, Moira. "International *Velvet* Mines Glam's Riches." *Billboard* 110, October 3, 1998, p. 22. A report on the film *Velvet Goldmine,* which was based on the lives of Bowie and Iggy Pop.

Mendl, Hugh. Liner notes to *Days of Future Passed.* 33–1/3 rpm LP. Deram DES 18012, 1967.

Milano, Brett. "*Heathen.*" *Sound & Vision* 67, September 2002, p. 121. A review of Bowie's *Heathen* album.

Milano, Brett. "Popular Music." *Stereo Review* 62, April 1997, p. 81. Includes a review of Bowie's *Earthling.*

Miles, Barry. *David Bowie Black Book.* New York: Quick Fox, 1980. Also published London: Omnibus Press, 1984. A biography and discography through the end of Bowie's Berlin period.

Mitchell, Emily. "Swan Songs." *Time* 135, May 21, 1990, p. 73. According to this report on Bowie's 1990 tour, it will be the last time the musician will be performing his old hits.

Molenda, Michael. "Production Values: Audio Visionary." *Electronic Musician* 11, October 1995, p. 36. This conversation with Tony Visconti finds the record producer discussing his work with musicians such as David Bowie, Paul McCartney, and the band T. Rex.

Morganstern, Steve. "Updates: Bowie Goes Binary." *Rolling Stone* no. 816–817, July 8, 1999–July 22, 1999, p. 34. A report on *hours...* and Bowie's work writing and recording music for the video game *Omikron.*

Morgenstern, Hans. "Classic David Bowie Albums Get Remastered." *Goldmine* 25, December 3, 1999, pp. 106ff. A report on the Virgin compact disc reissues of 17 of Bowie's 1969–1989 albums.

Morgenstern, Hans. "David Bowie: Best of Bowie." *Goldmine* 29, May 16, 2003, p. 59. A favorable review of the CD and DVD releases of *Best of Bowie.*

Morgenstern, Hans. "David Bowie Book Review: *Moonage Daydream: The Life and Times of Ziggy Stardust* by David Bowie and Mick Rock." *Goldmine* 29, August 22, 2003, p. 32. A favorable review.

Morgenstern, Hans. "David Bowie CD and DVD Reviews." *Goldmine* 29, July 25, 2003, p. 71. Includes reviews of the reissues of *Alladin Sane,* the two-CD album *The Rise and Fall of Ziggy Stardust and the Spiders from Mars,* and the DVD of the concert film *The Rise and Fall of Ziggy Stardust and the Spiders from Mars.*

Morgenstern, Hans. "Reissues: David Bowie." *Goldmine* 30, July 23, 2004, p. 44. A favorable review of the reissues of Bowie's *Outside, Earthling,* and *hours....*

Morgenstern, Hans. "Reissues: David Bowie—*Black Tie White Noise.*" *Goldmine* 20, June 11, 2004, p. 55. A favorable review of the double CD/DVD reissue of *Black Tie White Noise.*

Morgenstern, Hans. "Reissues: David Bowie—*Bowie at the Beeb.*" *Goldmine* 27, February 9, 2001, pp. 96–97. This collection is called "probably one of the greatest retrospective collections on the legendary musician available."

Morgenstern, Hans. "Reissues: David Bowie CD/DVD Box Set Review." *Goldmine* 30, April 2, 2004, 60. A review of the reissues of *Sound Vision* Box Set and *Best of Bowie.*

Morris, C. "David Bowie Pops Up on Another Iggy Album." *Billboard* 98, September 27, 1986, p. 20. A report on Bowie's extensive work on Iggy Pop's 1986 album *Blah, Blah, Blah.*

"Music: David Bowie Straight Up." *The Village Voice* 34, June 27, 1989, pp. 79–80.

Nash, Kim S. "Ch-Ch-Ch-Ch-Changes." *Computerworld* 33, January 4, 1999, pp. 8ff. An interview with Bowie in which he discusses his use of computer technology, as well as music distribution over the Internet.

Nashawaty, Chris. "*Heathen.*" *Fortune* 145, June 10, 2002, p. 218. *Heathen* is described as Bowie's "most haunting, honest record since *Scary Monsters.*" The author describes Bowie's dance, electronica, and pop work of the 1980s and 1990s as a mistaken attempt "to be hip."

"New Albums: *Station to Station.*" *Melody Maker* 51, January 24, 1976, p. 26. A review of the Bowie album.

"New David Bowie BMG Set Spawns Int'l Art Contest." *Billboard* 108, February 24, 1996, p. 11. An announcement of the art competition related to Bowie's *Outside* album. Note: The eventual winner of the competition would be Philippine art student Joseph Lee Alviar, who received a $25,000 scholarship to continue his art education.

"New Release: *Hours...*" *Goldmine* 25, December 3, 1999, 114. A review of the Bowie album.

Newcomb, Peter. "James Bonds? David Bowie Has His. Why Not Other Artists and Stars?" *Forbes* February 23, 1998, p. 43. A report on the issuance of the Bowie Bonds.

Newcomb, Peter. "The Key to David Bowie's Heart." *Forbes* 145, March 5, 1990, pp. 106–110. A report on Rykodisc, Inc., which was handling the compact disc reissues of Bowie's old RCA albums.

Newman, Melinda. "Bowie's BMG/Virgin Album Boasts Radio-Friendly Beats." *Billboard* 108, December 28, 1996, p. 15. A favorable review of Bowie's *Earthling* album. Bowie discusses the spirituality of the album and how he nearly joined a Tibetan monastery in Scotland in 1967.

Newman, Melinda. "David Bowie Returns to Drama." *Billboard* 107, August 19, 1995, pp. 8–9. A detailed report on Bowie's *Outside*.

Newman, Melinda. "First Bowie Set in 6 Years Is Black-Tie Event." *Billboard* 105, March 27, 1993, pp. 12ff. A detailed report on Bowie's *Black Tie White Noise*.

Newman, Melinda. "Savage Sues David Bowie, BMG for Breech of Contract." *Billboard* 108, January 13, 1996, pp. 10ff. A report on Savage's lawsuit pursuant to its 1993 failure shortly after releasing Bowie's *Black Tie White Noise*.

Newman, Melinda. "Toyota Wants Its MPG." *Billboard* 118, January 28, 2006, pp. 48–49. Among other things reported in this article is that David Bowie will receive the Academy of Recording Arts and Science's 2006 Lifetime Achievement Award.

Norris, Chris. "Golden Years." *Spin* 15, November 1, 1999, p. 120. A report on Bowie's happiness with the fact that he is still an active musician, even though he "wasn't born to be a rock star."

"Note." *Publishers Weekly* 251, May 10, 2004, p. 19. A brief report on Bowie's children's book and sing-along CD *Musical Storyland*.

Nugent, Benjamin. "Space Slacker." *Time* 159, June 17, 2002, p. 76. According to this review of *Heathen*, "the only two really good songs...are the covers."

*The Official Footprints in the Sand Page.* http://www.footprints-inthe-sand.com/. Accessed November 29, 2006.

"The 100 Top Music Videos." *Rolling Stone* no. 667, October 14, 1993, pp. 82, 87, 94. Rolling Stone's survey of the top 100 music videos includes the Bowie offerings "Ashes to Ashes," "China Girl," and "Jazzin' for Blue Jean."

Orshoski, Wes. "Bowie Enjoying His Newfound *Reality*." *Billboard* 115, October 11, 2003, pp. 15–16. A discussion of Bowie's new record deal, which will allow him to release albums on his own ISO label.

Orshoski, Wes. "*Reality*." *Billboard* 115, September 20, 2003, p. 46. A generally unfavorable review of Bowie's *Reality*. While "She Drives the Big Car" is called the strongest cut, most of the "songs feel thin and not always memorable."

Orshoski, Wes. "Wembley Honors Bowie." *Billboard* 116, January 17, 2004, p. 33. A brief report on Bowie receiving the 2003 Wembley Male Artist of the Year award. His November 2003 performances at Wembley sold 23,000 tickets "almost instantly."

"The *Outside* Story: David Bowie and Brian Eno Explain It All for You." *Musician* no. 204, November 1995, pp. 30ff. A feature on Bowie's *Outside* album.

Palmer, Robert. "Walk on the Wild Side." *Rolling Stone* no. 718, October 5, 1995, pp. 45ff. This excerpt from Palmer's book *Rock & Roll: An Unruly History,* deals with punk and alternative rock of the late 1960s and early 1970s; specifically, the work of Bowie, Iggy Pop and the Stooges, the MC5, and the Velvet Underground.

Paoletta, Michael. "*Best of Bowie.*" *Billboard* 114, December 7, 2002, p. 66. A favorable review of the *Best of Bowie* DVD.

Paoletta, Michael. "*Heathen.*" *Billboard* 114, June 15, 2002, p. 22. A favorable review of *Heathen.* The album is described as a "soul-searching set" that recalls Bowie's great 1970s albums "*Heroes*" and *Scary Monsters (And Super Creeps).*

Pareles, Jon. "Pop Review: Once More the Outsider, David Bowie Turns 50." *The New York Times* January 11, 1997, p. 11. A review of a concert performance by Bowie and a discussion about how Bowie continues to integrate newer pop music styles into his work.

Paytress, Mark and Steve Pafford. *Bowiestyle.* London: Omnibus, 2000. This book includes photographs, prints, paintings, and sketches by Bowie.

Pegg, Nicholas. *The Complete David Bowie,* 3rd ed. London: Reynolds & Hearn, 2004. A reference work on Bowie's career.

Peisner, David. "David Bowie: *Reality.*" *Rolling Stone* no. 928, August 7, 2003, p. 23. A brief report on Bowie's return to a harder-edged rock style for his *Reality* album.

Perone, James E. *The Sounds of Stevie Wonder: His Words and Music.* Westport, CT: Praeger Publishers, 2006.

Pesselnick, Jill. "Musicians Use Net to Capture Fans." *Billboard* 113, January 20, 2001, p. 84. Includes a report on Bowie's BowieNet Internet service provider.

Pitt, Kenneth. *David Bowie: The Pitt Report.* London: Design Music, 1983. Also published London and New York: Omnibus, 1985. A biography of Bowie.

Pitts, George. "Start: Live: Karma Chameleon: David Bowie." *VIBE* 11, March 2003, p. 90. A favorable review of Bowie's performance at Jimmy's Bronx Café in New York City.

Plagens, Peter and Ray Sawhill. "The Late Great Tate." *Newsweek* 131, April 20, 1998, p. 62. A report on a hoax that Bowie and 21 Publishing apparently perpetuated to coincide with April Fool's eve. The hoax involved a publication party Bowie threw for author William Boyd, author of the book, *Nat Tate: An American Artist, 1928–1960;* Tate never existed.

Pond, S. *Rolling Stone* no. 587, September 20, 1990, pp. 51ff. David Bowie is included as one of the important figures who defined rock music in the 1970s.

"Pop Music." *New York* 28, September 11, 1995, p. 92. A report on Bowie's work with the industrial band Nine Inch Nails.

"Pop 100: 38—David Bowie: Changes." *Rolling Stone* no. 855, December 7, 2000, p. 84.

Powers, A. "Music: Sarong Number." *The Village Voice* 38, May 4, 1993, p. 70.

Puterbaugh, Parke. "Music." *Sound & Vision* 70, June 2005, p. 101.

Puterbaugh, Parke. "*A Reality Tour.*" *Sound & Vision* 70, February–March 2005, p. 108. A review of Bowie's DVD, *A Reality Tour.*

Puterbaugh, Parke. "Tracking Surround." *Sound & Vision* 68, June 2003, p. 102. A report on new music releases that were remixed for release on digital videodisc, including Bowie's *Heathen.*

"*Q* Review: *hours...*" *Q* no. 158, November 1999, p. 120. A review of the Bowie album.

Quantick, D. "'Now Where Did I Put Those Tunes?'" *Q* no. 157, October 1999, pp. 88ff. An interview with Bowie.

Randall, M. "The Sidemen: Reeves Gabrels and Carlos Alomar on Bowie, Eno and *Outside.*" *Musician* no. 204, November 1995, pp. 36–37. A report on the reactions of guitarists Gabrels and Alomar to Bowie and Eno's *Outside* project.

"Record Reviews: *Low.*" *Down Beat* 44, May 19, 1977, p. 33. A review of the Bowie album.

"Record Reviews: *Tonight.*" *Musician* no. 74, December 984, pp. 98–99. A review of the Bowie album.

"Records: '*Heroes.*'" *Crawdaddy* no. 80, January 1978, pp. 70–71. A review of the Bowie album.

"Records: '*Heroes.*'" *Creem* 9, February 1978, p. 59. A review of the Bowie album.

"Records: '*Heroes.*'" *High Fidelity/Musical America* 28, February 1978, p. 119. A review of the Bowie album.

"Records: '*Heroes.*'" *Rolling Stone* no. 256, January 12, 1978, p. 56. A review of the Bowie album.

"Records: *Let's Dance.*" *Creem* 15, August 1983, p. 54. A review of the Bowie album.

"Records: *Let's Dance.*" *Rolling Stone* no. 396, May 26, 1984, pp. 59+. A review of the Bowie album.

"Records: *Lodger.*" *High Fidelity/Musical America* 29, August 1979, pp. 107–108. A review of the Bowie album.

"Records: *Never Let Me Down.*" *Rolling Stone* no. 501, June 4, 1987, pp. 129–130. A review of the Bowie album.

"Records: *Scary Monsters.*" *Creem* 12, January 1981, p. 56. A review of the Bowie album.

"Records: *Scary Monsters.*" *Rolling Stone* nos. 333–334, December 25, 1980–January 8, 1981, p. 102. A review of the Bowie album.

"Records: *Stage.*" *Creem* 10, January 1979, p. 78. A review of the Bowie album.

"Records: *Stage.*" *Rolling Stone* no. 279, November 30, 1978, p. 66. A review of the Bowie live album.

"Records: *Station to Station.*" *Creem* 7, April 1976, pp. 58–59. A review of the Bowie album.

"Records: *Station to Station.*" *Rolling Stone* no. 209, March 25, 1976, pp. 60ff. A review of the Bowie album.

"Records: *Tonight.*" *Creem* 16, January 1985, p. 50. A review of the Bowie album.

"Records: *Tonight.*" *Rolling Stone* no. 434, November 8, 1985, pp. 71ff. A review of the Bowie album.

Reed, Lou. "The 50th Anniversary of Rock: The Immortals—39: David Bowie." *Rolling Stone* no. 946, April 15, 2004, pp. 128–129. In the section of this issue of *Rolling Stone* entitled "The Immortals," singer-songwriter Lou Reed discusses David Bowie's significance in music history. Reed discusses, among other things, Bowie's vocal range and the way in which he brought sophistication to rock music. *Rolling Stone* named Bowie the 39th most important person in the history of rock music.

"Reissues: *Bowie at the Beeb.*" *Goldmine* 27, February 9, 2001, pp. 96–97.

Resnicoff, M. "Tin Machine's Progression of Perversions." *Musician* no. 155, September 1991, pp. 46ff.

"Reviews." *Spin* 15, November 1, 1999, p. 179. Includes a review of Bowie's *hours…* album.

"Reviews: *Bowie at the Beeb.*" *Guitar Player* 34, December 2000, p. 112. A review of the Bowie album.

"Reviews: *Let's Dance.*" *High Fidelity/Musical America* 33, July 1983, p. 90. A review of the Bowie album.

"Reviews: *Let's Dance.*" *High Fidelity/Musical America* 34, October 1984, pp. 64ff. A review of the Bowie album.

"Reviews: *Let's Dance.*" *Trouser Press* 10, August 1983, p. 40. A review of the Bowie album.

"Reviews—Popular Music: *Outside.*" *Stereo Review* 60, December 1995, p. 106. A review of the Bowie album.

Richardson, Ken. "Tracking Surround." *Sound & Vision* 69, February-March 2004, p. 116. Includes a review of the compact disc reissue of Bowie's *The Rise and Fall of Ziggy Stardust and the Spiders from Mars.*

Roberts, C. "Tin Machine." *Melody Maker* 67, September 7, 1991, pp. 10–11.

Robinson, L. "Bowie." *Spin* 6, August 1990, pp. 56ff.

"Rock Gender-Benders." *Stereo Review* 50, April 1985, pp. 52ff. Bowie is included in this feature on musicians whose personae emphasized androgyny.

"Rock Musician/Singer." *Rolling Stone* no. 498, April 23, 1987, pp. 74ff. A feature-length interview with Bowie on his style, various rock styles from the 1960s through the 1980s that influenced him, and his career as a singer-songwriter and actor.

"Rock-Pop Recordings: *Outside.*" *Audio* 79, December 1995, p. 94. A review of the Bowie album.

"*Rolling Stone* 500 Greatest Songs of All Time: David Bowie—'Changes.'" *Rolling Stone* no. 963, December 9, 2004, p. 120. Bowie's "Changes" was chosen as no. 127 among *Rolling Stone*'s greatest songs of all time.

"*Rolling Stone* 500 Greatest Songs of All Time: David Bowie—'Heroes.'" *Rolling Stone* no. 963, December 9, 2004, p. 102. Presents the story of how Bowie was inspired to write "Heroes" after seeing a couple rendezvous near the Berlin Wall. The song was chosen as no. 46 among the magazine's 500 greatest songs of all time.

"*Rolling Stone* 500 Greatest Songs of All Time: David Bowie—'Young Americans.'" *Rolling Stone* no. 963, December 9, 2004, p. 162. Bowie's "Young Americans" is listed as no. 481 among the magazine's 500 greatest songs of all time.

"*Rolling Stone* 500 Greatest Songs of All Time: David Bowie—'Ziggy Stardust.'" *Rolling Stone* no. 963, December 9, 2004, p. 137. Bowie's "Ziggy Stardust" was selected as no. 277 among the magazine's 500 greatest songs of all time.

"*Rolling Stone* Music Awards 1983." *Rolling Stone* no. 417, March 1, 1984, pp. 18–19. *Rolling Stone*'s readers selected Bowie as Male Vocalist of the Year for 1983.

Roseberry, Craig. *"Ziggy Stardust and the Spiders from Mars." Billboard* 115, April 5, 2003, p. 39. A favorable review of the DVD reissue of Bowie's concert film *Ziggy Stardust and the Spiders from Mars.*

Rowland, Mark. "David Bowie/Brian Eno." *Musician* no. 204, November 1995, p. 30. An interview with Bowie and Brian Eno on electronic music trends and "postmodern creativity."

Rubin, Philip. "Turn and Face the Strange." *The Chronicle of Higher Education* 52, September 23, 2005, pp. C2–C3. I include this article as an example of the extent to which David Bowie is a well-known cultural icon. The author describes his experiences interviewing for jobs in academe, including an experience in which he alienated a prospective employer by comparing the interviewer to David Bowie.

Ruhlmann, William. *"The Buddha of Suburbia." All Music Guide.* http://allmusic.com/cg/amg.dll?p=amg&sql=10:cqn8b5b4nsqj. Accessed October 28, 2006.

Sanford, Christopher. *Bowie: Loving the Alien.* London: Little Brown, 1997. New York: Da Capo Press, 1998. A biography of Bowie.

Santos-Kayda, Myriam. *David Bowie: Live in New York.* New York: PowerHouse Books, 2003. Contains photographs of Bowie in performance.

Scaggs, Austin. "The Music Q&A: David Bowie." *Rolling Stone* no. 932, October 2, 2003, p. 41. An interview with Bowie, in which he states that his earliest musical memory was the hymn "O for the Wings of a Dove," and that John Lennon was "hands down" his favorite Beatle. Bowie also states that the most emotionally moving music he knows is Richard Strauss's *Four Last Songs.*

"Scene." *People,* August 19, 2002, pp. 72–73. A report on Bowie and electronic rocker Moby being New York City neighbors.

Schneider, Mitch. "David Bowie Recovering." *New York Times,* July 10, 2004, p. B16. A report on Bowie's emergency angioplasty to clear a blocked artery in his heart and subsequent recuperation.

Seguin, Denis. "A *C.R.A.Z.Y.* Situation." *Canadian Business 78,* November 21, 2005, pp. 11–12. A report on the difficulties the Canadian film *C.R.A.Z.Y.* is having being accepted in the United States. Bowie's "Space Oddity" is included in the soundtrack.

Serwer, Andy. "Wall Street's Green Genie." *Fortune* 148, August 11, 2003, pp. 155–156. A report on the so-called Bowie Bonds, and affects that music downloading on the Internet has had on the value of the bonds.

Sexton, Paul. "Bowie Simulcasts *Reality." Billboard* 115, September 20, 2003, p. 6. A report on the simulcast of Bowie's September 8, 2003 performance of the *Reality* album in London.

Shapiro, Anna. "Films." *The Nation* 236, May 21, 1983, pp. 648–649. Includes a review of the film *The Hunger,* which starred Bowie and Catherine Deneuve.

Sheffield, Rob. "David Bowie." *Rolling Stone* no. 940, January 22, 2004, p. 75. A favorable review of Bowie's recent performance at New York's Madison Square Garden.

Sheffield, Rob. "Life After Ziggy." *Rolling Stone* no. 970, March 24, 2005, p. 81. A review of Bowie's *David Live* and *Stage* albums. According to the author, *Stage* is a far superior performance.

Sheffield, Rob. "RS Library." *Rolling Stone* no. 808, March 18, 1999, p. 66. A highly favorable review of Bowie's *Hunky Dory,* which highlights the impact that the album had, right up into the late 1990s.

Sheffield, Rob. "*Ziggy Stardust and the Spiders from Mars.*" *Rolling Stone* no. 923, May 29, 2003, p. 73. An unfavorable review of the DVD release of Bowie's concert film *Ziggy Stardust and the Spiders from Mars,* which is described as "one long technical glitch."

Simels, Steve. "David Bowie." *Stereo Review* 36, January 1973, p. 90.

Simels, Steve. "Stagey Bowie." *Stereo Review* 42, January 1979, p. 122.

Simmons, D. "Music: David Bowie Straight Up." *The Village Voice* 34, June 27, 1989, pp. 79–80.

Sinclair, David. "Station to Station." *Rolling Stone* no. 658, June 10, 1993, pp. 56ff. A profile of Bowie's career and a favorable review of Bowie's *Black Tie White Noise* album. This article contains some of the most revealing autobiographical statements from Bowie on subjects including his sexual orientation (he states that he considered himself to be a "closet heterosexual"), his famous 1970s recordings, and his feelings about fame.

Sischy, Ingrid. "The Music Who Dares to Keep Ch-Ch-Ch-Changing." *Interview* October 2003, pp. 164ff. A feature-length interview with Bowie.

Smith, Kyle. "*Heathen.*" *People* 57, June 17, 2002, p. 41. A review of Bowie's *Heathen* album in which his writing is labeled "apocalyptic." The author finds fault with the general lack of melodiousness on the album.

Smith, Kyle. "*Reality.*" *People* 60, September 22, 2003, p. 47. A generally favorable review of Bowie's *Reality* album. "Bring Me the Disco King" is singled out as the weakest track.

Smith, M. B. "25 Essential Rock 'n' Roll Albums of the '70s." *Goldmine* 25, March 12, 1999, p. 104.

Smith, Tierney. "Book Reviews." *Goldmine* 24, March 13, 1998, p. 134. A favorable review of George Tremlett's *David Bowie: Living on the Brink.*

"The Soul of the New Machine." *Rolling Stone* no. 616, October 31, 1991, pp. 74ff.

"*Sound +Vision* Boxed Set Reissue." *Advocate* no. 905, December 23, 2003, p. 54. A brief favorable review of the compact disc reissue of the Bowie compilation collection.

"Spins: *Earthling.*" *Spin* 12, March 1997, p. 102. A review of the Bowie album.

"Spins: *Outside.*" *Spin* 11, October 1995, pp. 116–117. A review of the Bowie album.

Stahl, Jerry. "Bowie Light." *Esquire* 119, May 1993, p. 118. A profile that asks the question, "Will true love spoil David Bowie" in relation to his marriage to Iman. The article also explores the mental illness in Bowie's family background and his use of image projection as a means of hiding from his true self.

Stahl, Jerry. "David Bowie." In Sean Manning, *The Show I'll Never Forget* (Cambridge, MA: Da Capo Press, 2007), pp. 258–262.

"Stardust Memories." Rolling Stone no. 498, April 23, 1987, pp. 74ff.

Strauss, Neil. "David Bowie: *Sound Vision.*" *New York Times,* November 30, 2003, p. 33. A report on the compact disc reissue of Bowie's *Sound +Vision* compilation.

"Style." *People,* August 24, 1998, pp. 121ff. This article reports on Ole Henriksen, who had helped to rejuvenate the skin of a variety of celebrities, including Bowie.

Sutherland, Sam. "Bowie: Boys Keep Swinging." *Melody Maker* 66, March 24, 1990, pp. 24–26.

Sutherland, Sam. "Bowie: Ch-Ch-Ch-Ch-Ch-Changes?" *Melody Maker* 66, March 31, 1990, pp. 14–15.

Sutherland, Sam. "Tin Machine: The Industrial Blues." *Melody Maker* 65, July 1, 1989, pp. 28–30.

Sutton, Terri. "Records." *Spin* 12, March 1, 1997, p. 99. Includes a review of Bowie's *Earthling* album.

Tate, Greg. "The Time of His Life." *Rolling Stone* no. 824, October 28, 1999, p. 100. A favorable review of Bowie's *hours...* album, which is said to sound modern while also making references to Bowie's great albums of the 1970s.

Taylor, Chuck. "Reviews & Previews: Singles." *Billboard* 111, November 20, 1999, pp. 25–26. Includes a generally favorable review of Bowie's single, "Thursday's Child." The entire *hours...* album is described as "a class act rich in single material."

"Ten Albums that Shaped a Decade: *The Rise and Fall of Ziggy Stardust and the Spiders from Mars*." *Melody Maker* 54, November 10, 1979, p. 36. The Bowie album is included in the magazine's list of the 10 most significant albums of the 1970s.

"The Ten Most Underrated Albums of All Time." *Spin* 6, February 1991, 17.

Thompson, Dave. "Bowie in the '80s." *Goldmine* 23, June 6, 1997, pp. 16ff. This article contains details on Bowie's recordings through the 1980s.

Thompson, Dave. *David Bowie: Moonage Daydream*. London: Plexus, 1987. A biography with a listing of performances, songs, filmography, and discography.

Thompson, Dave. "The Bewlay Brothers." *All Music Guide*. http://allmusic.com/cg/amg.dll?p=amg&token=&sql=33:hu67men39fco. Accessed June 21, 2006.

Thompson, Dave. "'The Pretty Things Are Going to Hell.'" *All Music Guide*. http://allmusic.com/cg/amg.dll?p=amg&sql=33:wc6xlf3e5ccq. Accessed November 27, 2006. A favorable review of the song.

Tiven, Jon. "Darling David Bowie." *Stereo Review,* May 1974, p. 82.

Tremlett, George. *David Bowie: Living on the Brink*. New York: Carroll & Graf, 1997. A biography of Bowie. Among the more important revelations from this one-time business associate of Bowie is the claim that Bowie used homosexuality as a public relations ploy.

Tremlett, George. *The David Bowie Story.* New York: Warner Paperback Library, 1975. A biography of Bowie.

Truman, J. "Riffs: Phase IV Bowie Damage." *The Village Voice* 28, April 26, 1983, p. 64.

"Turn and Face the Strange: David Bowie Looks Back." *Musician* no. 141, July 1990, pp. 60–70.

"20 Years of Tommy." *People* 64, September 26, 2005, p. 118. An interview with designer Tommy Hilfiger in which Hilfiger acknowledges Bowie's sense of style.

"Two for the Show." *People* 58, August 19, 2002, pp. 72ff. A feature report on Bowie's area2 tour with Moby. According to Moby, "With David, it doesn't feel nostalgic. He's still in his prime."

Udovitch, Mim. "Q&A: David Bowie." *Rolling Stone* no. 825, November 11, 1999, p. 43. Bowie discusses the influence of Buddhism on his *hours...* album, among other topics.

Udovitch, Mim. "Q&A: David Bowie." *Rolling Stone* no. 902, August 8, 2002, p. 30. An interview with Bowie, which deals in part with Bowie's *Heathen* and his reasons for quitting smoking (his young daughter, primarily).

Valentine, P. "Living up to Bowie." *Creem* 10, November 1978, pp. 36ff.

Varga, G. "Praise from the Rock: Rockers on Jazz." *Jazztimes* 30, March 2000, pp. 43ff.

Verna, Paul. "Spotlight." *Billboard* 107, October 14, 1995, p. 71. Includes a mixed review of Bowie's *Outside*, which "stumbles on long-spoken segments that advance the plot line but hold little musical interest." The reviewer notes, however, that the album "stands a chance of reestablishing Bowie as a vital artist," provided that the listener "cherry-pick" their way through it.

Verna, Paul. "Spotlight." *Billboard* 109, February 22, 1997, p. 80. A favorable review of *Earthling,* which Verna labels as Bowie's "most inspired, most cutting-edge, and most promising effort since *Let's Dance.*

Vernadakis, George. "If They Could See Me Now...They'd Be on the Web." *Inter@ctive Week* 5, July 20, 1998, p. 60. This article deals with the use of celebrity names for Web sites, including BowieNet.

"The Vibe 100: *Station to Station.*" *Vibe* 7, December 1999-January 2000, p. 164.

"The Vinyl Countdown—the *Maker*'s Albums of the Year: 1970–1995." *Melody Maker* 73, April 27, 1996, pp. 51–53. Bowie's *The Rise and Fall of Ziggy Stardust and the Spiders from Mars* (1972) and "*Heroes*" (1977) are both included as among the past 25 winners of the magazine's *Melody Maker*'s Album of the Year award.

Waddell, Ray. "Arenas Await Q4 Tours." *Billboard* 115, September 27, 2003, pp. 7ff. Included is information on ticket sales for Bowie's upcoming concert tour. Bowie's tour producer is quoted as saying that Bowie's appeal is regional in the United States, with his greatest popularity found in the Northeast.

Waddell, Ray. "Bowie's Back." *Billboard* 115, June 21, 2003, pp. 1ff. A feature article detailing Bowie's *Reality* Tour.

Waddington, R. "Ziggy the Crooner!" *Melody Maker* 51, February 14, 1976, p. 13.

Waldrep, Shelton. *The Aesthetics of Self-Invention: Oscar Wilde to David Bowie.* Minneapolis: University of Minnesota Press, 2004. Based on the author's doctoral dissertation.

Walls, Jeannette. "BBC Buddha Goes Begging in the U.S." *New York* 26, September 20, 1993, pp. 13ff. A report on the BBC television series *Buddha of Suburbia,* for which David Bowie wrote original songs and instrumental music.

Walsh, Christopher. "Studio Monitor." *Billboard* 114, August 31, 2002, p. 71. A feature on Tony Visconti's recording and production techniques on Bowie's *Heathen* album.

Walters, Barry. "*Aladdin Sane:* 30th Anniversary 2CD Edition." *Rolling Stone* no. 926, July 10, 2003, p. 72. A generally favorable review of the 2003 compact disc reissue of Bowie's *Aladdin Sane.*

"War Child Scandal." *Q* no. 174, March 2001, pp. 14–15.

Watts, M. "Bowie: Funereal in Berlin." *Melody Maker* 52, January 29, 1977, p. 36. A report on Bowie's *Low.*

Watts, M. "From Brixton to Berlin." *Melody Maker* 53, February 18, 1978, pp. 33–35.

Welch, C. "Bowie, Myths and Mystique." *Melody Maker* 52, March 12, 1977, p. 14.

Welch, Chris. *David Bowie: We Could Be Heroes: The Stories Behind Every David Bowie Song 1970–1980.* New York: Thunder's Mouth Press, 1999.

West, Rowan. "Review of *Sound + Vision Inc.*," January 26, 2004, p. 60. A highly favorable review of the Bowie compilation album.

White, Timothy. "David Bowie: *Sound & Vision* for 1990." *Musician* no. 138, April 1990, p. 7.

White, Timothy. "Rock *Buddha:* The Singular Bowie." *Billboard* 105, November 20, 1993, p. 5. A report on Bowie's music for the BBC2 television series *Buddha of Suburbia* and the release of *Bowie: The Singles 1969 to 1993.*

Wild, David. "Bowie's Wedding Album." *Rolling Stone* no. 648, January 21, 1993, p. 14. A report on Bowie's *Black Tie White Noise* album.

Wild, David. "The Soul of the New Machine." *Rolling Stone* no. 616, October 31, 1991, pp. 74ff. A feature article on Tin Machine.

Wild, David. "Tin Machine Gears Up." *Rolling Stone* no. 612, September 5, 1991, p. 17. A review of *Tin Machine II,* an album which "offers no shortage of worthwhile material."

Woodard, J. "Getting Low with David Bowie and Philip Glass." *Musician* no. 176, June 1993, pp. 40ff. A detailed report on Glass's *Low Symphony,* based on the music of Bowie's *Low* and *"Heroes"* albums.

Woods, Vicki. "Rock of Ages." *Vogue* December 1999, pp. 370ff. A report on David Bowie and Mick Jagger's ability to remain powerful figures in pop music by ever changing, while retaining the characteristics that set them apart from the rest of the rock world.

Wykoff, D. "Box Set Full of *Sound + Vision,* Signifying Bowie." *Billboard* 101, August 19, 1989, p. 57. A review of the compilation.

"The Year in Records: *Never Let Me Down.*" *Rolling Stone* nos. 515–516, December 17–31, 1989, p. 177.

"The Year in Records: *Sound + Vision.*" *Rolling Stone* no. 567–568, December 14–28, 1989, p. 220. A review of the compilation.

Young, C. M. "Bowie Plays Himself." *Rolling Stone* no. 256, 12 January 1978, pp. 11ff. An interview with Bowie.

Young, P. "Bodies in Collision." *Maclean's* 102, November 6, 1989, pp. 90ff. A profile of the Montreal-based modern dance troupe La La La Human Steps, which had collaborated with David Bowie on the production *New Demons.*

"Your Guide to the 21st Century." *Success* 46, January 1, 1999, p. 54. Among other topics covered in this article is Phil Leggiere's issuance of Bowie Bonds, which are tied to David Bowie's future earnings.

# Index

## About the Author

JAMES E. PERONE is the series editor for The Praeger Singer-Songwriter Collection. He is Professor of Music at Mount Union College, where he teaches American music, music theory, and clarinet. Perone is the author of *The Sound of Stevie Wonder: His Words and Music* (2006), and *The Words and Music of Carole King* (2006), both in the Singer-Songwriter series. He is also the author of the Greenwood Press books *Music of the Counterculture Era* (2004) and *Woodstock: An Encyclopedia of the Music and Art Fair* (2005).